Beyond Compare

Beyond Compare

St. Francis de Sales and Śrī Vedānta Deśika
on Loving Surrender to God

Francis X. Clooney, SJ

Washington, D.C. / Georgetown University Press

Cover photos: (Top) Image of Śrī Vedānta Deśika from his birthplace in Thoopul, Tamil Nadu, India, courtesy of www.sudarasimham.org. (Bottom) Nicolas Brenet (1728–92). St. Francis de Sales. Oil on canvas. Réunion de Musées Nationaux/ Art Resource, New York.

Georgetown University Press, Washington, D.C. www.press.georgetown.edu

Library of Congress Cataloging-in-Publication Data

Clooney, Francis Xavier, 1950–
Beyond compare : St. Francis de Sales and Śrī Vedānta Deśika on loving surrender to God / Francis X. Clooney.
p. cm.
Includes bibliographical references and index.
ISBN-13: 978-1-58901-211-0 (alk. paper)
1. Venkatanatha, 1268–1369. Rahasyatrayasara. 2. Francis, de Sales, Saint, 1567–1622. Traité de l'amour de Dieu. 3. Sri Vaishnava (Sect)—Relations—Catholic Church. 4. Catholic Church—Relations—Sri Vaishnava (Sect) 5. Visistadvaita. 6. Love— Religious aspects. 7. God (Christianity)—Worship and love. 8. Spiritual life—Comparative studies. I. Title.
BL1288.592.V46R3433 2008
261.2'45—dc22

2007050882

∞This book is printed on acid-free paper meeting the requirements of the American National Standard for Permanence in Paper for Printed Library Materials.

15 14 13 12 11 10 09 08 9 8 7 6 5 4 3 2
First printing

Printed in the United States of America

Dedicated to my fellow Jesuit, likeminded scholar, best of friends,

Ronald Anderson, SJ

(1950–2007)

Contents

Preface

This book seeks to be a commentary on two works rooted in different traditions: the *Essence of the Three Auspicious Mysteries* by Śrī Vedānta Deśika and the *Treatise on the Love of God* by St. Francis de Sales. Several of the personal things that I might say in a preface are in chapter 1, specifically with respect to this book's genesis in my earlier writing, in questions that lingered after that writing, and in personal choices I have made over the years. I deliberately write from a personal perspective in chapter 1 because I do not want it to appear that more personal and confessional observations on the genesis of this project should be kept at a distance from the project itself, as if the personal is merely a catalyst for and prelude to objective scholarly work. Personal insights and motivations do and should deeply affect scholarly writing, particularly in a project such as this, in which how we read and write are topics of keen interest. Indeed, the whole point of the classic texts written by St. Francis de Sales and Śrī Vedānta Deśika, and of their reception over the centuries by anticipated and unexpected readers, is that the intellectual, imaginative, and affective are inseparable, each intensifying the other in a way that in the end must really be personal. And so it is in chapter 1, and not in this preface, that I draw my reader into my project as a kind of personal quest that begins in memories and in unanswered questions regarding my work from a decade ago, and in acknowledgment of testimonies of loving surrender, literary and personal. So this preface can be brief, a place to note some occasions on which I tested the ideas in this book and to offer thanks.

I was happy to test the theme and method of this book in a variety of settings, including an October 2005 lunchtime seminar of the Project on Religion, Political Economy, and Society at the Weatherhead Center at

Harvard University and an October 2006 conference on the Comparative Philosophy of Religion at the University of Calgary. I was able to discuss my project more in depth in a seminar called "Reading Hindu Texts Interreligiously" in the spring of 2006 at Harvard Divinity School, and to present a more developed version of chapter 2 in the Miller Endowment Lectures at the University of Madras in February 2007. Since comparative theology is a balancing act that in this project employs Indological, literary, religious, and theological practices, all within the double reading of two classic texts, I welcomed the opportunity to present the methodological issues at stake in this volume in seminars at the University of Hawaii in January 2007 and at the University of Oxford in May 2007. An essay for the *International Journal of Hindu Studies* was devoted entirely to Deśika's exegesis of the Dvaya Mantra; ideas, translations, and choices of texts that eventually became part of chapter 4 of this book were first articulated in that context. I was happy to develop the implications of this study with respect to multiple religious belonging, in a presentation in the Christian Spirituality Group at the American Academy of Religion annual meeting in San Diego in November 2007.

Most notable, in terms of time commitment, was the other book project that occupied me during my sabbatical year of 2006–7: *The Truth, the Way, the Life: Christian Commentary on the Three Holy Mantras of the Śrīvaiṣṇava Hindus,* a commentary on the three holy mantras that figure in this book too, read first in accord with Vedānta Deśika's insights and then from an explicitly Christian perspective. In a world where readers would have great patience along with interest in my work, *The Truth, the Way, the Life* would be taken as the groundwork of a project completed in this book, as close reading is resolved and fulfilled in a recognition of the act of loving surrender as a value not constrained within solitary religious boundaries. If all these seminars, lectures, and publications overlap in content and approach, this is inevitable because they all grew out of my need to put into words what Vedānta Deśika taught so powerfully, and then also to receive his erudite teaching in my own Catholic tradition by a fresh discovery of St. Francis de Sales. I am indebted to all those who provided opportunities in which my interconnected projects could grow, each project with its own character but (as my "forthcoming" entries in the bibliography shows) relying on the others as well. And yet, I hope, *Beyond Compare* is the most mature fruit of this extended exploration.

I am grateful to those who took the time to read my manuscript in its earlier stages: Dr. Anuradha Sridharan, associate editor of *Nrsimhapriya* in Mylapore, Chennai; Professor Amy Hollywood at Harvard University;

and my Harvard students Michael Allen, Dominic Longo, and Ilyse Rian Morgenstein. All were most generous in their willingness to read the manuscript and give me their detailed comments. On various parts of the project and its underlying research, Mangalam R. Parameswaran, retired professor of the University of Manitoba, gave me invaluable advice on details, context, and the underlying academic concerns. With the help of these friends and colleagues, I have avoided some of the smaller and larger mistakes I would otherwise have made; had I the opportunity to read for a long period of time with them and other teachers, the remaining imperfections too would have been diminished.

I am grateful to Harvard Divinity School for the 2006–7 sabbatical, and to my new colleagues there for encouragement in my somewhat distinctive writing projects. I owe a special debt to my Jesuit brothers at Boston College, where I continued to live during the writing of what has turned out to be the last project completed during my twenty-three years there. I dedicate this book to Ronald Anderson, SJ, a scholar and my friend and housemate for more than twenty years, who died as this book neared its completion.

Chapter 1

Two Spiritual Classics and the Possibilities They Present

> Perhaps the ideal reader can be described as someone who reads like a *prapanna*—like someone who does *prapatti*, who surrenders completely, somewhat desperately, having run out of strategies and plans: surrendering to the text and its meaning after attempting and abandoning every skillful strategy by which to make something certain and safe of it. The *prapanna* would speak and write from this simple, clear, unadorned learning. This is a spiritual possibility, to be sure, but it can also be described as a carefully cultivated intellectual virtue which extends the scholar to the limit and which can profitably inform the whole comparative exercise.
>
> Clooney, *Seeing through Texts*

I. On Writing as a Scholar beyond Himself: 1996

When I wrote these words in 1996 near the end of *Seeing through Texts*, I was enchanted by the one hundred songs of the medieval Hindu devotional classic *Tiruvāymoḻi*, which I had been studying for more than a decade. I was deeply touched by Śaṭakōpaṉ's intense devotion, the literary and spiritual worlds he so vividly evoked, his bold act of taking refuge (*prapatti*) with his Lord Nārāyaṇa and the Goddess Śrī, a moment of loving surrender commonly seen as enacted with this verse:

> "I cannot be away even for a moment,"
> says the Lady of the flower

who dwells on Your chest;
You are unmatched in fame, owner of the three worlds, my ruler,
O Lord of holy Veṅkaṭam where peerless immortals and crowds of sages delight:
with no place else to go, this servant has entered right beneath Your feet.[1]

This verse has inspired Śrīvaiṣṇava Hindus for more than a millennium, and, for better or worse, I felt I understood it from the first time I translated it. I was moved even by the traditional commentaries that strove, often in (what seemed to me) initially very difficult terms, to spell out the great drama of desire and love that energized *Tiruvāymoḻi*, the extraordinary composition of this person who had indeed lovingly surrendered to God and thus become entirely dependent (*prapanna*). In writing the words that begin this chapter, I sought to capture, in completing the project, the condition and manner of the reader trying to engage such texts with so open a mind and heart.

In my reflection, I was attempting to imagine the situation of an attentive reader who could be described by three features. First, ideally, she or he would have the requisite historical, cultural, and linguistic expertise and would be persistent in the interrogation of philosophical and theological ideas and even underlying faith positions. Second, she would also be open to the full powers of the text, vulnerable to being changed in the reading, and determined to write in accord with truths discovered in the reading, and with new purpose after this radical shift in perspective. Third, she would also, as expert, speak and write this rich learning in a way that would benefit a much wider audience. Expertise, after all, is never simply for the satisfaction of the experts; it is also for the much wider community that needs and seeks clearly composed and insightful writing. In the end, such a person might well be won over by the text and to the purposes of its author and community—thereby moving from the status of observer and even "scholar" to that of partially or completely persuaded practitioner who at some level would convert to this new tradition, surrendering in love. In the limit case described in *Seeing through Texts*, such a person surrenders completely in an act that is both religiously recognizable as a leap into the mystery of God and most easily described in terms of what is lost rather than what is gained, as customary religious beliefs and practices retreat to the background, and as God seems farther away and not readily available in expected terms.

As I was estimating the texts and the surrender of which they spoke,

I was also mindful that I, a Roman Catholic, was learning from a South Indian Śrīvaiṣṇava Hindu text. This added complication contributes to a transfigured intellectual and spiritual situation that is new and complex, and that few of us can understand or find words for. Even if this reader is determined to adhere faithfully to the tradition into which she or he has been born, loving God in familiar, sanctioned ways, such simple loyalties are more difficult after learning across religious boundaries. Such interreligious learning cannot but take shape in accord with new norms, new images, and new words that are more easily recognizable in some other tradition. Neither the home tradition nor the visited tradition is likely to understand this situation, and neither will be pleased by the intrusion, in this person, of the other. This person-reader-scholar–surrendered person may then stand at a distance from both traditions because of this double reading that sins by taking *both* of them seriously. But remembering her or his past commitments as well, such a reader also refuses to move to a higher viewpoint or to claim a special, insider language, instead remaining committed to careful and competent reading in several traditions at once, in a double reading that is necessarily unruly because unanticipated by the traditional readers of either text, both now subjected to a double take, reception from the inside and from without.

I certainly did not, in 1996, take up the topic of radical transformation simply as an interesting topic that merited scholarly inquiry. As I have already indicated in my preface, the boundary between the personal and the academic ought not to be neatly definable. A key point, indeed, was and is to call into question any such boundaries between the personal and the scholarly. For even in writing *Seeing through Texts,* I was also (re)discovering dimensions of my own experience, finding in Śaṭakōpaṉ's text a way to come to terms with "surrender to God" as an intellectual and religious commitment that does, or should, still have meaning in the twenty-first century. My concern was also personal in a particular way, since loving surrender to God was a value deep in my own tradition. The words of Jesus can of course be taken as normative for all Christians:

> If you would be perfect, go, sell what you possess and give the
> proceeds to the poor. You will have treasure in heaven;
> and come, follow Me. (Matt. 19:21)

and,

> Father, into Your hands I commit my spirit. (Luke 23:46)

In reading Śaṭakōpaṉ's songs of desire and loving surrender, I had also to look a little deeper into my own Jesuit tradition, recalling the prayer I recited aloud as the vow formula by which a new Jesuit commits himself to God in the Society of Jesus.[2] The words are meant to be uttered as a very personal statement, even if redolent of imagery and sentiments centuries old:

> Almighty and eternal God, I understand how unworthy I am in Your divine sight. Yet I am strengthened by Your infinite compassion and mercy and am moved by the desire to serve You. I vow to Your divine majesty, before the most holy virgin Mary and the entire heavenly court, perpetual poverty, chastity, and obedience in the Society of Jesus. I promise that I will enter this same Society to spend my life in it forever. I understand all these things according to the Constitutions of the Society of Jesus. Therefore by Your boundless goodness and mercy and through the blood of Jesus Christ, I humbly ask that You judge this total commitment of myself acceptable; and, as You have freely given me the desire to make this offering, so also give me the abundant grace to fulfill it.[3]

I remembered too these still older words near the end of the *Spiritual Exercises* of Ignatius Loyola, a prayer that is propaedeutic to any Jesuit commitment:

> Take, Lord, into Your possession, my complete freedom of action, my memory, my understanding and my entire will, all that I have, all that I own: it is Your gift to me, I now return it to You. It is all Yours, to be used simply as You wish. Give me Your Love and Your Grace; it is all I need.[4]

Both of these Ignatian texts and the dedication they announce were familiar to me before I studied Hinduism, but they came to resonate with what I learned from Śaṭakōpaṉ, his prayer of refuge, and how it was read in his Śrīvaiṣṇava tradition.

All these texts, Christian, Jesuit, Hindu, resonate well, but the meaning of the resonance has remained unclear. What does a complete, loving surrender to God mean? What are its intellectual, imaginative, and affective implications? And where does this new affinity lead us, intellectually and religiously? How texts mediate the power and possibility of surrender is a mystery, as is the very idea of living out the act of surrender into God's hands for the rest of one's life. I have remained deeply interested in the confident and passionate certainties underlying surrender, this total self-giving to God with no safety net, a choice disruptive of the attitudes, habits, and self-conceptions that shape ordinary life, a choice from which there is supposed to be no return. I remained curious how this seemingly implausible and imprudent decision retains its (fragile, marginal, nearly erased) place among an array of attractive and mundane choices that religious people make.

Because (for me at least) all of this is deeply intertwined in the reading of texts that promote this state and that provide the words of its enactment, the powers latent in proper reading have stayed in the forefront of my concern. How have authors been able to put the ideal of loving surrender into writing sufficiently eloquent and persuasive to inspire readers to live by these ideals? Most believers grow up in a tradition, and only later discover its texts. But in a world where many of us encounter religious traditions other than our own *first of all* through written words, it seems that the text can also introduce effective ways of religious living, and not just arise in that context of that living. And so I have continued asking what it means when a reader comes to understand and then be attracted to an ideal and exemplar of loving surrender—either inside one's own tradition or outside it, in a tradition constructed even through that reading.[5] The ideal and its provocations have stayed with me, as I have sought to find a way to remain religiously committed to my own Roman Catholic tradition, but also be the kind of person who could be won over by the words of a new religious tradition, here the Śrīvaiṣṇava Hindu tradition—while yet also remaining a member in good standing of the academic community, able to teach and write respectably within that community.

I was facing such questions in 1996 as I completed *Seeing through Texts*, but I was unable to deal with them adequately there or in subsequent writings. Over the years, I have tried other theological entrées into the study of Hinduism, studies with one or another thematic focus.[6] But in this current work, I am circling back to probe more directly the potent imaginative and affective dimension of intellectual work, the intense engagements to which a careful reader is vulnerable as she or he learns to live differently after taking the ideal of loving surrender seriously. In the pages to follow, I explore whether the profile of this reader can be more adequately refined, accounting for this affective power and yet too shedding more light on how to study religions with a "post-objective" empathy and engagement. In a sense, this book is an extended commentary on my 1996 claim and quandary, a commentary in which I let a Catholic author and a Hindu author do most of the talking.

II. Reading Loving Surrender across Religious Boundaries

I focus narrowly on just two learned, well-ordered, and highly rhetorically charged texts of spiritual theology, one by a Hindu and one by a Catholic: the *Śrīmadrahasyatrayasāra* (*The Essence of the Auspicious Three Mysteries*, henceforth *Essence*) of Veṅkaṭanāta (1268–1369; more commonly named Vedānta Deśika ["The Teacher of Vedānta"]); and the *Traité de l'Amour de Dieu* (*Treatise on the Love of God*, henceforth *Treatise*) of Francis de Sales (1567–1623).[7] I now introduce each text in turn.

1. *Vedānta Deśika, His Śrīvaiṣṇava Tradition, and the* Essence

Vedānta Deśika was born in Tuppul, near Kanchipuram in today's state of Tamil Nadu, into an orthodox Śrīvaiṣṇava Hindu family.[8] Śrīvaiṣṇavism is an ancient South Indian tradition devoted to worship of Nārāyaṇa as the sole God, along with his consort, Śrī (Lakṣmī). It draws on the Sanskrit and Tamil language traditions, explicating their truths and defending the coherence of a single creed expounded over the centuries in two languages. According to the earliest South Indian accounts, Deśika had a traditional upbringing, which included a rigorous education in Tamil and Sanskrit sources, and was propelled by his deep faith and erudition to become a teacher and scholar. Early on, he was recognized for his extraordinary spiritual and intellectual capabilities, his vigorous defense of Śrīvaiṣṇava tenets, and his exemplary personal devotion and manner of living. He matured into a leading Śrīvaiṣṇava Hindu theologian deeply rooted in the tradition of Śaṭakōpaṉ, and he taught in certain key locations of Śrīvaiṣṇava culture in South India. He eventually settled in Śrīraṅgam, the temple town that is even today the center of Śrīvaiṣṇava piety and practice; it is was at Śrīraṅgam that Deśika composed the *Essence*. He is considered the leading teacher of the "northern" (*vaṭakalai*) school of Śrīvaiṣṇavism.[9]

Śrīvaiṣṇavism is a tradition that prizes great learning and expects much of its leading representatives. It traces itself to the learned teacher Rāmānuja,[10] to his great predecessors Āḷavantār and Nāthamuni, and beyond them to the poet saints known as the āḻvārs, most notably Śaṭakōpaṉ. In fidelity to the Rāmānuja tradition, Deśika also drew upon the Vedānta Sanskrit heritage, with the Upaniṣads, the Bhagavad Gītā, the Brahma (*Uttara Mīmāṃsā*) Sūtras and a much wider body of related Sanskrit sources.[11] As Singh, Patricia Mumme, and K. K. A. Venkatachari have indicated, Deśika is a most highly respected synthesizer who gave to his tradition, so complex in its multiple linguistic and cultural resources, a solid coherence that would serve it well in intellectual and spiritual matters. Though on any given issue his sharply stated views might provoke some debate, his status and value are indisputable. As Singh states rather boldly in arguing for Deśika's preeminence:

> He is the only Srivaisnavacarya who was equipped with a great dialectical acumen. He is the only Visistadvaitin who combines logic with poetry, intellectualism with emotionalism and ritualism with spiritualism. . . . He is the only sectarian leader of his days who was liked, even for his conservatism, by the people. He is the only religious leader of his times who commanded the respect of his rival-religionists.[12]

According to Singh, Deśika's unique contribution is evident in many fields:

> Unlike any other post-Ramanuja teacher it was he alone who possessed the real synthetic sense, the key-note of the Visistadvaita Vedānta. It was he who carved, first of all, a prominent niche for Prapatti in the midst of the Vedic Sadhanas or the Brahma Vidyas. It was he alone who gave, first of all, a sound metaphysical background to Sri Vaisnavism. It was he alone in the host of his contemporaries or successors who utilized the services of poetry for the spread of the ideals of Visistadvaita and Sri Vaisnavism. The Vadagalais and the Tengalais both looked up to him for upholding the cause of Visistadvaita against the attacks of the Sankara-Vedantins, the Madhva-logicians and the other diverse critics of Ramanuja.[13]

As an orthodox Hindu, Deśika has inherited a tradition of practice (*karma*) and meditation (*jñāna*) that cannot be merely dispensed with. Even devotion (*bhakti*) takes an orthodox form as a highly respected efficacious path, an arduous one requiring practice over a long duration. Although respecting these three ways (*yoga*) and insisting that devotion can lead to liberation and union with God, Deśika and important predecessors such as Piḷḷai Lokācārya (1205–1311) and his brother Aḻakiya Maṇavāḷa Perumāl Nāyanar̲ (1207–1309) sought to create an intellectual justification as well as practical space for the simpler, more effective act of loving surrender at the feet of the Lord. If devotion is successful in bringing the devotee to God, it might seem that the "rival" path of taking refuge, so easy and simple, could undercut devotion and all the virtues and practices that accompany it. Deśika is in the mainstream of Śrīvaiṣṇavas who praise taking refuge as the easiest, most effective path, even if devotion is permitted its honored and traditional place amid the enduring obligations of the orthodox way of life. The shift from ordinary, honored devotion to the more radical act of taking refuge is a key theoretical and practical theme in the *Essence*, a matter that clearly requires justification, since loving surrender might seem a threat to the very idea of enduring orthodox obligations: All is God's work, and of us nothing is possible or required.

The *Essence* is by tradition one of Deśika's last works, his erudition in full flower, and yet by style, presentation of ideas, and practical intent, it is also meant for a wide popular (though literate) audience.[14] Like other teachers of this tradition, but most brilliantly, Deśika draws with ease on Tamil and Sanskrit sources, introducing abundant citations from each language tradition as needed. In the prefatory *Essence of the Lineage of Teachers* (*Guruparaṃparāsāra*; henceforth, *Lineage*) that sets the tone for the entire *Essence*, Deśika repeatedly emphasizes the need to be connected to the tradition, writing from it and in gratitude to it, not as an independent thinker. At the start of the *Lineage*, for instance, Deśika confesses in verse that his insights are simply those of the āḻvārs, who rendered in clear Tamil the obscure teachings of the Sanskrit Veda:

> The sage Poykai, Bhūtattār, Peyāḻvār, Kurukeśan̲[15] who appeared
>   at the cool Tāmiraparaṇi River, Viṣṇucittan̲,
> pure Kulaśekharan̲, our Pāṇanāthan̲, Toṇṭaraṭippoṭi,
> the light arising in Maḻicai,
> the prince of Maṅkai carrying the sword and spear,
> that the Veda might shine throughout the world:
> with delight they recited beautiful garlands of Tamil,
> and we in turn sing them with clarity
> now understanding clearly the unclear parts of the Vedas.[16]

He also takes care in enumerating the lineage of teachers, beginning with Nāthamuni who revived the tradition by retrieving and reviving the seemingly "lost" heritage of Nammāḻvār (Śaṭakōpaṉ):

> Among these teachers, Nāthamuni, son of Īśvaramuni, graciously composed the instructive text known as the *Nyāyatattva* and also the *Yogarahasya*. Through the lineage of the tradition beginning with Maturakavi, by his own recitation of *Tiruvāymoḻi*, Nammāḻvār, who appeared to him when he was in a yogic state, was his teacher.

He precisely details the lineage as it proceeds from teacher to student:

> Nāthamuni's son was Īśvara Bhaṭṭāḻvāṉ. To Īśvara Bhaṭṭāḻvāṉ was born Āḷavantār, whose eight texts were the *Āgamaprāmaṇya*, *Puruṣanirṇaya*, the *Siddhitraya* comprised of the *Ātmasiddhi*, *Īśvarasiddhi*, and *Samvitsiddhi*, the *Śrī Gītārthasaṃgraha*, the *Stotra Ratna*, and the *Catuḥślokī*.[17]

After further detail regarding the students of Nāthamuni and Āḷavantār, Deśika focuses on the most revered teacher, Rāmānuja, himself a beneficiary of the lineage of teachers.[18] But then, after meticulously listing so many names, he is generously inclusive with respect to the post-Rāmānuja period, allowing for local traditions that need not be certified by himself: "The names of the chief disciples of Rāmānuja may be learned in accord with the respective local tradition of each (student)."[19] As for himself, Deśika reaffirms that his most important learning is what has been passed down to him by his own teacher, a wisdom reenacted in his own loving surrender to the Lord:

> I take refuge with him who graciously bestowed on me my life,[20]
> and in turn I reverence the lineage of his teachers, and after that
> by grace I place before me Rāmānuja,
> the flood that rose in Perumpūtūr, along with
> Periyanampi, Āḷavantār, Maṇakkālnampi and
> Uyyakoṇṭār who taught him the good path,
> Nāthamuni, Śaṭakōpaṉ, Senānāthaṉ, and
> the auspicious Lady Śrī of sweet ambrosia—and putting this one first,
> I take refuge at the holy feet of my Lord.[21]

At the end of the preface, three verses proclaim Deśika's adherence to the teaching of the three great teachers, Rāmānuja, and his predecessor, Āḷavantār, and Āḷavantār's grandfather, Nāthamuni.[22] Deśika humbles himself before these esteemed predecessors, and makes it clear that he intentionally and firmly stands in their lineage. It is essential to Deśika's approach that he—and his readers—should continually trace true teachings back to these masters, powerful defenders of the truth; in their teachings and persons, he finds guidance and personal inspiration that transforms how one adhering to the tradition is to think, speak, act. We return in chapter 2 to appreciate more deeply how Deśika's estimate of the *Essence* as a work of tradition shapes his thinking and writing. Here it suffices to note that he does not boast of originality or independence; what matters most is that he belongs to a tradition in which he was a humble learner before daring to teach. His own singular contribution, paradoxically, is to be nothing but the handing down of what others taught before him. In this way, of course, he establishes his authority as one authentic in his transmission of all that he received.

As a constructive text deeply indebted to tradition, the *Essence* is first of all an exegesis of three holy (sacred, *rahasya*) mantras central to Śrīvaiṣṇavism's theology, piety, and commentarial production. They are short, totaling twenty-seven "commentable" units; compared with many other mantras, they are also straightforward, simple words. They praise Lord Nārāyaṇa, the Lord's invitation to the devotee to surrender completely, and the devotee's unqualified act of taking refuge in Nārāyaṇa with the Goddess Śrī:

> The Tiru Mantra: *Aum namo Nārāyaṇāya*—Aum, obeisance to Nārāyaṇa.
>
> The Carama Śloka: *Sarvadharmān parityajya mām ekaṃ śaraṇam vraja ahaṃ tvā sarvapāpebhyo mokṣayiṣyāmi, mā śucaḥ*—Having completely given up all modes of righteousness, to Me alone come for refuge. From all sins I will make you free. Do not grieve.
>
> The Dvaya Mantra: *Śrīmannarayanacaraṇau śaraṇaṃ prapadye Śrīmate Nārāyaṇāya namaḥ*—I approach for refuge the feet of Nārāyaṇa with Śrī; obeisance to Nārāyaṇa with Śrī.

The mantras chart the human acknowledgment of dependence on God, the divine and human exchange of commitments, and the divine promise of liberation and ultimate peace. They are considered by the Śrīvaiṣṇava tradition to contain, in a particularly condensed and essential fashion, all that needs to be said about the human condition, the goal of life, the way to that goal, and obstacles thereto.[23] Elucidated with the commentator's acute eye, they condense the ancient, large body of revelation (*śruti*) and revered tradition (*smṛti*), offering a succinct distillation of teachings that in turn can be expanded at great length.

Deśika invites Śrīvaiṣṇavas, including readers of later generations, to understand, feel, and enact all necessary religious truths and values through the ideas, words, and actions inscribed in the three mantras. Their theology is an implicit creedal formulation, and traditional teachers found the interpretation of them to be an effective catechesis, in summary of the faith and practice of the tradition: To recite the mantras is to say and pray all that is necessary. They are more than containers for ideas; they are also effective with respect to the pedagogy and psychology of devotion. They are, or can be, prayers appropriate for devout recitation, regular moments in individuals' and communities' ongoing relation with the divine couple: praise, invitation to trust, and loving surrender.[24] In Sanskrit, they distill a very orthodox tradition; meant for the widest of audiences, they return Sanskrit learning to the whole community. A reflective appropriation of the mantras opens the way for the transformation of the life of a person who takes them to heart.

For one thousand years or more the three mantras have been read together, complementing and reinforcing one another. The textual evidence for this goes back at least to the time of Parāśara Bhaṭṭar (twelfth to thirteenth centuries), whose *Āṣṭaślokī* is the oldest commentary we have. Soon thereafter we have the *Parantappaṭi* and *Nigamanappaṭi* of Periyavāccaṉ Piḷḷai (1167–1262). Piḷḷai Lokācārya wrote a number of commentaries on the mantras. His *Mumukṣuppaṭi* is considered authoritative for many Śrīvaiṣṇavas, especially with the commentary of Maṇavāḷamāmuni (1370–1443); similarly, his *Śrīvacanabhūṣaṇam*, also with Maṇavāḷamāmuni's commentary, is also dedicated to fostering the attitudes and life intended by the mantras.

Deśika, very much aware of his predecessors and the virtues of their work, followed their example in composing a number of small commentaries on the mantras. But his *Essence* is the most comprehensive of all commentaries on the mantras. It is an exegesis that pays explicit contextual attention to the accompanying philosophy and theology, the religious practice and communal values of south Indian Śrīvaiṣṇavism.

The thorough exegeses of the Tiru Mantra, Dvaya Mantra, and Carama Śloka occur only in chapters 27, 28, and 29, and this is balanced and enriched by the prose narratives of chapters 3–19. Chapters 3–6 offer philosophical and theological underpinnings for the entire project; chapters 7–12 offer the logic and psychology of taking refuge; and chapters 13–19 spell out the manner and motive of a life lived in accord with the mantras (table 1.1). We thus have a series of intersecting perspectives: exegesis (chapters 27–29), doctrine (chapters 3–6), psychological-spiritual context (chapters 7–12), ethical implications (chapters 13–19), and the transmission of tradition (chapters 30–31). Thus the truth, the beneficial way, and the goal—geared respectively to the Tiru Mantra, Dvaya Mantra, and Carama Śloka—are explained variously throughout the *Essence,* seen over and again from different perspectives. As a result, the attentive reader learns the truths to be affirmed, the practices to be undertaken, and the goal that concludes life's journey.

Inclusive in tone and relatively accessible in terms of the learning expected of readers, the *Essence* marks Deśika's determination to fashion a consensus for all Śrīvaiṣṇavas regarding the meaning and implemen-

Table 1.1 A Thematic Overview of the *Essence*

The Teaching	Expository Chapters	Mantra	Exegetical Chapters
Preface: On the lineage of teachers *chaps. 1-2 Introduction*			
Tattva (truth, reality of total dependence on God)	3–6	Tiru Mantra	27
hita (the beneficial: Nārāyaṇa and Śrī as means to salvation)	7–12	Dvaya Mantra	28
Puruṣārtha (the goal, living in service, for the Divine Couple and the community)	13–19	Carama Śloka	29

chaps. 20–22 Eschatology
chaps. 23–26 Further consideration of disputed topics
chaps. 30–31 The duties of the teacher and the disciple (on the importance of tradition)
chap. 32 Summation and conclusions

tation of the mantras in the life of the community. He emphasizes common ground and appeals to scriptures and treatises widely honored by all Śrīvaiṣṇavas; he roots his interpretations in the teachings of revered predecessors, including Āḷavantār, Rāmānuja, Parāśara Bhaṭṭar, and his own uncle and teacher, Appuḷḷār. He does not attack Śrīvaiṣṇava rivals by name but rather presents his ideas as logical developments that fill out, without contradiction, what had been said previously. His goal, in the long run, is to enhance the inner power of his tradition by a complete and clear presentation of it. Though quite argumentative in other writings, here he has little time for polemics.[25]

Deśika is clearly orthodox, and his thought seems definitely aimed at a scrupulously faithful presentation of the tradition he has received. Yet we cannot ignore the fact that there is no text quite like the *Essence*: It is so full, complete in every way, in inscribing the mantras in a notably multidimensional framework. It is a work that shows both the self-effacement and the distinctive brilliance of its author. In a sense, Deśika finds creativity in reliance on tradition. Indeed, his coherent presentation of the orthodox worldview—culminating in the case for loving surrender to God as an alternative to be preferred over the well-established, proven paths of religious practice and wisdom—is a cautious radicalism, traditional theology at the service of real change.

In studying the *Essence* over the past five years—having first read the English translation nearly thirty years ago—I have been duly impressed at how this formidable work of scholarship serves to instruct minds and touch hearts so deeply and acutely that readers might well put into practice what they have read.[26] It interests me as a site where reason, imagination, affective intensification, and radical religious commitment come together powerfully. I have been fascinated by Deśika as a religious intellectual who, by his choices in writing, makes his erudite tradition effectively present, a vast store of learning geared to the benefit of a wide range of readers. Or to draw on his terminology to predict the nature of my own book: Truths and doctrine (*tattva*) are only the beginning of learning and as such cannot be our primary object. More to the point is the beneficial path by which we undertake the transformation of our lives (*hita*), a path that includes attention to how we are to think rightly (chapter 2) and how, again by careful reading, we are to expand our imaginations and cultivate our emotions (chapter 3). But all this is for the sake of where we are to end up (*puruṣārtha*), at the brink of loving surrender, before God (chapter 4).

2. Francis de Sales, His Catholic Tradition, and His Treatise

Given my Christian upbringing and current commitment, and my hope to exemplify an intelligent response to today's pluralistic environment wherein no religion stands alone, I have chosen to intensify my reading of the *Essence* by drawing it into a more complex double reading with St. Francis de Sales' *Treatise*. The *Treatise* is a classic of Christian spiritual theology that like the *Essence* focuses in practice on loving surrender to God. In important ways, the *Treatise* manifests the same intelligence and passion as Deśika's text, reinforcing in the reader the disposition to recognize loving surrender as a real possibility.

As in my original choice of Deśika, at the base of my choice of de Sales' text is my instinct as a reader about what works well in an interreligious reading. It would be an interesting but very different project to choose texts that do not read well together, do not fruitfully compare. My choice of de Sales is not a neutral one: After reading Deśika's *Essence*, I considered a number of possible analogues in my own tradition and found in the *Treatise* a Catholic text that promised to read well with and in light of the *Essence*.[27] Even if the Catholic tradition de Sales and I share deeply affects how I have received his text, readers are advised not to think that I was familiar the *Treatise* before turning to the *Essence*; rather, the reverse was true. Given the manner of my choice, reflection on the *Treatise* and *Essence* ought not to be taken as the basis for proving something larger about the Christian and Hindu traditions; the value of my choice should become evident in the actual reading, but not as a theoretical matter on a larger conceptual terrain where one might try to prove something about the nature of religions, devotion, and so on. This book is simply an exercise in reading two powerful religious classics together, with great interest in the fact that this double reading enhances each text's effect upon the reader in ways neither author could possibly have anticipated.

Francis de Sales was the bishop of Geneva-Annecy, renowned as teacher and preacher and spiritual guide during his busy lifetime. He was canonized a Roman Catholic saint in 1665 and was declared a doctor of the church in 1877. His *Treatise* aims to instruct and inspire readers, leading them on a reflective journey from the simplest material forms of desire and love to the highest manifestations of a love immersed, surrendered, in the depths of God. Like Deśika, de Sales was a versatile religious leader for whom writing was part of a larger, fully lived intellectual and spiritual vocation in service to his community. Despite his many duties, he devoted much time also to a serious exploration of the subtleties of the spiritual life, that he might help seekers advance more quickly. He saw the *Treatise* as a tool for the spiritual guidance of the Catholic community in Geneva and throughout the French-speaking world (and beyond, with early translations). Even if the *Treatise* is a challenging text most suited for those who are both literate and advanced in the spiritual life, it is, like the *Essence*, meant for the whole community and not reserved for ascetic meditators.

What we know of the history behind de Sales' writing of the *Treatise* goes beyond the minimal internal information we have regarding Deśika's writing of the *Essence*; numerous scholars have rehearsed the story of de Sales' life and the creation of the *Treatise*. But for our purposes, a few comments must suffice. The *Treatise* appeared in print in 1616, but de Sales referred to the project as early as 1607, even before the 1609 appearance of his more famous *Introduction to the Devout Life*. The *Treatise* was first envisioned as a "Vie de sainte Charité," to appear in a smaller format. Thus in 1609 de Sales reported his plan for two small treatises, one on the love of God, grounded in the first three of the Ten Commandments, and a second on the love of neighbor, grounded in the remaining seven commandments. The idea for a second treatise was never followed through, but the first took fruit in the *Treatise*, furthered by his regular service of spiritual direction for the nuns at the newly founded Visitation Sainte-Marie.[28] Out of his exchange with the nuns there resulted, as André Ravier suggests in his preface to the *Oeuvres de Saint François de Sales*, "a spiritual doctrine integrating the most elevated and humblest states of the soul."[29] He announced the work to be finished—in draft form—in 1614, and it was published two years later.[30]

As Antanas Liuima indicates near the beginning of his *Aux Sources du Traite de L'Amour de Dieu de Saint François de Sales*, over the ten years when de Sales was writing the *Treatise*, it became also a record of his own history during that period:

> The history of the *Treatise* is also the history of his soul. It was little by little, in the course of multiple redactions, and after multiple revisions, that its idea developed. In 1609 he spoke of a book on the love of God in practice. Later, the idea came to him to add a few theoretical chapters which are now joined together in the first two books. After ten years of prayer, reflection, study, and experience, the "little book" that had been discretely mentioned appeared as a veritable treatise full of erudition and personal insights.[31]

Though de Sales, like Deśika, does not dwell on his personal experience, we do well to keep in mind the foundation of the *Treatise* in his own discernment of God's will and the meaning of divine love.

Here is a brief overview of the *Treatise*, by way of the themes announced in the titles of its twelve books. Books 1 through 4 offer the philosophical and theological grounding of de Sales' understanding of love and its growth:

1. Containing a Preparation for the Whole *Treatise*
2. The History of the Generation and Heavenly Birth of Divine Love
3. Of the Progress and Perfection of Love
4. Of the Decay and Ruin of Charity

Beginning with book 5, de Sales focuses on practices likely to be fruitful within the stated theological and psychological framework, particularly practices leading to greater conformity to the will of God:

5. Of the Two Principal Exercises of Holy Love Which Consist in Complacency and Benevolence
6. Of the Exercises of Holy Love in Prayer

Books 7–9 move quickly to the climax of de Sales' reflection on the logic of love:

7. Of the Union of the Soul with Her God, Which Is Perfected in Prayer
8. Love of Conformity, by Which We Unite Our Will to the Will of God, Signified unto Us by His Commandments, Counsels, and Inspirations
9. Love of Submission, Whereby Our Will Is United to God's Good-Pleasure

The final three books, perhaps additions to the *Treatise* as originally conceived, have to do with living the Christian life:

10. Commandment of Loving God above All Things
11. Sovereign Authority Which Sacred Love Holds over All the Virtues, Actions, and Perfections of the Soul
12. Containing Certain Counsels for the Progress of the Soul in Holy Love[32]

De Sales, at a quickening pace as the *Treatise* progresses, guides the reader spiritually into an intensification of love that is also an increasingly pure submission to God's will. As such, the *Treatise* begins with the same kind of theoretical foundations as the *Essence*, tends practically to the same spiritual goal as Deśika's, and highlights too problems of ethics in regard to how life is to be lived in the community after the act of loving surrender. Thus, although the chapters and books of course do not line up exactly, and key portions of each text are not mirrored in the other, it is helpful to notice a certain parallelism (table 1.2).[33]

As for the wider context: Of course, de Sales too was not writing in a vacuum or simply for the sake of a lovely exposition of the spiritual life. In his preface, Ravier sketches the difficult social and political situation in which de Sales worked as bishop, theologian, and reformer in Geneva-Annecy, given the religious politics of Savoie in the time of the Catholic Reformation.[34] From his position of authority, de Sales was concerned with nourishing Catholic identity in Geneva-Annecy by implementing the reforms of the Council of Trent. Although the *Treatise* does not directly inform us about debates current in the larger world of the church in de Sales' time, scholars rightly assume that it was written in light of the intellectual challenges of seventeenth-century Geneva and Reformation debates about grace and free will: All is dependent on God and surrendered to God, yet human freedom and dignity remain important. I return to this balance in chapter 4.

Like Deśika, de Sales too makes his case by synthesizing traditional sources in support of a coherent and healthy life that is both intelligent and spiritual. In his survey of the theories of the rational and sensitive appetites and passions in seventeenth- and eighteenth-century French thought, Anthony Levi stresses the importance of de Sales to a wide range of participants in debates during his era and later.[35] Although de Sales was not a systematic theologian or philosopher, we cannot overestimate his importance in drawing together key elements from the tradition for a coherent understanding of human nature:

> The significance of Francis de Sales in any study of the French moralists of this period derives primarily from his transitional ethic. On the one hand, he belongs to the homogeneous tradition of non-scholastic moral writing which highlighted truly religious values and which derives from Ficino. . . . On the other hand his authentic Augustinianism relates him to another series of moralists including Bérulle, Saint-Cyrian, and many of the authors associated with Port-Royal. These, too, are frequently beholden to the Neoplatonist tradition of Florence. But Francis de

Sales, much more successfully than Charron, by exploiting the tiered structure of the soul itself, unites the Neostoic and the Augustinian traditions of moral writing in a way which is itself sufficient to call in question some of the conventional views on the antithetic nature of the two traditions.[36]

Table 1.2 A Comparative Overview of the *Essence* and *Treatise*

The *Essence*	The *Treatise*
The *Lineage*, on the teaching tradition	The preface, placing the *Treatise* in the context of earlier spiritual and theological classics
Chapters 1–2: Introduction to the Content and Purpose of the *Essence*	Book 1. Containing a Preparation for the Whole *Treatise*
Chapter 3: On the Dependence of All Things on God	
Chapter 4: On the Five Things to Be Known	Book 2. The History of the Generation and Heavenly Birth of Divine Love
Chapter 5: On the Three Realities	Book 3. Of the Progress and Perfection of Love
Chapter 6: On the Identity of the Supreme God	Book 4. Of the Decay and Ruin of Charity
Chapters 7–12: On the Theology of the Taking of Refuge in Relation to Other Religious Practices, and on the Psychology and Enactment of Surrender to God	Book 5. Of the Two Principal Exercises of Holy Love Which Consist in Complacency And Benevolence Book 6. Of the Exercises of Holy Love in Prayer Book 7. Of the Union of the Soul with Her God, Which Is Perfected in Prayer Book 8. Love of Conformity, by Which We Unite Our Will to the Will of God, Signified unto Us by His Commandments, Counsels, and Inspirations Book 9. Love of Submission, Whereby Our Will Is United to God's Good-Pleasure
Chapters 13–19: On How One Is to Live after Taking Refuge with Nārāyaṇa and Śrī	Book 10. Commandment of Loving God above All Things Book 11. Sovereign Authority Which Sacred Love Holds over All the Virtues, Actions, and Perfections of the Soul Book 12. Containing Certain Counsels for the Progress of the Soul in Holy Love

Though he acknowledges the "eclectic" and "uneven" nature of de Sales' contribution to explaining the passions, Levi insists that "the synthesis attempted by Francis de Sales was to be of great importance for the history of vernacular writings on morals in the first half of the seventeenth century."[37] De Sales, like Deśika, provided a deep and sure foundation for intelligent spiritual practice in generations after him—even if he was a transitional figure, whereas Deśika powerfully fixed his "northern" Śrīvaiṣṇava tradition in the form it holds even today. To read de Sales or Deśika is to catch hold of the interwoven broader conversation of the author's time.[38]

In his own preface, de Sales readily acknowledges his debt to earlier authors:

> Now it is true that many writers have admirably handled this subject. Above all those ancient Fathers, who as they did very lovingly serve God so did they speak divinely of his love. O how good it is to hear St. Paul speak of heavenly things, who learned them even in heaven itself, and how good to see those souls who were nursed in the bosom of love [*dilection*] write of its holy sweetness! For this reason those amongst the schoolmen that discoursed the most and the best of it, did also equally excel in piety. St. Thomas has made a treatise on it worthy of St. Thomas; St. Bonaventure and Blessed Denis the Carthusian have made diverse, most excellent ones on it under various titles, and as for John Gerson, Chancellor of the University of Paris, Sixtus of Sienna speaks of him thus: "He has so worthily discoursed of the fifty properties of divine love which are described in the course of the *Song of Songs*, that he alone would seem to have taken proper account of the affections of the love of God." Truly this man was extremely learned, judicious and devout.[39]

Even his comments on women writers show him to be progressive (for his era) and attentive to what counts most in spiritual writing:

> And that we may know this kind of writings to be made more successfully by the devotion of lovers than by the learning of the wise, it has pleased the Holy Ghost that many women should work wonders in it. Who has ever better expressed the heavenly passions of sacred love, than St. Catherine of Genoa, St. Angela of Foligno, St. Catharine of Siena, St. Mechtilde?[40]

The implied tension between "the devotion of lovers" and "the learning of the wise" is strong, and we shall return to it in chapter 2.

De Sales goes on to mention the writers "in our age," appearing to make a courteous tour of religious orders: "Louis of Granada, that great doctor of piety . . . Diego Stella, of the Order of St. Francis . . . Christopher Fonseca, an Augustinian . . . Louis Richeome of the Society of Jesus . . . John of Jesus Maria, a discalced Carmelite . . . that great and celebrated Cardinal Bellarmine . . . M. Camus . . . Laurence of Paris, a Capuchin preacher . . . [and] lastly the Blessed Mother Teresa of Jesus." He then makes an estimate of his own contribution, professing humility and inviting his readers to see for themselves where his work stands:

> And although, my dear reader, this *Treatise* which I now present you, falls far short of those excellent works, without hope of ever running even with them, yet have I such confidence in the favor of the two heavenly lovers to whom I dedicate it, that still it may be in some way serviceable to you, and that in it you will meet with many wholesome considerations which you would not elsewhere so easily find, just as again you may elsewhere find many beautiful things which are not found here.[41]

He concludes somewhat obscurely, but with clear emphasis on the distinctiveness of his practice: "Indeed, it even seems to me that my design is not the same as that of others except in general, inasmuch as we all look towards the glory of holy love. But of this your reading will convince you."[42] Indeed, after the preface, the mass of bibliography and erudition slips into the background, and de Sales rarely if ever cites any of the authors he praises as masters of such "excellent works." In reading de Sales, we must therefore be mindful of the wide learning behind the *Treatise* and the connectedness of his writing to the literary and ecclesial tradition, yet also recognize his determination to write in his own voice, without undue explicit reliance on older sources. In the same way, Deśika's interactions with his own revered teachers and with other learned teachers in his adulthood deeply enrich his writing and its insights—even as he composed a text with a distinctive, even unique character to it. For both authors, it is in the text itself, written in a most original way, that tradition comes alive.[43]

And to what effect are we then to read? De Sales makes clear that he hopes for divine activity in the hearts of his readers:

> Ah! I conjure you by the heart of your sweet Jesus, King of hearts, whom your hearts adore—*animate my heart, and all hearts that shall read this writing*, by your all powerful favor with the Holy Ghost, that henceforth we may offer up in holocaust all our affections to his divine goodness, to live, die, and live again for ever, *amid the flames of this heavenly fire*, which Our Lord your son has so much desired to *kindle* in our hearts, that he never ceased to *labor and sigh for* this until "death, even the death of the cross."[44]

This intense and ardent devotion is also the ardor of ideal reading; the *Treatise* offers and intensifies the states of which it speaks, serving as an instrument of divine action.

As we have seen, this is true for Deśika too, whose own words can be traced, in his mind and that of his original readers, to divine wisdom and divine teaching. However we estimate the inspiration guiding both authors, our readings and double reading put us in touch with traditions, truths, and manners of expression of extraordinary pedigree and power that are intended to change attentive readers. If, therefore, I say less than might be said regarding a multiplicity of possible conceptual comparisons, it is because I have placed priority on de Sales' larger goal—*animate my heart, and all hearts that shall read this writing*—and the eventuality of loving surrender toward which he writes, what Deśika terms the beneficial way (*hita*) and the goal (*puruṣārtha*).

3. *Vedānta Deśika and Francis de Sales, Brought into Conversation*

Neither of our authors has much to say about the historical and social situation in which he is writing; each prefers that we focus on his words and submit to the educative process that constitutes the activity of his treatise. Deśika and de Sales are both traditional and creative; though each is indebted to his predecessors, neither relies on some previously developed, complete model for his work. Both are deeply concerned with communicating a practical message that will bear practical implications in their readers' lives—and for this, they write highly original and effective treatises that promise to transform all who would read them carefully. Deśika's *Essence* is an integral treatise that is deeply practical, aiming to draw in readers by illumining their minds and making them realize the incongruity of their current situation such that they become all the more inclined to act in accord with the worldview of loving surrender. For loving surrender is indeed a plausible option that they can only with difficulty avoid choosing once their minds and hearts are cleared of distorted images and disordered emotions with respect to their own identities and how they stand before God. De Sales' *Treatise* is a similarly integral and practical work, likewise meant for a well-disposed audience. He too aspires to a transformation in his readers while insisting that his own role is minimal, a matter of human words that can channel divine power. The fundamental life change that both Deśika and de Sales aim to inspire cannot be fully apprehended or assessed conceptually, even if the reader's analysis proceeds by lucid and logical arguments. Imagination and intuition are at stake, and the reader is required likewise to reflect on her or his own reading, discerning shifts in her own sense of what is possible and desirable in the presence of God.

My work here responds in kind; it is primarily a rather simple but extended exercise in reading together these two brilliant and compelling texts, in order that we might notice how attentive readers, possibly including ourselves, are educated and made vulnerable to the power of the ideals our authors propose. This exercise requires that we move from reading at a distance, with a professional control that correctly and necessarily prizes detachment, toward a submission to these texts, immersion finally in a double reading that makes us vulnerable to the realities of God and self as imagined by the authors. In this process, I suggest, not only do we learn much about each author and his tradition and its underlying spiritual theology; but, in the freedom engendered by our necessarily uncharted double reading, we also gain a vantage point from which to see how the presentations of loving surrender, consisting of their many ideas, images, stories, appeals, and rhetorical charges to the reader, create a community of readers competent in both texts and susceptible to their power.[45]

Our best practice, then, is to attend to the *Treatise* and the *Essence* as the effective communicative acts they were intended to be, as it were catching them in the act, in three moments. First, we discover a reconsideration of how and for what purpose we think and then write and read religiously; their confidence in productive writing is operative even as they see clearly the limits of the power of words and utility of books with respect to spiritual advancement (chapter 2). Second, we discover a new sensitivity to spiritual writing as deeply educative and productive of fresh imaginative and affective resources that change how individual readers (re)act with respect to possible religious goals; with humility and a conception of themselves as instruments of tradition, they make a place and give voice to potent ideas, sentiments, and personal insights that long preceded them (chapter 3). Third, we discover a reappropriation of the case for loving surrender as a real life choice; all of this opens the way for actual transformation, and loving surrender to God, as an event that cannot be produced by any text and yet is made intensely present in the words of their *Essence* and the *Treatise* (chapter 4). By going directly to the texts and these movements that infuse their reading and writing, I hope to draw my readers right into the middle of de Sales' and Deśika's creative worlds, mirroring in my text the dynamic of their writing, as we ourselves begin to face the prospect of loving surrender and all that follows from it.[46]

4. *"Loving Surrender" as the Key in This Double Reading*

Though the core of this book lies in the dynamic of a double reading of the *Essence* and the *Treatise,* I am also making this claim: "Loving surrender is the value and practice at the core of both texts." I have used the term "loving surrender" many times in the preceding pages, and the theme recurs everywhere in the chapters to follow. Thus a preliminary clarification is in order regarding the advantages and costs of the choice I have made to use this term, which is found explicitly in neither text, as a key to my reading of both.

"Surrender," if we can put aside connotations inevitably associated with military victories and defeats, can be taken to capture what is at stake in the Catholic Christian and Śrīvaiṣṇava Hindu ways of relation to God. As the *Oxford English Dictionary* puts it, to surrender is "to give up, resign, abandon, relinquish possession of, especially in favor of or for the sake of another," "to abandon oneself or devote oneself entirely to," and even, in an older usage, "to render, return (thanks)."[47]

Deśika speaks at length of the giving over of oneself to God: *prapatti* (approaching the Lord humbly), *śaraṇāgati* (taking refuge), *bharanyāsa* (laying down the burden of self-protection). By this act, a person reshapes her or his way of life, so that God and not self is at the center of her actions and of her plan for survival, flourishing, and liberation; and it is an approach and entrustment to the divine Nārāyaṇa—and to the Goddess Śrī—who are known to be loving, approachable, and eager to receive people in need. I have attempted to capture in English something of this commitment that is both radical and secure, by reference to a "surrender" that is "loving"—rooted in love, an enactment of loving trust. To say that surrender is "loving" rules out factors of violence, demeaning fear, or sheer compulsion, highlights the freedom and intelligence that are intrinsic to this surrender, and draws attention to the trust, recognition, and reciprocity that make self-abandonment possible. If we admit that loving surrender is a radical choice, then we also rule out the easier notion of a choice that would be merely one among many choices autonomous agents make. Rather, this is an irrevocable self-giving that cannot be taken back.

As for the comparable theme central to de Sales' *Treatise*, here too we find repeated and increasing mention of a dramatic transformation of life, a self-giving into the hands of God, a commendation and an abandonment. Since this self-giving is exemplified by the words of the dying Jesus on the cross—*Into Your hands I commend my spirit*—it is by no means to be imagined tame. Surrender is radical, transformative; it is all about permitting a revision of one's life in accord with God's often mysterious, sometimes terrible will. Yet as the title of de Sales' text suggests, all of this is about *love*, God's love and the drawing of human desire, pleasure, and love up into the divine fullness. Here too, then, it seems that "loving surrender" serves reasonably well as a key to the *Treatise*. As we read, however, it will be worthwhile to keep in mind the distinctive nuances of each text and its theme.

I find the term "loving surrender" and the values underlying it to be powerful and attractive. As will be increasingly clear in the following pages, I am committed primarily to a positive and sympathetic presentation of the ideal of loving surrender posed by both authors, such that we will be able to appropriate both texts and reflect on them with real understanding and empathy. Yet I admit the need for a critical eye in an era when religious extremism as a kind of sacred abandon is a great worry and when people may all too confidently speak of extreme choices as "the will of God." Our reading requires balance and patience: balance, because throughout we remain necessarily on the boundary between insider sympathies and more distanced questioning; patience, because more useful critiques are those posed by individuals understanding the complexities of positions regarding which they have doubts. De Sales and Deśika themselves are not far from such a balance; indeed, they write both to reinforce the deepest values passed down to them, and to correct, more or less gently, errors that have diminished loving surrender and its accompanying values. But if readers wish to take a much more critical approach than I, that too will help move our project forward.

III. Some Cautions as We Look Ahead

I close this chapter by highlighting five issues implicit in the preceding pages that condition the work of following chapters, its constraints, and the results likely to issue from it.

First, context is of course important, and it is noncontroversial to admit that one does well to research in detail the intellectual and literary, social, and religious factors defining the spaces in which authors such as Deśika and de Sales write. There is no value in imagining a stark choice between historical and social contextualization on the one hand, and close reading on the other. Yet the order and priority of one's interests remain a question. We cannot do everything at once, or in a reasonably sized book, and rightly have to make choices. The close reading of texts seems often deferred for the sake of the study of an external context, and on occasion actual close reading occurs only belatedly if at all. Moreover, reading together two texts from different traditions rarely occurs. It seems fair, then, to admit a distinctive emphasis in this book, with distinctive priorities. The recovery of the dynamic of loving surrender in an interreligious context requires that we remain close to the dynamics of our two texts as they are written and tell us of their worlds and that we discipline ourselves to think within the boundaries of this writing. It is not the traditions as social and historical phenomena, nor any given theme, nor comparative methodology, that is of primary concern, but rather the *Essence* and *Treatise* as texts that draw readers into a transformative process. And so I work from the inside out, as it were. But although I do not aim to contribute significantly to our understanding of the historical and cultural contexts of either author and his book, this does not mean that I have written only for specialist readers who already know those contexts and have read the relevant secondary literature. Rather, my goal is to draw us quickly into the middle of things, so as to begin learning the traditions and how those traditions might act upon us in these particular classic texts. From this specifically defined inner place, any number of acts of contextualization might be taken up later.

Second, that we may indeed find ourselves in the middle of things, I seek to compose an "intratextual" space comprising abundant quotations from both texts; I seek to position myself and my readers as incipient commentators dedicated to prolonged reflection on the *Essence* and the *Treatise* as we read them carefully. Though my own book cannot replace the texts about which I write, I do intend at every point to allow the *Essence* and the *Treatise* to intrude upon our reading. Myriad quotations, carefully chosen, break the flow of my writing and force upon the attentive reader a slower assimilation of the text. I seek to write in such a way that my words defer to theirs and make no sense without theirs. In this, I am simply imitating de Sales and Deśika, both of whom cite their sources liberally in hopes of drawing readers into the traditions from and for which they humbly wrote.

Third, I privilege the productive convergence of these texts—chosen in part for their affinity—and locate the primary meaning of my study in their interplay when read together and its ability to produce new challenges for their readers. Since, as I said earlier, I read and studied the *Essence* first and only thereafter found my way to the *Treatise* as an equally powerful text, I decided early on that the texts can be read together fruitfully, intensifying our theme of loving surrender. With this admitted bias, the present book cannot be enlisted as neutral scholarship demonstrating the similarity of religions. Another scholar might just as well choose two very different texts, to rather different effect, or might choose simply to read the *Essence* and *Treatise* against each other to accentuate differences. Some readers might notice more differences than I draw attention to, and that too can be a fruitful extension of the experiment undertaken here.

But distinctiveness does matter greatly with respect to styles and shared ways of producing an awareness conducive to choosing loving surrender. As we read the *Treatise* and the *Essence* attentively, we are flooded with the names, ideas, beliefs, images, texts, and practices of two independent traditions and have to shift gears continually, moving from Deśika's crisp analytic discourse to de Sales' more intuitive, expansive narrative, and from Deśika's clarification of our thinking to de Sales' igniting of our hearts. Though the texts do not clash in any single intellectual and emotional space by contrary claims that would stymie further reading, the texts do instruct and affect us distinctively, and we should become all the richer, unsettled and released, by the back-and-forth process of reading them together.

And yet as we read the *Essence* and the *Treatise* carefully, we will find that it is very difficult to read them together. These texts inscribe complete religious worlds and resonate with fuller traditions, Catholic and Śrīvaiṣṇava, that do not easily tolerate alternative religious conceptions of the world. The two texts occupy whole mental spaces and cannot suddenly be said to exist in some broader encompassing space. Reading one of these texts tends to shadow and marginalize the other, and for many readers through the centuries, just one of these texts is quite sufficient for a lifetime. If we are to read the texts together, our reading has to take on the characteristics of an agile dance, as the texts are made to defer to one another, each read for a moment before the other steps again into the foreground. What these powerful texts tell us of God and loving surrender lies, I suggest, partly in their resistance to each other, the interplay of their forces, intensified through the fact of the double reading. The entirety of this book may be taken as the cultivation of a kind of Derridean *différance* wherein we learn in the persistent, unsettled, and unsettling double reading to tease out the presences and absences our two texts impose upon each other and the quite possibly confused reader. In this context no reader should imagine herself or himself standing back so as to make neat comparisons of selected themes or methods; rather, we are exercised within, inside, the encounter of texts, pushed along (I would say) toward the ideals of loving surrender they promote.

Fourth, it is in light of the preceding points that the meaning of this book's title becomes evident. *Beyond Compare* does not seek to be a comparative study in the sense that one might systematically compare the theologies and spiritualities of de Sales and Deśika on such themes as the nature of God, grace, sin, and the practice of loving surrender so as to highlight commonalities and differences in what the authors have to say. The words "comparison" and "comparative" occur rarely in the pages to follow, and the reader is advised not to think of this as a comparative study with a stable objectified context; even "loving surrender" is less a topic for comparison than, as I have explained, a key that unlocks our reading. And so I will be saying less about comparative method than readers who might hope to pick up a few ideas on comparison and comparative reading. To draw once again on Deśika's terms, this book is less about systematic truths than about what is in practice beneficial (*hita*) toward the finality (*puruṣārtha*) of spiritual reflection. This project is "beyond comparison"; it is concerned rather with the further step occurring when a reader (who may also become a writer) takes the texts of two traditions to heart, reading them together with a vulnerability to their power and purpose precisely so as to be doubly open to the transformations their authors intended to instigate in readers. If, in this light, we discover a new situation, *after* and *beyond* the myriad comparisons that occur along the way, we might nonetheless have achieved some fruitful comparative insight; but such is not the primary purpose of this engagement in a double reading of loving surrender.[48]

Fifth, despite the fact that my bookish project may seem rather far removed from the more immediate arena of actual interreligious dialogue, I see it as making a particular contribution to interreligious understanding, precisely in its intensive focus on particular texts. For example, my approach resonates well with "Scriptural Reasoning," an established project of dialogue and close textual reading in which Jews, Christians, and Muslims read together selected passages from the scriptures of the three traditions for the sake of deeper mutual understanding.[49] Scriptural Reasoning seminars are convened regularly in various settings, including the American Academy of Religion Annual Meeting, and in local venues around the world. Most pertinent for our purposes is the project's self-conception with respect to the sharing of traditions, and the benefits and risks we incur in venturing to take seriously the scriptures of another tradition. In his foreword to a recent issue of *Modern Theology* dedicated to Scriptural Reasoning, C. C. Pecknold highlighted the key dynamic at stake in an interreligious reading:

> Scriptural reasoning is a risky practice. It resists dominant modes of neutral public reasoning. It embraces inherited, embodied traditions of faith and judgment, particularly those traditions generated by the story of Abraham's God. It is a practice that is local and provisional and yet risks a long-term commitment to patient dialogical contestations and conversations on a scriptural plane.[50]

These risks, potent enough in the Jewish-Christian-Muslim context, may be seen as further intensified in the relatively uncharted realm of Hindu-Christian relations, where the openings made possible by this new exchange are not constrained by a shared story of history and human destiny, and where, from a certain perspective, the theological differences seem greater than any that occur in the Jewish-Christian-Muslim exchange.

In the same issue of *Modern Theology*, Ben Quash highlights four pertinent characteristics of Scriptural Reasoning. *Particularity* is the insistence "that responsible thought only ever proves itself by the quality of attention it is able to pay to the concrete and particular, by the adequacy of its descriptions of the world around it, just as by the adequacy of its descriptions of texts."[51] *Provisionality* is a sense that conclusions are always open to revision, elusive with respect to definitive formulation, and woven into the larger ongoing drama of life in encounter with God. Of *sociality*, he writes: "[Scriptural Reasoning] is an activity of irreducibly particular gatherings of people. . . . The interrogative, argumentative and collaborative patterns of SR study depend on there being groups rather than solitary individuals at work in response to the scriptural texts on the table." And of *surprise*: "The interrogation of one's own scriptures by other voices can have the effect of making the all-too-familiar texts of one's tradition 'strange' once again" as we thus become able to return to our own tradition with a fresh sense of possibilities. These four elements that are validated in the ongoing experience of Scriptural Reasoning are, I suggest, also operative in the differently configured dialogue that occurs when the *Essence* and the *Treatise* are read together. For our project too is highly *particular*, limited to a reading of these two texts; it is *provisional* in the sense that it is an exercise that can be repeated, extended, improved, and tested in other unanticipated circumstances with other texts; it is *social*, at least in the sense that the voices of two traditions must be heard throughout our study, neither generalized according to the expectations of the other; and it is likely to be *surprising*, since there is no already settled framework in which its meaning can be adjudicated or the outcome predicted.

Quash admits a value that arises in the conflict of texts discovered by participants in the Scriptural Reasoning seminars:

> Part of what stimulates the energetic labor of SR are the tensions that arise (or the gaps that open up) between the texts being studied. The texts—especially when read in each others' company—present difficulties of interpretation. But . . . SR tends to see the *inter*-scriptural challenges of reading across Jewish, Christian and Muslim traditions as signs of the generosity of our scriptural texts, and not simply as regrettable problems. . . . Debate over the texts creates a community of argument and collaborative reasoning. The texts are together *creative* of a community of discussants. And this may be a more desirable, flexible and time-sensitive "product" of the texts than any body of doctrine would be. The participants in SR are not asked to come to agreements that can always be summarized in propositional terms. They are not first and foremost concerned with agreement on "doctrines." High quality argument may in the end be a better "product" of SR . . . than any agreed statement would be, and a more desirable thing to transmit to those who enter the tradition which this practice generates.[52]

A similar tension is operative as the *Essence* and *Treatise* are read together, and the entirety of *Beyond Compare* is written along the fault line where the two great texts suddenly share a proximity that is difficult to decipher insofar as neither text is to be allowed to dominate the other, neither tradition's mode of reading is to be given absolute priority, and no higher academic perspective is to be permitted to decide what counts in the reading. As the reading deepens, the tension grows, especially when members of the other tradition reinterpret and reread for us the scriptures of our own tradition—and when, as in our reading of Deśika and de Sales, a growing understanding of and affinity for the "other" text changes our own relationship to a more familiar text of our own tradition, and thus begins to create a new community among those willing to engage in this reading.

Although Scriptural Reasoning is in harmony with the intentions of this book, three differences are noteworthy, even apart from differences in tradition and style already mentioned. First, as I have already suggested, my book offers primarily an interior dialogue constituted by my reading of Catholic and Hindu texts together. In a sense, the *sociality* of my project is minimal; I have been primarily reading books, and I have not been reading them with members of the Śrīvaiṣṇava tradition. However, I have been learning from the Hindu commentarial tradition and from Śrīvaiṣṇava friends over several decades, and several of them have generously read the manuscript of this book. De Sales and Deśika too write as members of long traditions; they can teach because they have listened to numerous older voices. In reading their works as works of tradition, we begin to engage, respectfully, the communities so deeply interwoven with such classics, and we become (at first unexpected) members of both communities, even as long-term guests.

Second, in my interior dialogue as reader (learning with Deśika and de Sales) and as writer (hoping for my own readers), my intention is not ultimately to read Hindu scriptures through Christian eyes nor to listen to Hindus speak of their scriptural and interpretive traditions. Rather, as a Christian reader and writer, I have read conscientiously and taken to heart a spiritual classic of a Hindu tradition and remained attentive to its ideas, affective states, and its decisive movement toward loving surrender. So too, my reading of the *Treatise* as a deeply Christian text is, I hope, irredeemably informed by the insights, strategies, affects, intentions, and practices of the *Essence*. In my project, boundaries are ideally blurred, references doubled, lineages interwoven. *Beyond comparison*, in a respectful sense this book is also *beyond dialogue* as ordinarily understood, since there are no longer settled groups of interlocutors, religiously identified, who come and constitute the expected sides of the dialogue.

Third, the *Treatise* and the *Essence* are not scripture, even if both are honored in their traditions as powerful classics deeply rooted in scripture. I, a theologian, read two theologians who are constructing in good faith what they hope to be effective renderings of the most important and transformative religious insights, utterances, practices, and experiences of their traditions. By attending to theological writings and not to foundational scriptures, I highlight more consciously what happens when we study religious intellectuals like ourselves, who stand at some distance from scriptural sources while yet making choices about how to use and extend scripture and inscribe its potent meanings in their own reflection. This book therefore complements, I suggest, the text-based conversations carried on under the rubric of Scriptural Reasoning. For this is another kind of dialogue that shares and contributes to the same long-term goals.

But now let us get into the project of actually reading our texts together, exploring the kind of reasoning that is appropriate, the manner of writing and reading that ensues, and the possible intensification of the goal that is loving surrender.

Chapter 2

Thinking, Writing, Reading

Finding a Path to Loving Surrender

> The book which de Sales composed about divine love is a masterpiece admired by those capable of judging it; but it is certain that in order to know its value, one must necessarily be very devout and very learned; these are two qualities rare enough when separate, and still more rare when conjoined.
>
> Claude Favre de Vaugelas

> We are at the feet of the White Horse who is our Teacher; what was written inside us we then put on a palm leaf: So what are we in all this?
>
> Desíka, *Essence*

I. The Problem of Reason in Interpreting Religious Truths

The *Essence* and the *Treatise* deal with mysteries central to the Śrīvaiṣṇava and Catholic faiths, respectively. Both are classics of spiritual theology, erudite discourses that skillfully place the call to loving surrender before receptive readers, and in a way that provides new images and more intense affective states to the reader. In this way, the texts make at least imaginable a real transformation of life in the act of loving surrender. They are written to engage and win over those among the faithful who choose to read with attention and piety and who are open to spiritual transformation. All of this is presented in works that are elegantly written and well reasoned—and yet de Sales and Deśika remain deeply ambivalent about reason's role in religious matters and about the value of human words in speaking of the mysteries of God; accordingly, they are ambivalent about their own texts as well.

This chapter and the next one explore how Deśika and de Sales balance potential and limitation in their projects. Because they are wise enough to know that they must employ theory, argument, and logic even for their practical and spiritual purposes, Deśika and de Sales launch no broad attacks on reason. Rather, they commit themselves to a diagnosis of reason's ailments, flaws that are evident in the reasoning and speech of those who lack proper formation in accord with tradition, instead thinking, questioning, and determining values on their own. De Sales and Deśika consider arguments produced by a logic that is not deferential to tradition's wisdom harmful because they are clumsy, inadequate to the subtlety of tradition, and prone to lead people away from valid religious ideals. In their view, reason becomes "mere reason" only when stripped of its integrative (de Sales) and illusion-banishing (Deśika) roles, of its dynamism toward vision (Deśika) and love (de Sales). They have faith in reason that has not been so diminished and believe that it can play a moderate role in their project; as authors, they also trust the properly disciplined written word with respect to the larger spiritual goal of loving surrender. When reasoning is properly disciplined, it sheds a bright light on the human condition and discloses the incongruities of our ways of living; this clarity prompts a new assessment of those unreflective lives, now shown to be untenable in light of how we should live, in accord with who we are and who God is.[1] Similarly, words rooted in tradition work to this constructive purpose as well. All of this constitutes the subject matter of this chapter.

Chapter 3 explores the positive side of the matter: the value and power of texts such as the *Essence* and the *Treatise*. As a corrective to ordinary thinking and speaking, Deśika and de Sales recommend that religious people become deeply imbued with the language and images of scripture, its images and emotions, and imposing and inspiring examples of people who have lived concretely the ideals which scripture announces. Accordingly, Deśika and de Sales intend their texts to be resources wherein spiritual matters are not merely talked about but are made present and available for the reader's participation.

But in this chapter, the negative side is primary: We will see their sober analyses of the limitations even of their own reasoning and words, and how these resources are reconstituted to serve a spiritual purpose in writings such as their own treatises. First, we look at reason, its limits, and the remedy of proper contextualization. Second, we examine de Sales' and Deśika's understanding of the nature and role of conversion as a radical change of life rooted in a critical reevaluation of possible ways of living; here, reason plays a limited but crucial role. Third, we can then identify de Sales' and Deśika's understanding of themselves as writers, as they assess their role in the larger plan intended by God. Fourth, I extend these reflections to a consideration of the duties of the attentive reader, in light of the categories of philosophy as religious reading and spiritual exercise.

1. *Reason's Limits and Potential in the* Treatise

The *Treatise* is not a work of systematic theology, and de Sales presupposes with reverence the truth of the teachings of the Roman Catholic Church; indicative of his reverence for ecclesial tradition and authority are his dozen appeals to the authority of the Council of Trent. Although he focuses on the spiritual effects of correct thinking on how Christians live, de Sales is resolute in providing an adequate intellectual grounding for his effort to inflame the hearts of his readers, and so he devotes the first four books of the *Treatise* to such foundations:

1. A preparation for the whole *Treatise*
2. The history of the generation and heavenly birth of divine love
3. Of the progress and perfection of love
4. Of the decay and ruin of charity

Though hardly abstract, these first books are expository, providing context for all that follows, a framework wherein love and its practical dynamism toward God can be properly understood. But in his preface, even de Sales hesitates regarding the efficacy of this theorizing and, more practically, regarding the likely reception of the four books:

> Some perhaps will think that I have said too much, and that it was not requisite to go so deep down into the roots of the subject, but I am of the opinion that heavenly love is a plant like that which we call Angelica, whose root is no less odoriferous and wholesome than the stalk and the branches. The first four books and some chapters of the rest might without doubt have been omitted, without disadvantage to such souls as only seek the practice of holy love, yet all of it will be profitable unto them if they behold it with a devout eye: while others also might have

> been disappointed not to have had the whole of what belongs to the treatise of heavenly love.[2]

The problem is not simply the reader's tolerance level but, more deeply, the inability of human words to express adequately the great mystery that is God. At the beginning of book 2, de Sales reflects on the nature of God and the correlative limits of human comprehension. He first reflects on the brilliance and steadiness of the sun, the light of which we can endure only in lesser intensities and in reflected, less intense forms. Similarly, he says, what we can know and say about God is limited and partial:

> In like manner we discourse on God, *not so much according to what he is in himself,* as according to his works, by means of which we contemplate him; for according to our various considerations we name him variously, even as though he had a great multitude of different excellences and perfections.[3]

For example, appreciating some single aspect of the divine perfection, we may then wish to call God just, merciful, or wise, even if God is perfectly possessed of all such perfections, all the time, and in the simple wholeness of his being:

> He is himself one most single, most simple and most entirely unique perfection: for all that is in him is but himself, and all the excellences which we say are in him in so great a diversity are really there in a most simple and pure unity.[4]

Our words, implicated in the plurality of things that constitute our world, always fall short, particularly when we would speak of a supreme unity we cannot know and express:

> Now to assign a perfect name to this supreme excellence, which in its most singular unity comprehends, yea surmounts, all excellence, is not within the reach of the creature, whether human or angelic; for as is said in Revelation: *Our Lord has a name which no man knows but himself* [Rev. 19:12] because as he only perfectly knows his own infinite perfection he also alone can express it by an adequate name.[5]

This truth about God and the limits of human language should chasten humans who venture to speak authoritatively about God:

> *Whence the ancients have said that no one but God is a true theologian,* as none but he can reach the full knowledge of the infinite greatness of the divine perfection, nor, consequently, represent it in words.[6]

Of necessity, we multiply words to catch something of the divine perfection:

> We are forced, then, *in order to speak in some way of God,* to use a great number of names, saying that he is good, wise, omnipotent, true, just, holy, infinite, immortal, invisible—and certainly we speak truly. God is all this together, because he is more than all this, that is to say, he is all this in so pure, so excellent and so *exalted a way,* that in a most simple perfection he contains the virtue, vigor and excellence of all perfection.[7]

But even these words are misleading:

> Nevertheless wretched creatures that we are, we talk of God's actions as though daily done in great number and variety, though we know the contrary. But our foolishness, Theotimus, forces us to this, for our speech can but follow our understanding, and our understanding follows how things ordinarily occur among us.[8]

How we speak of God tells us more about ourselves and our needs than about what God is like:

> When we behold so many different works, such great variety of productions, and the innumerable multitude of the effects of the divine power, it seems to us at first that this diversity is caused by as many acts as we see different effects, and we speak of them in the same way, *in order to speak more at our ease,* according to our ordinary practice and our customary way of understanding things.[9]

Writing about God is therefore a deeply problematic activity, and the more so for those who see the greatness of their topic and feel the inadequacy of their words. It is essential, in de Sales' eyes, that every writer and reader remember the fragile nature of such human words about God, even when still using words to speak of God and to aid people in their search for God: as we succeed, we still keep failing.

Much of book 2, however, is devoted to determining how it can still be useful to speak of God in imperfect human terms—speaking, for example, of a divine will that motivates and guides divine actions, or imagining God to be choosing now and again to work in the world for the sake of humans. Such language is imperfect, but not entirely misleading, since we can speak of the divine will insofar as it is manifest in the love that energizes and directs human life:

> Although God willed to create both angels and humans with free will, free with a true freedom to choose evil or good still, to show that on the part of the divine goodness they were dedicated to good and to glory, he also created them all in original justice, which is nothing but a most sweet love, which disposed, turned and set them on the way towards eternal felicity.[10]

This loving providence is not only the unchanging and universal disposition of God toward the world; it is also effective with respect to each person.

> Although our Savior's redemption is applied to us in as many different manners as there are souls, nevertheless love is the universal means of salvation which mingles with everything, and without which nothing is salutary.[11]

For God actively searches for each soul:

> But he is not content with announcing thus publicly his extreme desire to be loved, so that everyone may have a share in his sweet summons; he goes even from door to door, knocking and protesting that, *if anyone opens to me the door* [Rev. 3:20], he will come in to him, and will sup with him: that is, he will give him proof of all kinds of good will towards him.[12]

In this way de Sales shows himself to be satisfied neither with an uncritical confidence in words about God nor with a dysfunctional fear of language as necessarily a failure. Because God is determined to interact with the human race in ways that humans can comprehend, and so has created a "history of love," we can also speak of God and God's action by words that can successfully affect how we think of and relate to God.

De Sales proceeds then to describe the soul's innate movement toward this God who is always reaching out to humans. He proposes a nuanced understanding of human knowing and affective recognition, as rooted in a recognition of the complexity of the human soul. Introducing love in book 1, de Sales differentiates and organizes kinds of reasoning and various sources of knowledge:

> We have but one soul, an indivisible one; in that one soul there are various degrees of perfection, for it is *living, sentient* and *reasonable*; and according to these different degrees it has also different properties and inclinations by which it is moved to the avoidance or to the acceptance of things.[13]

The soul knows in accord with inclination and appetite and by gradations of a reasoned and volitional apprehension of the good:

1. Now this [first, instinctive] inclination does not proceed from any knowledge that the one has of the hurtfulness of its contrary, or of the advantage of the one with which it has affinity, but only from a *certain hidden and secret character* that produces this insensible opposition and antipathy, or this deep pleasure and sympathy.
2. Second, we have in us the sensitive appetite, whereby we are moved to seek and avoid many things by the sensitive knowledge we have of them. . . . In this appetite resides, or from it proceeds, the love that we call sensual or brutish but which properly speaking ought not to be termed love but simply appetite.
3. Third, inasmuch as we are reasonable, we have a will by which we are led to seek the good, according as by discursive reasoning we know or judge it to be such.[14]

With reference to this third way of knowing, de Sales further distinguishes in the rational soul two dimensions, the inferior and the superior, and consequently two modes of knowing:

> That is called *inferior* which reasons and draws conclusions according to what it learns and experiences by the senses. That is called *superior*, which reasons and draws conclusions according

> to an intellectual knowledge not grounded upon the experience of sense, but on the discernment and judgment of the spirit. This superior part is called the spirit and mental part of the soul, as the inferior is termed commonly sense, feeling, and human reason.[15]

Furthermore, these ways of reasoning typify kinds of people with lesser or greater inner capacity—either "according to natural light, as the philosophers and all those who have reasoned by empirical knowledge did," or "according to supernatural light, as do theologians and Christians, [who] establish their reasoning upon faith and the revealed word of God."[16] Although in both cases the person can be said to exercise reason, her or his thinking is distinguished by context, resources, and finality. By implication, of course, de Sales himself is ready to engage readers in accord with natural possibilities, while yet also helping them to rise to the higher, spiritual perspective.

De Sales uses the image of Solomon's great temple to picture more vividly the constitution of the soul and its orientation toward the higher mysteries:

> There were three courts in Solomon's temple. One was for the Gentiles and strangers who, wishing to have recourse to God, came to worship in Jerusalem; the second for the Israelites, men and women (since the separation of men from women was not made by Solomon); the third for the priests and the order of Levites; and finally, besides all this, there was the sanctuary or sacred house, which was *open only to the high priest, and that but once a year.*[17]

Analogously, "our reason, or, to speak better, our soul in so far as it is reasonable, is the true temple of the great God," and contains three courtyards marking three modes of reasoning:

> In the first we reason according to the experience of sense, in the second according to human learning, in the third according to faith.[18]

De Sales does not explain thoroughly how these three kinds of reasoning cohere in a single person; his purpose, more practical, is to help his readers to recognize how they reason, to have a better sense of possible kinds of knowing and, ideally, to ascend gradually through the three modes of knowing. But there is a further complication, for all this is a backdrop for a still deeper and more potent knowing beyond all three degrees of reason:

> This is a certain eminence or supreme point of the reason and the spiritual faculty, which is not guided by the light of discursive thought or reason, but by a simple intuition of the intellect and a simple movement of the will, by which the spirit acquiesces in and submits to the truth and will of God.[19]

Here reason defers to and embraces an intimacy it cannot account for by its own light:

> In this degree of the soul there is no discursive reasoning which sheds light. . . . Nothing enters but by faith, which produces, like rays, the sight and the sentiment of the beauty and bounty of the good pleasure of God. . . . *In this apex of the soul discursive reasoning enters not,* but *only the high, universal and sovereign feeling* that the divine will ought sovereignly to be loved, approved and embraced, not only in some particular things but in general for all things, nor only generally in all things, but also particularly in each thing.[20]

No longer insisting on a reasoned comprehension of its own destiny, the soul willingly submits to the great divine mystery in an experience that is best envisioned as a kind of tactile, sensate knowing:

> Vision in the supreme part of the soul is in some sort obscured and veiled by the renunciations and resignations which the soul makes, not desiring so much to behold and see the beauty of the truth and the truth of the goodness presented to her, [but rather] to embrace and adore the same, so that the soul would almost wish to shut her eyes as soon as she begins to see the dignity of God's will, to the end that not occupying herself further in considering it, she may more powerfully and perfectly accept it, and by an absolute deep pleasure unite herself to it without limit, and submit herself thereto.[21]

Though dependent and beyond itself in this higher and pleasing apprehension of God, reason does not fail entirely, since God teaches the soul in an intimate, even pleasurable communication:

> When God gives us faith he enters into our soul and speaks to our spirit, not by manner of discursive reason, but by way of inspiration, proposing in so sweet a manner unto the understanding that which ought to be believed, that the will receives there from a great and deep pleasure, so great indeed that it moves the understanding to consent and yield to truth without any doubt or distrust. Herein lies the marvel: God proposes the mysteries of faith to our souls amidst obscurities and darkness, in such a way that we do not see the truths but we only get a glimpse of them.[22]

In this awakening and pleasure, the soul grasps a fullness of truth well beyond its ordinary capacity and objects:

> And yet, when this obscure light of faith has entered our spirit, not by force of reasoned discourse or by show of argument, but solely by the sweetness of its presence, it makes the understanding believe and obey it with so much authority that the certitude it gives us of the truth surpasses all other certitudes in this world, and keeps the understanding and all its workings in such subjection that they have no credit in comparison with it.[23]

The next paragraph connects the languages of faith, love, and knowledge, and highlights the state of the self as ignorant yet wise, lost in shadow yet all the surer of itself:

> Faith is the chief beloved of our understanding, and may justly speak to human ways of knowing which boast that they are more evident and clear than she, as did the sacred spouse to the other shepherdesses. *I am black but beautiful*—O human reasonings, O acquired knowledge! *I am black*, for I am amidst the obscurities of simple revelation, which have no apparent evidence, and which make me look black, putting me well-nigh out of knowledge: yet *I am beautiful* in myself by reason of my infinite certainty; and if mortal eyes could behold me such as I am by nature they would find me all fair.[24]

The mind and heart must endure this quandary, lost and yet deeply connected at the same time. If we understand the dilemma we face before

God, we can in fact still find words appropriate to this situation—failed, imperfect, yet still effective—and move forward a process that can be completed only beyond our words, in faith:

> Pious discursive reasoning and arguments, the miracles and other advantages of the Christian religion, make it extremely credible and knowable, but faith alone makes it believed and acknowledged, enamoring men with the beauty of its truth, and making them believe the truth of its beauty, by means of the sweetness faith pours into the will, and the certitude it gives to their understanding.[25]

For both the author and the reader, heart leads, and the mind gropes for what it does not know. This situation is pleasurable, yet still a search into mystery, an abandonment and a fulfillment:

> For so our heart, by a deep and secret instinct, in all its actions tends towards, and aims at, felicity, seeking it here and there, as it were groping, without knowing where it resides, or in what it consists, till faith shows and describes the infinite marvels thereof. But then, having found the treasure it sought for—ah, what a satisfaction to this poor human heart! What joy, what deep pleasure of love! *O I have met with him, whom my heart sought for without knowing him!* [Song of Songs 3:5] O how little I knew whither my aims tended, when nothing contented me of all I aimed at, because, in fact, I knew not what I was aiming at.[26]

Later on, in book 6 of the *Treatise*, de Sales asks a rhetorical question that both undercuts the status of honored intellectual scholarship and commends a humble spiritual wisdom:

> Which of the two, I pray you, loved God more, the theologian Occam, held by some to be the most subtle of mortals, or St. Catherine of Genoa, an unlearned woman? He knew God better by knowledge, she by experience; and her experience conducted her deep into seraphic love, while he with his knowledge remained far remote from this excellent perfection.[27]

A scene in the same chapter dramatizes the simple faith before which erudition must defer:

> The Blessed Brother Giles, one of the first companions of St. Francis, said one day to St. Bonaventure: "O how happy you learned men are, for you understand many things whereby you praise God, but what can we unlearned people do?" And St. Bonaventure replied: "The grace to be able to love God is sufficient." "Nay, but Father," replied Brother Giles, "can an ignorant man love God as well as a learned?" "Yes," said St. Bonaventure, "and further, a poor simple woman may love God as much as a doctor of theology." Then Brother Giles cried out in fervor: "O poor simple woman, love thy Savior, and thou shall be as great as Brother Bonaventure." And upon this he remained for the space of three hours in a rapture.[28]

Like many a spiritual writer before and after him, de Sales almost necessarily honors simple faith, for which great learning by itself is no match. And like those of the other notables among such writers, his words render a paradox, for the person writing them was neither unlearned nor simple. To compose a work such as the *Treatise*, great erudition, skill, and passion must converge in the author, that she or he might produce effective words in search of readers who can rise to their possibilities.

Also in book 6 but more schematically, de Sales distinguishes a theology *about* God from a theology in encounter *with* God:

> The speculative treats of God with men and amongst men, the mystical speaks of God with God, and in God himself. The speculative tends to the knowledge of God, and the mystical to the love of God; that, therefore, makes its scholars wise, and learned, and theologians, but this makes its scholars fervent, and affectionate, lovers of God, a Philotheus or a Theophilus.[29]

It is to this mystical theology that de Sales himself aspires, with the goal of composing a text that reaches into the deeper recesses of readers' hearts, because its power arises from hearts already inspired by the Holy Spirit:

> O God! what a difference there is between *the language of the ancient lovers of the Divinity*—Ignatius, Cyprian, Chrysostom, Augustine, Hilary, Ephrem, Gregory, Bernard—and that of less loving theologians! We use their very words, but with them the words were full of fire and of the sweetness of amorous perfumes; with us they are cold and have no scent at all.[30]

De Sales surely hopes his *Treatise* will be similarly ablaze, in the sense that it is mystical and not speculative theology. Reason (though frail) and words (though inadequate) can, under the right conditions, be very effective.[31]

a. De Sales on Pagan and Christian Learning

We can understand more fully de Sales' attitude toward deficient and integral reasoning by noting his judgment on persons who fail to use their intellectual gifts in full honesty and openness before God. Early in the *Treatise*, he is highly critical of reasoning that lacks humility and refuses to subordinate itself to the divine will as manifest in the community. Because this selective and stubborn individuality lacks the benefit of learning within tradition, he is not impressed with people who are greatly learned but sporadic or self-contradictory in living out the consequences of their learning:

> Sin has much more weakened man's will than darkened his intellect. The rebellion of the sensual appetite, which we call concupiscence, does indeed disturb the understanding, but still it is against the will that it principally stirs up sedition and revolt: so that the poor will, already quite infirm, being shaken with the continual assaults which concupiscence delivers against it, cannot make so great progress in divine love as reason and natural inclination suggest to it that it should do.[32]

De Sales is willing to praise the Greek wisdom that stands for the best of "non-Christian" learning:

> Alas! Theotimus, what fine testimonies not only of a great knowledge of God, but also of a strong inclination towards him, have been left by those great philosophers, Socrates, Plato, Trismegistus, Aristotle, Hippocrates, Seneca, Epictetus![33]

But after singling out Socrates for special praise, as one who knew of the unity of God and was inclined to love God, de Sales laments all the more how exemplary Greeks such as him cut short the trajectory of their knowledge and denied the better instincts of their own hearts, which he attributes to an excessive regard for the opinions of others:

> But, O eternal God! those great spirits who had so much knowledge of the divine unity and so great propensity to love it were all wanting in force and courage to love it well. By visible creatures *they have known the invisible things of God*, yea *even his eternal power also and divinity*, says the Apostle, *so that they are inexcusable. Because that, when they knew God, they have not glorified him as God, or given thanks* [Rom. 1:20–21]. They glorified him indeed in some way, attributing to him sovereign titles of honor, yet they did not glorify him as they ought to glorify him, that is, they did not glorify him above all things. Not having the courage to destroy idolatry, but communicating with idolaters, *detaining the truth which they knew in injustice, prisoner in their hearts*, and preferring the honor and vain repose of their lives before the honor due unto God, *they grew vain in their reasoning* [Rom. 1:21].[34]

De Sales especially laments Socrates' unwillingness, at the time of his death, to stay true to his belief in one God. He complains similarly about Hermes Trismegistus and Epictetus, who knew better than to continue dabbling in polytheism but lacked the courage to draw the right conclusions and *act* differently. Their learning lacked the discipline of good living, and so they failed to live as they knew they should.

Much later, in book 9, de Sales contrasts pagan tenets with Christian doctrine by three principles that clearly mark it as comprising a whole way of life superior to the best that pagans can offer:

> The Stoics, especially good Epictetus, placed all their philosophy in abstaining and sustaining, bearing and forbearing; in abstaining from and forbearing earthly delights, pleasures and honors; in sustaining and bearing wrongs, labors and trials. But Christian doctrine, which is the only true philosophy, has three principles upon which it grounds its exercise: abnegation of self, which is far more than to abstain from pleasures, carrying the cross, which is far more than tolerating it, and following Our Lord, not only in renouncing our self and bearing our cross, but also in the practice of all sorts of good works.[35]

Rooted in these three principles is a Christian reasoning that is integral to a whole way of life, coherent with an honest person's moral and spiritual being; only when deprived of the discipline of integral learning within tradition does reason become infatuated with sense knowledge and worldly concerns, and hence unreliable as a guide to life.

For de Sales, then, proper reasoning has to do with much more than simply the logic of an argument or the deduction of proper conclusions from available evidence. It marks, rather, the way of thinking and proper living that is rooted in love, itself in a deep relationship to God. Reasoning then is a profoundly religious and even Christian activity, and a coherent, forcefully written religious essay or treatise will be a soundly reasoned document, helping to express for the writer and create for the reader the wholeness of a world in which religious values are lived properly and ultimately for the sake of loving surrender to God.

2. *Reason's Limits and Potential in the* Essence

Let us now draw Deśika into our discussion, noting how he understands the limitations and religious potential of reasoning. He too is unwilling to place full confidence in reason, his clear commitment to logic and argumentation notwithstanding. Like the *Treatise*, the *Essence* theorizes about God and self for pragmatic reasons, to enhance Deśika's spiritual agenda. He confirms that the finality of proper reasoning lies in its clarification of life's values and disorders and in that clarification's ability to open people up to changing their lives. Here too, thinking at its best is valued in relation to the larger project of spiritual transformation; at its worst, reason can be a destructive power that in its curiosity and questioning leads both thinker and audience astray.[36]

Deśika too lays a conceptual foundation at the beginning of his book, before moving to the affective and performative concerns that are of more urgent concern to him. In chapters 3–6, he presents key tenets of Śrīvaiṣṇava faith and philosophy as starting points that are simply to be taken as true: knowledge of world, self, and God, and the necessities and problems incumbent upon the human relationship to God, points made in older syntheses that are now collected in a single account:

> *Essence,* chapter 3, "The Distinctive Doctrine of Śrīvaiṣṇavism," refers to the soul-body relationship, etc., between the Lord and sentient beings and non-sentient things. . . . Everything exists as an inseparable specification of the Lord's proper being, and so their existence, etc., depend on the existence of Him on whom they depend. . . .[37] The state of belonging entirely to Him is common [to conscious and nonconscious beings], and so we need

> to meditate carefully on what distinguishes us in our free choice to act as servants of the Lord.[38]

The next two chapters offer two traditional ways of summarizing Śrīvaiṣṇava doctrine and practice. His chapter 4 describes the means and goal of the spiritual journey and the obstacles to be encountered on the path:[39]

> *Essence* chapter 4, "The Five Things to Be Known," describes God, self [as essentially free yet also deeply flawed], the means to liberation, the fruit that is liberation, and obstacles; the spiritual life is about overcoming obstacles to clarity of vision of and restoring union with the Lord whom one serves.

The Tamil and Sanskrit verses ending this chapter aptly exemplify the force inherent in a liberating and transformative knowledge of the divine persons:

> The whole enduring truth—
> the Lord of the lotus-born Maiden,
> the self who joins with His feet and loves only that one grace,
> the means by which to gain them
> and the result too, plus
> deeds and ignorance together—it is all so clear:
> those who know these five have made their truth clear,
> that my mind might suffer no more in darkness.[40]

Through learning that opens into worship, one regains what was lost—one's own self:

> I am ready to attain that which is to be attained, Brahman,
> the One to whom everything belongs entirely, the Highest;
> this is like inheriting a father's wealth,
> by nature I am meant for this, like the celestial beings—
> but alas, due to the notion of "I" and the wrong thinking rooted there,
> I lost Him—
> but now I have been taught that
> surrendering my burden to the Couple to whom all belongs
> is the way forward.[41]

Chapter 5, "The Three Realities," draws on another standard Śrīvaiṣṇava reckoning of the fundamental truths, this time stressing their cognitive rather than performative dimensions:

> Reality is composed of three essential realities: the Lord, sentient beings, and nonsentient beings; the latter two are dependent, ordered to the Lord; Deśika comments that such knowledge is important because "we must first put an end to the confusion of self with material nature and the confused view that the self is independent, and so too the underlying attraction to the position that there is no Lord."[42]

Chapter 6, "The Supreme Reality of the Deity," makes clear that the Lord to whom one is to surrender is Nārāyaṇa with Śrī, and no one else; only with this knowledge can one advance toward liberation.

In these early chapters, to which analogues can be found elsewhere in Deśika's writing, he makes clear that what is to follow in the *Essence* presumes proper doctrine: knowledge that is precise and compelling and also, when understood properly, potent in transforming the life of the person who thinks honestly. Knowledge about God, world, and self matters because it sets in place rules governing the practice of the divine-human relationship. Conversely, ignorance and misunderstanding skew one's relationship to self, world, and God, respectively by egoism, materialism, and conceptions of God as too much like us or too transcendent and distant.

Despite his clarity and his insistence on getting the basic truths right, Deśika too is suspicious of reason. He finds its questions and analyses to be unreliable guides to the spiritual life; those who live by reason very often go astray. Even in the *Essence*, which is focused on progress in the spiritual life, Deśika thinks it important to correct errors and criticize harmful thinking. As the Sanskrit verse at the end of *Essence*'s chapter 5 suggests, the undisciplined mind produces and transmits noxious teachings, whereas those who have patiently learned to see reality clearly banish illusions about life from their thinking. Ending the mirage that is ordinary life is like the sudden clarity of perception by which we dispel the illusion that a distant tree stump is instead the silhouette of a man:

> By unnecessary connections and divisions,
> by endless claims about this or that object

—"it exists" and "it does not exist"—
like the myriad images of a poet's mind,
out of control, people produce semblances of reasoning:
but the person who perceives reality has no equal,
capable all at once of dispelling all of those images, entirely;
when the Person is really seen,
no longer is there a tree stump to be seen.[43]

Similarly, argumentation is varied and unreliable, unable by itself to cure reason of its harmful ideas.

Verses in other chapters too warn of the dangers of logic and the contrasting value of humble learning from the wise. Contemplation of Nārāyaṇa with Śrī is the surer remedy recommended by our wise "forest-teachers," who propound the wisdom of the ancient Upanishads, texts associated with the asceticism of life in the forest.

> Lest debaters disturb the Veda by the usual haughty logic,
> lest good people be thoroughly upset
> when people teach this or that god as the first one,
> our forest-teachers propound our Ancient One
> who abides with His lovely Śrī, abiding in the lotus.[44]

Useless and harmful reasoning progresses easily, whereas correct reasoning is hard—so hard that for most people, a simple adherence to the Tiru Mantra ("the Eight" syllables) and the Dvaya Mantra ("the Two")[45] is the best option:

> If all this learning does not suffice and you desire still more,
> this world's eighteen burdensome arts are all around you,
> but all these are just details;
> and so it was the Eight and the Two—
> which the unsleeping immortals praise—
> that the teachers of our tradition gave us to learn,
> our unique, wise foundation.[46]

Humbly receiving the truths passed down from Rāmānuja ("king of ascetics") puts an end to a fruitless succession of arguments:

> If in this last age someone very wise
> should learn this unique doctrine taught by the king of ascetics,

the dawn dispelling the darkness of ignorance,
then right there, right then
the tumultuous waves of chattering arguments—
the caprice of those establishing this or that view—
subside, all at once.[47]

This "unique doctrine" is the distinctive Śrīvaiṣṇava insistence that the self is totally dependent on God, as if in a soul-body relationship. The arguments are quelled not by the teacher's fiat, says Deśika, but rather by the teaching itself, which is so clear that ignorance, and the quarrels that arise from it, dissipate naturally, like night before the rising sun.

The most concentrated critique of undisciplined and rootless reasoning occurs in chapter 23. Here, in a prelude to reiterating his own views on important but disputed doctrinal and practical positions, Deśika declares that reasoning on its own is inadequate to the most important truths. Three things, he says, soften the Lord's just determination to punish sinners: the prayer that leads to the taking of refuge, the grace of a wise and spiritual teacher, and participation in proper tradition. Erroneous thinking comprises wrong views about the identity of Nārāyaṇa and Śrī; for the weak, association with any person arguing wrong views is a danger, since these members of the believing community may be led astray.

Necessary truths have to be learned in a spiritual environment from teachers who combine virtue and learning and who are able, through the dynamics of their personal relationship with the student, to guide her or him by teachings formulated and communicated in ways that are directly useful. For most people, simple and straightforward instruction suffices, even if a few may find it "appropriate to inquire with proper arguments, for their own clear understanding and to bring clarity to those deluded by specious arguments."[48] But the dangers remain real, since there will always be people who have not learned to think in a religiously disciplined way:

> Such people do not understand clearly and by proper reasoning the meaning [of authoritative texts]. As it says,
>
> > Whosoever understands the seers' teaching of dharma
> > with the help of reasoning
> > not contrary to the Vedas and instructive scriptures[49]—
> > only that person understands dharma, no one else. [*Manu* 12.106][50]

> Mere reasoners, who have recourse to arguments inconsistent with the Vedas, strip away its authentic meanings. As it says,
>
> > The threefold dharma is fragmented by the Kāṇādas, the Buddhists, and the schismatics [*Atri Smṛti*].[51]

It seems that for Deśika, obviously "alien" communities are seen as a threat to Śrīvaiṣṇavas, but he is also wary about Śrīvaiṣṇavas who fail to live up to the standards he deems proper. Hence chapters 23–26 are given over to the meticulous correction of wrong or inadequate interpretation of matters debated inside the community. Believers who go astray are inevitably those who look to their own reasoning instead of authentic teachers who put the many words and ideas of scripture in a proper and salutary perspective.[52] For even the learned can go astray, when so many texts claim authority:

> Truly, the great seers have declared,
> Were there only one instructive scripture,
> knowledge could be free from doubt.
> But because there are many such scriptures in the world,
> the essential truth of knowledge is exceedingly difficult to obtain, [*Itihāsa Samuccaya* 33.99]
>
> and,
>
> Hari ever dwells in all those who are free from doubt, but
> Mādhava does not abide with those who doubt because of their reasoning. [Mahābhārata, *Śānti Parva* 359.71][53]

Even within the more learned circles of Śrīvaiṣṇavas and with respect to central issues such as the status of the goddess Śrī, only those whose knowledge has been properly inculcated can grasp "with their hearts" the technicalities of the tradition.[54] Without heart, it seems, people may gather many ideas, yet without acquiring wholeness and coherence.[55] By contrast, a properly disciplined mind accepts what is taught, regarding both the cognitive and performative dimensions of the tradition: "We have already stated that authoritative texts should not be set aside by mere reasoning."[56]

The concluding Sanskrit verse in *Essence* chapter 23 captures Deśika's sentiments about people who should know better but miss the obvious because they look for answers outside the tradition rather than deeper within it:

> Those who day and night keep looking outside
> may in fact be sleeping over a treasure,

> but even now they still do not see it
> since they lack the tradition of our teachers;
> they miss it even if, as is stated clearly in the revelatory texts,
> that treasure is itself the means for gaining itself,
> and is most near to those established in the truth.[57]

Here Deśika highlights rather than resolves the key paradox. People miss central and evident truths when they lack guides who can help them understand it coherently. This is so even if the treasure in question—truths such as the reality of Nārāyaṇa with Śrī as the way and goal of salvation—are available in revelation and should be obvious to believers in the first place. But people, even good people, may simply be looking in the wrong direction.

Similarly, at the beginning of chapter 28 Deśika cautions his readers not to scrutinize too deeply the meaning of the Dvaya Mantra, a holy mantra that exemplifies the deeper, most precious religious truth. True knowledge is gained humbly, and we must receive the truth and power of the mantra—known from scripture and tradition—without undue scrutiny or evocation of an extrinsic standard of plausibility. Even a well-meaning effort to rationalize the mantra bears no fruit:

> The inner power of even a single utterance [of the mantra] is easily grasped by the authoritative force of revelatory texts, etc. The cause of the mantra's power can be understood from confirmatory texts and from our tradition. One ought not to seek out reasons behind the meanings of the most sacred mysteries. That we must accept authoritative texts and have faith is stated in texts such as *Mahābhārata*, for example
>
> > Reasoning is of no use
> > regarding divine things and other hidden things, O Goddess—
> > a person desiring what is beneficial should act like the deaf
> > and blind. [*Mahābhārata, Ānuśāsana Parva* 206.60][58]

While this stark claim is to be read in the general context of Deśika's consistent, strong commitment to reason and learning, it is nonetheless striking that yet again he is advising readers to accept the most sacred truths simply on faith. The paradox—deaf, blind faith urged by the most erudite of authors—is a paradox we should keep in mind throughout, particularly as we find our way deeper into the learned simplicity of his *Essence*.

a. The Ascent of the Mind and Heart to God

Even if we grant that for Deśika independent, undisciplined reason is an unreliable ally for those on the path to liberation, we can still profitably ask where properly disciplined reason leads us. To illumine this positive purpose, Deśika evokes the rich narrative on knowledge familiar from the time of Rāmānuja and the subsequent era of great commentaries on Śaṭakōpaṉ's *Tiruvāymoḻi* taken as charting the saint's spiritual ascent.[59] In chapter 9, Deśika uses two sets of terms—the yogas of action, knowledge, and devotion (*karma yoga, jñāna yoga, bhakti yoga*), and the more intense and efficacious course of higher devotion, higher knowledge, and supreme devotion (*para bhakti, para jñāna, parama bhakti*)[60]—to trace the ascent to God and the interruptions one must allow for human frailty and divine grace.

Deśika envisions a religious practice and learning appropriate to the cognitive and affective potential of the human person as a being oriented to God yet incapable of attaining and seeing God under present conditions. Though in the end he will always emphasize the sheer gift of a knowledge that is infused by grace and not the result of religious, even meditative, practice, Deśika finds it important to trace the better way of higher devotion, higher knowledge, and supreme devotion against the background of the perfectly sound—but too indirect and difficult—way of the three yogas. So let us consider these two triads in turn.

The yoga of action consists of pious, unselfish acts, both ritual and in ordinary life. It is conducive to liberation, it discloses the clear light by which the self can be seen:

> Taking refuge becomes the means of attaining liberation either through devotion or directly, depending on differences among competent persons. In the same way, the yoga of action, with the help of yogic practice and its subsidiary parts, and either through the yoga of knowledge or directly, becomes the means to a vision of self.[61]

The yoga of knowledge extends the apprehension of self that was initiated in the yoga of action into a continuing contemplative act:

> For a person who has mastered the inner organs of knowledge by the yoga of action, then the yoga of knowledge is constant and uninterrupted reflection on the proper form of self which is a

> mode of the Lord who is entirely different from matter and the like. This self is related to Him as His body, is dependent on Him, is ruled by Him, and belongs entirely to Him.[62]

Those who persevere in the yoga of action and the yoga of knowledge are no longer distracted by world or self, and accordingly ascend to a clear vision of and deeper union with God:

> If a vision of self occurs by yoga, that is, by the yoga of action and the yoga of knowledge, and if the yogi is not entangled in that pleasure of self-experience that causes distaste for all sense-pleasures, he next becomes immersed in the practice of the yoga of devotion, the means to the supreme goal, experience of the Lord.

This person sees first the human self in its true form and then peers through the self toward the Lord who dwells within:

> The person competent for the yoga of devotion first engages in seeing the individual self who is the Lord's body—just as one sees the pouch before seeing the gem inside it—and thereafter becomes competent for the wisdom that is vision of the inner controller.[63]

This yoga of devotion is in turn extended in an ongoing meditation that has as its object the Lord's proper form, and is experienced as an unsurpassable pleasure; it is "in the form of a continuous stream of knowledge, an uninterrupted remembering like oil streaming down continuously, a clarity tantamount to direct manifestation, a special continuity in knowing that is practiced every day," even until death.[64]

Although the three yogas taken together form a complete and ascending spiritual path that in theory is quite attractive and well attested in scripture and tradition, Deśika treats this path as a very difficult option that is honored more as theory than as a real option. It is ultimately only background to a still higher way, generated out of a still more intense interplay of knowing and loving, desire and deferred realization, such as leaves the seeker in a state of desperation:

> *Higher devotion* produces an eager desire to see the Lord directly, making the person cry out,

> Lord of yoga, show me Your imperishable self! [Bhagavad Gītā 11.4]
>
> and
>
> Graciously grant that I may see You! [*Tiruvāymoḻi* 8.1.1]
>
> and
>
> May I see You one day! [*Tiruvāymoḻi* 6.9.4]
>
> By this desire alone comes the specific grace of the Lord who rewards this person with full and direct manifestation within a specified time. This manifestation is *higher knowledge*. Thus is born an abundant and unsurpassed pleasure, like that of a man, suffering from great thirst, who sees a tank of water. This abundant pleasure is *the supreme devotion*.[65]

When the person seeking God realizes that there is no reasonable way actually to reach God, no matter how skilled one might be in the three yogas, the alternative is the realization accessible only to the person who, like Śaṭakōpaṉ, so desperately desires God that all established means are set aside:

> Śaṭakōpaṉ is unable to endure except by way of an unrestricted experience; as it says in his verse,
>
> Silent sage, Four-faced Brahmā, Three-eyed Śiva,
> You are a flawless jewel, Your lips like fruit, Your eyes like lotuses,
> my thief, full self for me who have no other—
> You have come upon my head,
> and now I will not let You go:
> so do nothing to surprise me." [*Tiruvāymoḻi* 10.10.1][66]
>
> In his desire he cries out "with an oath that cannot be ignored . . ." [*Tiruvāymoḻi* 10.10.2] and so arouses in the Lord an overabundant eagerness to give Śaṭakōpaṉ immediate liberation, enabling him to attain liberation, finally quenching his great desire.[67]

Like de Sales, Deśika maps the spiritual world and the path of spiritual progress very clearly; for him too, human knowing, acting, and feeling are all affirmed, yet subordinated to faith and the still more intense demands of the spiritual ascent. Indeed, as soon as the path to God is explained as a series of steps to be taken, the truly helpless and desperate person sees that she or he cannot travel steps that might be quantified as higher devotion, higher knowledge, and supreme devotion. A path that is reasonable and in accord with human nature has a truth and legitimacy to it, but fulfillment is elsewhere, dependent rather on an elusive vision only God can give. It is therefore necessary, in a text such as the *Essence*, to explain clearly the nature and practice of authentically human spiritual advancement—and then to allow for an entirely different conclusion, by grace, a way that reasoning cannot explain or predict.[68]

II. Conversion: Reason and the Leap Beyond

How reasoning still matters even with respect to larger spiritual realities beyond reason's grasp becomes clearer if we attend to how de Sales and Deśika understand "conversion," by which I mean the event of spiritual awakening and self-appropriation in which a person comes to see that her life must be lived very differently if what she believes is true. In this moment, reason, affect, and the deepest religious insights intersect intensely, all for the sake of transforming the entirety of a person's life.[69] In conversion, a person comes to see and appropriate the truth about self, world, and God, grows dissatisfied with the incongruity between these truths and ordinary ways of living, and then (slowly and quietly or dramatically and all at once) devises a radically different relationship to world, self, and God. Beginning simply with honest reasoning and examining the world closely, we begin living a life in a way that leads toward deeper commitment to God.[70]

1. *Deśika on Conversion*

Deśika discusses conversion most clearly in *Essence*'s chapter 7, which marks the fruition of the preceding expository chapters. It is by design a transitional chapter, a pivot between the expository discourses of chapters 3–6 and the intense psychological inquiries that occupy chapters 8–12 on the wherewithal and practice of loving surrender.[71] At this point, correct knowledge becomes useful knowledge as the awakening person begins to see that loving surrender to God is the most advisable path to proper living. As Deśika explores the change in attitude required if one is to become free of this world and one with the Lord, the chapter links reflection on human nature and the human condition with attention to the scriptural view of self and world, meditation on the truths of the holy mantras of the tradition, and reflection conducive to spiritual goals.

The opening verse of chapter 7 highlights how proper knowledge operates to make the status quo unbearable:

> The rotations of time, prime matter and its modifications,
> faults arising from the pleasures of desire,
> sufferings resulting from sin, experienced like the burning pit,
> the established order of self and other as they really are,
> the divine place, this body as a prison—
> who can know all this and still tolerate such bondage?[72]

Clear-minded reflection on time, matter, desire, and the human condition reveals the unreflective life to be a kind of bondage. People who learn this from the instructive scriptures become able to see the deeper, true self:

> They see how the self has a self-illumined proper nature, how it is a knower, doer, enjoyer, and possessed of a body, how it is atomic in size, eternal, without parts, not liable to cutting, burning, or suffering, how it is devoid of increase or decrease, etc., and thus how it is different from the body, senses, etc., which specify that self.[73]

The self is "atomic" in the sense that it has a material aspect (as all beings must) but only the most minimal (that is, atomic) spatial extension. By contrast, God is "pervasive" (*vibhu*) of all reality. Instructive scriptures make it possible to know self as it really is, and this instigates a program of change, a growing illumination and rectification of desire, purified of attachment to lesser goods:

> Thus determining that it is worthwhile to gain a different body and ascend to His higher world, they become suited for those universal human goals that extend beyond this world. They become afraid of the pains of further births, such as falling again into hell, etc., and so they cease from the actions that cause such woes. They also determine that the self is distinguished as needing a foundation, as subject to injunction, existing entirely for the sake of another, paltry in power, atomic in size, suited to ignorance, doubt, reversals, sorrow, etc. It is therefore the very abode of all that is inauspicious, and different from the Lord whom such selves specify.

This proper knowledge, acutely refined, makes possible a deeper, wiser desire that becomes a way of life:

> People who know all this become ready to desire the glory pertaining to the self's own proper form; this takes the form of service to the Lord.[74]

Deśika cannot forgo citing a sarcastic comment on those who fail to seize this opportunity to see and change:

> Ignoring this fruit, people become objects of ridicule:
> When the tail of a dog does not cover his loins or chase flies and stinging insects, it is useless—
> and just like this is learning bereft of righteousness.[75]

In sharp contrast, those who truly make knowledge their own are the ones who profit from it:

> Quite different are those who hasten to employ the means to the highest human goal, means appropriate to their own selves and in accord with what is heard in scripture. As it says,
> In keeping with their age, deeds, and purposes,
> as something learned and something innate,
> let people in this world bring harmony to their appearance, word, and action [*Laws of Manu* 4.18].[76]

Religious action leading to liberation is the expected, correct consequence of proper understanding; anything less is needless disappointment. The reader who attends closely to what she or he reads and takes it to heart will feel increasingly awkward in the world, such that a change of life becomes almost necessary.

I close this consideration of Deśika's sense of conversion with a passage from early in the *Essence* indicating that human transformation is ultimately an act of God. In chapter 1 Deśika tells the basic and familiar tale of a person who loses his place and identity but unexpectedly recovers both. A king's son is lost in the jungle and, without knowledge of his true identity, is raised by hunters in a lifestyle very different from that of the palace. Finally relatives discover the boy, bring him home, and teach him who he is and how he should act as the heir to the throne. Deśika's simple point is that we are like that: On our own, we likewise lose our way, forget who we are, and need to be rescued. And so teachers are sent to instruct the individual self lost in this world:

> Teachers reveal the innate relation existing between this individual and Nārāyaṇa, the Lord of Śrī, who with His scepter
> rules without the least exception the entire earth
> surrounded by the turbulent ocean and the world of Heaven
> too.[77]

Such teachers are deeply loving and skilled in employing words that fulfill their compassionate intent:

> They try earnestly to help the person who is trying out the means for attaining this Lord. They find his attainment of the glory of liberation to be as delightful as ruling the golden world and the whole earth. Loving him as a cow tenderly gives milk to her calf right from the day of its birth, they teach him succinct and flawless verses, removing from the self its ignorance, doubts, and mistaken ideas.[78]

That the teaching of the *Essence* replicates their teaching is shown by a summary that could just as well summarize key elements of Deśika's text:

> They teach this person the proper form, way of being, and relationship of the Lord to the things ruled by the Lord, pleasure and heavenly attainment, what is to be rejected and what is to be taken up, the means to each of these, their paths and modes, and the expressed and unexpressed obstacles that obstruct liberation. These are the things that must be known by a person seeking liberation.[79]

Deśika concludes *Essence* 1 with two verses highlighting the great liberation that is to take place. In Tamil, he praises the same learned teachers who make this potent wisdom available to us in our dire straits, showing us the way to Nārāyaṇa (Tirumāl) and Śrī (Tiru):

> Along with Tiru
> a lustrous gem[80] came to abide near the heart of Tirumāl, and
> like that, we manage to touch His lotus feet;
> lest we disappear into that flood of deeds
> started even in the womb,

> the learned ones, knowing the five subtle truths,
> make this knowledge all we need.[81]

In the Sanskrit verse, Deśika emphasizes how the person saved then becomes able to transmit the tradition:

> On the rotating wheel of deeds, ignorance, and such things,
> by the varied, beginningless flow specific to each individual,
> the time comes for every kind of fruit,
> and so all schools agree:
> but at just the right moment someone is grasped by the First Teacher's compassion
> and becomes wise, a repository of riches right up to sovereignty and liberation.[82]

Such persons are saved, and in them tradition flourishes. The trick, then, in Deśika's calculus, is to help ordinary people think and react to their situation in such a way that they come to see it very differently and begin to avail themselves of possibilities they had not previously envisioned. It is the work of the teacher—and writer—to help bring about this new situation.

2. De Sales on Conversion

Ever the pragmatist, de Sales is concerned primarily with the practical implications of the philosophical, psychological, and theological distinctions he makes along the way, particularly early on in the *Treatise.* In his study of de Sales, Liuima emphasizes that de Sales writes precisely to guide readers spiritually: to help them understand, be free with respect to, and change the pattern of their spiritual lives. Though well versed in tradition and in sophisticated theological arguments, and respectful of right thinking, de Sales is most interested in the spiritual transformation of his reader. He is more a director of souls, less an expositor of doctrine.

Change is possible if people can understand and gain freedom with respect to their own experience. This is why, according to Liuima, de Sales writes from his own experience, that he might unfold and deepen the experience of his readers:

> The reason for his success is that he does not speak of things he had not himself tested. No mere theory, not a single abstract word; everything comes from his heart, from his own experience,

> and everywhere he always reaches down to the roots. His whole life is summed up in the *Treatise on the Love of God*. This work is the history of his own soul.[83]

His writing is grounded in his primary reflection on his own life's movements:

> He does not write during ecstasies of the understanding or will, but in the ecstasy of his life; that is, every action of grace expresses itself first by its works, penetrating his own living of truths, and then suggesting to him reflections, the search for explanations, systems, and formulas.[84]

De Sales himself to some extent confirms Liuima's viewpoint. Though without direct reference to himself, he praises experience as a manner of knowing that is more potent than intellectual discourse:

> In your opinion, Theotimus, who would love the light more—the one born blind, who might know all the discourses that philosophers make about it and the praises they give it, or the ploughman, who by a clear sight feels and realizes the agreeable splendor of the fair rising sun? The first has more knowledge of it, but the second more fruition, and that fruition produces a love far more lively and affective than a simple knowledge by discursive reasoning; for the experience of good makes it infinitely more agreeable than everything we might know about it.

This experience, an intimate knowing, opens into great desire, love:

> We begin to love by the knowledge which faith gives us of God's goodness, which afterwards we relish and taste by love; love whets our taste and our taste refines our love. Just as we see the waves, under the stress of winds, roll against one another and swell up, as if in envy meeting one another, so the taste of good strengthens our love of it, and love increases our taste for it, as divine Wisdom says: *They that eat me, shall yet hunger: and they that drink me shall yet thirst* [Wisdom 24:29].[85]

And yet the way forward is not clear because self-knowledge is not easy, and people do not know where to begin changing their lives. Because we have the greatest difficulty knowing ourselves, we also have great trouble in ordering our lives to God:

> God alone is he, who, by his infinite wisdom, sees, knows and penetrates all the turnings and windings of our hearts: he understands our thoughts from afar, he finds out our paths, evasions, and detours; his knowledge therein is admirable, surpassing our capacity and reach. Even if our spirits could turn back upon themselves by reflection and by reconsideration of their acts, we should enter into labyrinths from which we should find no exit; and it would require an attention quite beyond our power, to think what our thoughts are, to consider our considerations, to observe all our spiritual observations, to discern that we discern, to remember that we remember: these acts would be mazes from which we could not deliver ourselves.

Even the learning that is possible is so demanding that without guidance we are likely to get lost:

> [In this learning] so many different interior movements take place that to express them all is impossible, not only by reason of their number, but also for their nature and quality, which being spiritual, they cannot but be very rarefied, and almost imperceptible to our understanding. . . . We oftentimes lose the sight and knowledge of our own hearts in the infinite diversity of motions by which it turns itself, in so many ways and with such promptitude, that one cannot discern its wanderings.[86]

Because the soul is a mysterious reality wherein we easily get lost, a guide is almost essential; thoughts and words by themselves are unlikely to change us.

So how does a human author write, or plan to write, this mystical theology? According to Ravier,[87] de Sales avoids grand words about the divine nature—recall above his cautions on reason that strives for abstract clarity—and instead seeks to root his work on love in human experience. For this reason he prefers *amour* to *charité*, since the latter word might be interpreted as cordoning off "love of God" from other kinds of love and desire.[88] Rather, it is in the intricacies of human love that the mystery of divine love can first be discerned. Love in its manifold possibilities ranges from the material and multiple all the way to an intensely focused love of God, in God, who is the God of the human heart:

> As soon as man thinks with even a little attention of the divinity, he feels a certain delightful emotion of the heart, which testifies that God is God of the human heart; and our understanding is never so filled with pleasure as in this thought of the divinity, the smallest knowledge of which, as says the prince of philosophers, is worth more than the greatest knowledge of other things; as the least beam of the sun is more luminous than the greatest of the moon or stars, yea is more luminous than the moon and stars together. And if some accident terrifies our heart, it immediately has recourse to the Divinity, protesting thereby that when all other things fail him, It alone is good to him, and that when he is in peril, It alone, as his sovereign good, can save and secure him.[89]

Thus divine love is not to be separated from human love: "[De Sales] will try—and in our opinion he will succeed—in showing how love of God engages the human heart in the adventure of lived faith."[90] The *Treatise* is also about traveling this path of love; it is practical, designed "to guide the devout soul"—through itself—"toward the perfection and plenitude of devotion."[91]

All of this occurs in the particular, concrete details of the lives of writer and reader. In his preface, de Sales quite aptly describes his project as *une histoire*: not a theoretical treatise on love, but a detailed record of what happens in "the history of the birth, progress, decay, operations, properties, advantages and excellences of divine love." Accordingly, his aim is to illumine what has happened and is now happening in the heart of his reader:

> Truly my intention is only to represent simply and naïvely, without art, still more without false colors, the history of the birth, progress, decay, operations, properties, advantages and excellences of divine love.

Conversion begins in a careful and attentive reading of the self and its movements toward and away from God; as such, it is a highly intelligent process, yet more than that too. To write with an eye toward enabling readers to change their lives at the deepest level is to see the work of discernment as a fruit of the learning process. Such writing is necessarily and fundamentally reflective, both the author and ideal reader "turning with" through their work with and in the text.

To understand more specifically how conversion "works" and what a text like the *Treatise* might have to do with it, it is helpful to bring in the parallel notion of *repentance,* a practice that is both reasonable and affective, a natural operation and a sheer product of grace. According to de Sales, "repentance" marks the reflective process in which a person begins to recognize, honestly and with regret, that she or he has sinned and violated God's will, and then, in honesty, ventures to rectify what went wrong. How this comes about may vary. We may simply realize that we have offended God by breaking the commandments and wish to stop acting this way. We may be dismayed at the punishments before us or the prospect of losing the joys of heaven. Or we may see and become appalled at "the ugliness and malice of sin, according to what faith teaches us," so that we finally see how we have lost our dignity and are deserving of great punishment. Such moral and religious insights are intensified when we ponder, even in reflective reading, the disparity between our rather dreary lives and the beauty of lives instilled with virtue:

> We are provoked to repentance by the beauty of virtue, which brings as much good with it as sin causes evil; further we are often moved to it by the example of the saints. For who could ever have cast his eyes upon the exercises of the incomparable penitence of Magdalen, of Mary of Egypt, or of the penitents of the monastery called "Prison," described by St. John Climacus, without being moved to repentance for his sins? *The reading alone* of this history arouses those who are not entirely insensible.[92]

But de Sales quickly adds that even this richly textured process of honest reflection on one's life can be fruitful because God intervenes in the innermost life of the penitent, in a potent chemistry of love and tears:

> Theotimus, amongst the tribulations and remorse of a lively repentance God often puts in the bottom of our heart the sacred fire of his love, and this love is converted into the water of tears; and those, by a second change are converted into another and greater fire of love. Thus the famous penitent lover [Magdalen] first loved her Savior; her love was converted into tears, and

> those tears into an excellent love; whence Our Savior told her that *many sins were pardoned her because she had loved much* [Luke 7:47].[93]

Careful attention to one's personal plight is preparatory to the deeper, transformative experience of repentance. When sin is exposed and God moves intimately within the attentive soul, love becomes nearly irresistible, like fire, like a torrent of tears. As the sun gradually warms a mirror to a power "so strong that it begins to burn before it has yet well produced the fire, or at least before we have perceived it," so too the Holy Spirit sets us on fire, casting

> into our understanding the consideration of the greatness of our sins, in that by them we have offended so sovereign a goodness, and our will receiving the reflection of this knowledge, repentance little by little grows so strong, with a certain affective heat and desire to return to God's grace, that finally this movement comes to such a height, that it burns and unites even before the love be fully formed, though love, as a sacred fire, is always at once lighted, at this point.[94]

In the end, this newly kindled desire for a return, for repentance, amounts to something far greater than a modest resolve to behave well, as it becomes a conflagration wherein God consumes the whole person. As a result:

> Repentance never comes to this height of burning and reuniting the heart to God, which is her utmost perfection, without finding herself wholly converted into fire and flame of love, the end of the one serving as the beginning of the other; or rather, the end of penitence is within the commencement of love. . . . The beginning of perfect love not only follows the end of penitence but even cleaves and ties itself to it; and to say all in one word, this beginning of love mingles itself with the end of penitence, and in this moment of mingling, penitence and contrition merit life everlasting.

One survives this new love by repeating prayers expressive of repentance, and in turn these intensify the experience of repentance. Reasonable reflection makes vulnerability to divine action more likely; self-scrutiny is neither sufficient nor dispensable in the process of change. We must act with an awareness of God acting upon us.

A passage from book 2 captures the drama of conversion that God instigates deep in the penitent's heart:

> And truly we should well deserve to remain abandoned of God, when with this disloyalty we have thus abandoned him. But his eternal charity does not often permit his justice to use this chastisement; rather, exciting his compassion, it provokes him to reclaim us from our misery. This he does by sending us the favorable wind of his most holy inspirations, which, blowing upon our hearts with a gentle violence, seizes and moves them, raising our thoughts, and moving our affections into the air of divine love.
>
> Now this first stirring or motion which God causes in our hearts to incite them to their own good, is effected indeed in us but not by us; for it comes unexpectedly, before we have either thought of it or been able to think of it, *seeing we are not sufficient to think anything towards our salvation of ourselves as of ourselves, but our sufficiency is from God* [2 Cor. 3:5], who did not only love us before we were, but also to the end we might be, *and might be saints* [Eph. 1:4]. For this reason he comes to us first with the *blessings of his* fatherly *sweetness* [Ps. 20:4], and excites our souls, in order to bring them to holy repentance and conversion.[95]

Although all of this reaches beyond the capacity of reason, we nonetheless benefit from clarity about the human condition and an attentive awareness of the small, nearly imperceptible workings of God within the human heart, and a reasoned recognition of how then we are to respond and change our lives. Once reason finds its particular place, it also finds its importance as an intelligent spiritual force that aids us in seeking to understand and change how we live.

At the very end of the *Treatise*, de Sales couples intense devotion to the suffering Christ with a hope that his writing will guide readers to a most radical choice, for Christ Crucified:

> Love and death are so mingled in the Passion of Our Savior that we cannot have the one in our heart without the other. Upon

> Calvary one cannot have life without love, nor love without the death of Our Redeemer. But except for there, all is either eternal death or eternal love: and all Christian wisdom consists in choosing rightly; and *to assist you in that, I have made this treatise, my Theotimus;*
>
> It is necessary to choose, O mortal,
> in this mortal life,
> either love eternal,
> or death eternal;
> the ordained plan of our great God
> leaves no middle ground.[96]

Written somewhere between love and death, the *Treatise* provides a place where the reader can travel in letting go of the erroneous notion that there is a safe middle ground, and on that basis finally make an honest choice about how to live before God.

III. The Self-Understanding and Intentions of Deśika and de Sales as Writers

We have thus far traced the limits and possibilities of reason in the *Essence* and the *Treatise*, and saw that even if reasoning is ineffective when not guided and disciplined by tradition, nevertheless the processes of careful analysis, learning, and critical judgment all matter greatly: Radical change of life is possible, and its instigation has a substantive intellectual component. In this light, we can now ask still more deliberately: If reasoning and words bear the power and suffer the limits Deśika and de Sales think them to have with respect to the transformation of life, then how do they assess their own writing—the *Treatise* and the *Essence*—as contributory to the desired conversion of life for the reader who will ostensibly surrender to God? What kind of writing do Deśika and de Sales ambition, with what authority and to what effect?[97]

1. *Why de Sales Writes, and with What Authority*

The *Treatise* uses words that aim to reach beyond what words can easily communicate. It is a work about love and of love, written for the sake of Christians already serious about progress into greater intimacy with God. Like Deśika, de Sales is reticent about his own authority and why his writing should have a role in spiritual transformation, but it is possible to tease out his sense of himself and his writing in God's larger plan.

In the dedicatory prayer that begins the *Treatise*, de Sales consecrates his composition to Mary and Joseph, elaborating his hope for what he writes: that a divine fire might enkindle both his heart and his readers' hearts such that his words might summon a power beyond their own in effect.

> Of old the lamps of the ancient temple were placed upon golden lilies [1 Kings 7:49]. O Mary and Joseph, couple without peer! Sacred lilies of incomparable beauty, among which *the well-beloved feeds himself* [Song of Songs 6:2] and feeds all his lovers! Ah! if I may give myself any hope that this *love-writing*[98] may *enlighten and inflame* the children of light [Luke 16:8], where can I better lay it than amongst your lilies? Therein did the Sun of Justice, *the splendor and brightness of the eternal light* [Wisdom 7:25–26], so sovereignly re-create himself that there he fulfilled the delights of the ineffable love of his heart towards us? Ah! I conjure you by the heart of your sweet Jesus, King of hearts, whom your hearts adore: *animate my heart, and all hearts that shall read this writing*, by your all powerful favor with the Holy Ghost, that henceforth we may offer up in holocaust all our affections to his divine goodness, to live, die, and live again for ever, *amid the flames of this heavenly fire*, which Our Lord your son has so much desired to *kindle* in our hearts, that he never ceased to labor and sigh for this *until death, even the death of the cross* [Phil. 2:8].[99]

Also it is instructive that his preface begins with reference to the work of the Holy Spirit, who inspires all fruitful speech and action in the church:

> The Holy Ghost teaches that the lips of the heavenly Spouse, that is The Church, resemble *scarlet* and the *dropping honeycomb* [Song of Songs 4:3, 11], to let every one know that all the doctrine which she announces consists in sacred love; of a more resplendent red than scarlet on account of the blood of the spouse whose love inflames her, sweeter than honey on account of the sweetness of the beloved who crowns her *with delights* [Song of Songs 8:5]. So this heavenly spouse when he thought good to begin the promul-

gation of his law, cast down upon the assembly of those disciples whom he had deputed for this work a shower of fiery tongues, sufficiently intimating thereby that the preaching of the gospel was wholly designed for the inflaming of hearts.[100]

Just as nature is varied, the Church is rich in all manner of ways of manifesting the divine wisdom:

> The Church is indeed adorned with an excellent variety of teachings, sermons, treatises and spiritual books, all very beautiful and pleasant to the sight by reason of the admirable mingling which the Sun of Justice makes of his divine wisdom with the tongues of his pastors, which are their feathers, and with their pens, which sometimes hold the place of tongues, and form the rich plumage of this mystic dove. But amongst all the diverse colors of the doctrine which she displays, the fine gold of holy love is everywhere spread, and makes itself excellently visible, gilding all the knowledge of the saints with its incomparable lustre, and raising it above every other kind of knowledge. All is love's, and in love, for love, and of love, in the holy Church.[101]

To claim that the *Treatise* too is a fruit of the Church's teaching tradition, this is not simply to assert that it is a text with ecclesial approval; it is to say that it is a work of the Holy Spirit communicating love through the manifold resources that constitute the church.

Given the pervasive presence and power of the Holy Spirit in Christian teaching and writing, it is striking that de Sales rather soberly narrows his audience in recognition of the demanding nature of his writing and his great hope for *some* readers:

> This *Treatise* then is made for a soul which is already devout, that she may be able to advance in her design. Hence I have been forced to say many things somewhat unknown to most people, and which will therefore appear rather obscure. The depths of knowledge are always somewhat hard to sound, and there are few diverse who care and are able to descend and gather the pearls and other precious stones which are in the womb of the ocean. But if you have the courage fairly to penetrate my writing, it will truly be with you as with the diverse, "who," says Pliny, "see clearly in the

> deepest caves of the sea the light of the sun." For you will find in the hardest parts of this discourse a good and fair light.[102]

Thus people already initiated into the spiritual life and committed to its practice form the audience for this *Treatise*. "My purpose here is to speak to souls that are advanced in devotion."[103] A comment by Claude Favre de Vaugelas, the grammarian and literary scholar, during de Sales' canonization inquiries aptly captures the intensity and selectivity generated by the *Treatise*:

> The book which he [de Sales] composed about divine love . . . is a major work admired by those capable of judging it; but it is certain that the price for knowing it well is necessarily to be very devout and very learned; these are two qualities rare enough when separate, and still more rare when conjoined.[104]

And yet de Sales does not dwell on scholastic complications, as he might were he content with readers who are merely learned; rather, the direct communication he practiced in preaching undergirds his writing as well, enabling him to find words likely to nourish those receiving his word:

> I have touched on a number of theological questions, proposing simply, not so much what I previously learned in disputations, as what attention to the service of souls and my twenty-four years spent in holy preaching have made me think most conducive to the glory of the Gospel and of the Church.[105]

Part of our task is to understand how one is to write in a way that "speaks to advanced souls" while yet also transforming theological subtleties into a living word that nourishes rather than perplexes the reader.[106]

Given his experience in preaching and spiritual direction, de Sales the author would not despair of communicating a potent vision of a way of life entirely geared to divine love. Skeptical of the reach of his own words, he was also convinced that the Holy Spirit could indeed choose to work through writers like him for the sake of a transformation that could never actually be produced by words such as his.

2. *Why Deśika Writes, and with What Authority*

Deśika does not promote himself as an independent thinker who succeeds by reliance on his own reasoning or even his own grasp of scripture. The ideal teacher is never original, an initiator of tradition. He is always a student who gratefully passes on what he has received from his own teachers. This true teacher is one who has already been set free—rescued from the jungle, as it were—because he received from earlier guides the instructive wisdom he needed.

Deśika is not expansive about his personal goals in composing the *Essence*, but we can glimpse his intentions in some verses from the beginning and end of the *Essence*. The prefatory *Lineage* begins with three declarative verses that highlight the importance of having a teacher. The opening verse sets the tone:

> We make obeisance to our teachers and their teachers too;
> in the very beginning, we invoke the Couple that rules the worlds.[107]

To honor the teachers is not a separate practice, something apart from honoring the divine couple, because teachers human and divine share a single teaching mission. Writing a work such as the *Essence* is an activity to be understood in that same context, as words and ideas received from past generations.[108] Consequently, one must be mindful of the lineage, in all learning activities, whether one is studying, teaching, or writing:

> These points have been made so as to indicate that those desirous of liberation should meditate on the line of teachers, right up to the supreme Lord.[109]

Deśika goes on to elaborate these claims, naming many of his illustrious predecessors, and by a longer theological reflection showing the Lord himself to be the guarantor of the proper transmission of tradition in every generation.[110] Although Deśika may seem fresh and original to readers today, he would doubtless have preferred to be thought of as a faithful servant who passed along what he had received. Passing along ancient tradition in a fresh voice is of course easier said than done, and we shall notice several of Deśika's successful writing practices in chapter 3.

The conclusion of the *Lineage* reemphasizes obligation to one's teacher and responsibility to care for the mantra received from the teacher:

> It follows that in all circumstances a person should glorify his teacher by overflowing devotion for that teacher. It is also settled that the mantra should be watched over, not revealed merely for

> financial considerations to fickle persons lacking the complete set of qualities prescribed for a disciple. In this way, its great value, like that of a ruby casket containing precious jewels, will not be disturbed, nor one's own firm establishment in the mantra.[111]

Deśika concludes with a reaffirmation of right practice:

> It is stipulated then with injunctive force that whenever a person meditates on these mysteries, he should meditate on the lineage of teachers as well.[112]

As we noted in chapter 1, the *Essence* is in a sense a prolonged meditation on the three mantras, and so the writing of it must be rooted in remembrance and deference to tradition. Consequently, reading it should ideally begin and end in that same grateful recollection of the ancient sources of the text's wisdom.

At the end of the *Essence*, in chapters 30 (on the teacher) and 31 (on the disciple), Deśika returns to the theme of the transmission of knowledge and reflects on the duties of learned Śrīvaiṣṇavas to receive the tradition, cherish it, and share it wisely with the next generation. If the bulk of the *Essence* is about the content of the teaching, its multiple dimensions and their integral interconnection, these final instructive chapters emphasize again the need for exact, faithful transmission to ensure the efficacy of what is taught and written. Thus, at the end of chapter 30, he speaks of the teachers' power to illumine our darkened world:

> That the world might end its ignorance,
> for the sake of joy in heaven,
> that we might adorn our heads with the Lord's feet
> and thus become most wealthy in wise service—
> our teachers, free of darkness,
> by their gracious reflection
> have lit this undying lamp among the best.[113]

They teach out of compassion, just as the Lord, the first teacher, had taught them, that both student and teacher are saved:

> By the unrestrained waves of the divine ocean of his boundless compassion,

the teacher disciplines his students through continuing instruction
and the inculcation of many good qualities;
such a teacher, mindful of the successive commands of the Teacher
who is not last [but first],
protects not only them, but in that guise himself as well.[114]

The *Essence* is but a moment in a much longer story, a single fruit of the divine teacher's continuing presence to a tradition of teachers.

The Sanskrit verse at the end of chapter 31 identifies the ideal human teacher with the divine teacher who intervenes repeatedly in the world, and so both divine and human teachers implicitly authenticate Deśika's own teaching, since he himself writes only in reception of that tradition:

The teacher's tongue is the lion throne
where the Horse-faced Deity[115] sits;
we consider no other deity to be higher than this teacher
whose form Nārāyaṇa himself once took without losing His own form,
to carry across the ocean of existence beings drowning there.[116]

Indeed, if the tradition is a divine word and God is the primal teacher—Hayagrīva, God in the form of the horse—the human teacher, though in a way unimportant, is not a mere secondary transmitter of knowledge; in the teacher's person and word, divine illumination occurs in the world. This becomes personal, as the transmission occurs within Deśika himself, as if a happening out of his control:

We are at the feet of the White Horse who is our teacher;
what was written inside us we then put on a palm leaf:
so what are we in all this?[117]

What is required, then, is a kind of double take on the *Essence* and its authority: Though Deśika claims no divine authority, he sees the *Essence* as the fruit of an ancient and still contemporary divine intervention in human reasoning and writing.

The seal on Deśika's commitment to proper transmission is found in chapter 31, where he starkly contrasts proper learning with the efforts of would-be teachers who lack the purity, discipline, and authority of the lineage:

> If a person who teaches the mysteries related to the self lacks tradition and teaches what he has read on a palm leaf or heard by scaling a wall,[118] he is like someone who wears a jewel he has stolen, afraid of all who see him. He comes to a bad end, as it says:
>
> When by chance a mantra is heard
> by a person in hiding, or by deception, or learned merely from what is seen on a palm leaf,
> it has no value, but surely causes misfortune. [*Padma Saṃhitā* 23.81]
>
> How to hear and speak has been explained by this text,
>
> Know this by prostration, by posing careful questions, and by service;
> those who have knowledge and have seen the truth will impart knowledge to you, [Bhagavad Gītā 4.34][119]
>
> and by this one,
>
> Having prostrated himself and offered respectful salutations,
> Maitreyi carefully posed questions to Parāśara
> who had completed the rites prescribed for the earlier part of the day. [*Viṣṇu Purāṇa* 1.1.1][120]
>
> A person who learns and teaches in deviation from this proper way is like a person who wears a death effigy—loathed by everyone.[121] Such teaching surely brings misfortune:
>
> The person who does not teach in accord with dharma,
> and the one who asks questions not in accord with dharma:
> one of them dies, or they become enemies. [*Mahābhārata, Śānti Parva* 335.51]
>
> One is to teach only after learning in the proper way; but even then, if one teaches without glorifying his teacher first, all his ideas will lack grounding, like a parasitic, rootless plant. Such teaching arouses nothing but great suspicion in the student, and will be disregarded.[122]

Likewise, no writing can aid a reader who has not learned properly from a teacher; indeed, great disrespect may be shown, and harm done.[123] Even the carefully composed *Essence,* the work of a peerless teacher, is an insufficient guide to the truths and values it proposes, if one merely reads it "in print," off a palm leaf or from a modern printed version. Personal relationships among those in the community who are dedicated to the ideal of refuge are required. So, oddly enough, if we read carefully and take the *Essence* to heart as the teaching of a foremost teacher, we learn not to take it as a final word, for it points beyond itself.

Flawless recitation—and likewise, flawless writing and reception of a text—requires alertness and dedication, remembrance and gratitude; originality is less important. Deśika himself received the tradition; his writing is effective because it is an act of reproduction, a memorization and faithful replication of what was already given over and again:

> I heard all the preceding and following verses about the three mysteries as the word of Maṭaippaḷḷi—known in tradition as Vedānta Udayana—just as he had heard them from his teacher. Kiṭāmpi Appuḷḷār made this servant learn as a parrot learns, just as the Lord, in accord with the mercy, had shed light on all this and made it clear in Kiṭāmpi Appuḷḷār's own heart. That I might not forget, he made me speak these verses without error.[124]

The *Essence*—as verses and as prose explication around the verses[125]—is nothing but the fruit of tradition. Conversely, though, Deśika can still speak of a primal moment when the Lord—Mādhava—taught him personally:

> When I did not know the Eight and the Two,
> my [Lord] Mādhava made me know them,
> He gave me that place beyond our grasp,[126]
> and aiming to do away with my whole mass of karma,
> He said, "Do not be afraid," and by that lovely, strong word,
> I gained the state of no anxiety.[127]

The *Essence* arises from that transformative learning, yet also simply records what had been said in previous generations. As authentic text—authentic because of the tradition—it is also the voice of God heard now, in the words of Deśika and in his writing.

By weaving the *Essence* seamlessly into a tradition that traces itself back to Nārāyaṇa, the divine teacher, Deśika invests his work with a very high degree of authenticity and potency. The paradox is real but simple: Readers who take the *Essence* too seriously as a unique authorial contribution have to be corrected, taught to see that it is not important in itself. But readers who appreciate the living tradition of which the *Essence* is simply a part can then value it as a powerful and immediate point of contact with that tradition and even with the divine intentions. As an author, Deśika has therefore to write with a kind of carefree responsibility, as if his carefully chosen words do not of themselves matter at all. In turn, readers must be very diligent, yet free enough to allow the emergence of truths, emotions, and relationships that such a text itself could not produce.

We have in the *Essence* and *Treatise* two instances of the skillfully conceived and composed text that is both reasonable and affectively charged, able to draw readers into a religious possibility—loving surrender—that is beyond easy ideas and words. Their effect can be felt, however, only in accord with the discipline and dedication of both the author and the reader. Both must in a sense be conduits of the divine power latent in the text, its writing and reading. As brilliant authors, de Sales and Deśika are central to their texts and their meanings, yet only by a kind of de-individualization, as the "author ego" is erased for the sake of the writing itself. Deśika presents himself as a nearly invisible, barely heard and noticed transmitter of an older, authentic tradition that goes back to the beginning. De Sales highlights the importance of a positive, rich experience that has to be more than reasoned discourse, and yet he tells us little of his own experience; his own and his readers' transformations are the work of the Holy Spirit, after all. In suggesting that the best theology is mystical theology—such as truly transforms people—de Sales is also pointing to a writing that in a sense gets quickly out of (his) hand, beyond what any author can really manage; and in this dynamic, he echoes Deśika's differently nuanced yet harmonious position on tradition and its serial expositors. By different imaginative paths, each of our authors succeeds in writing beyond himself, prizing yet questioning the powers of reason, word, and self for the sake of a more potent communication that occurs in this very ambivalence. As the reader likewise reads and reflects on what she or he has read, this must be done with a willingness to find in the *Essence* and *Treatise* a power beyond what most texts contain; and for this power to have its effect, this reader must risk being fully engaged in the reading, open to the possibility of a conversion of mind and heart. All of this comes to a head in the theme that is central to their writing and to this book, loving surrender to God. For this is an ultimate state beyond ordinary conceptions of how to live and beyond the words we apply to our lives, and yet, according to de Sales and Deśika, surrender is an intelligent choice a reflective reader can make in reaching beyond herself or himself.

IV. From Writer to Reader: On the Exercise of Religious Reading

At the end of chapter 1, I offered some initial reflections on the kind of focused reading the *Essence* and *Treatise* requires of us, and I indicated some of the choices I felt necessary to make in writing a book dependent on these texts. At that point, my observations were entirely provisional; I admitted that to justify this particular intellectual-spiritual reading of de Sales and Deśika, I needed to say more about their understanding of the weaknesses and dangers—and possible virtues—of how we think, speak, and write, and on the promising though constrained virtue of disciplined reflection, words, and writing with respect to something so potentially demanding as loving surrender to God. This chapter's exploration of the authors' self-understanding and the choices they made in writing (with the expectation that their frail human words might nevertheless channel religious power) allows me to say a bit more about the correlative reading that will do justice to such texts.

Although reading does not take the place of reasoning, an attentive reading very aptly symbolizes the dependent intellectual activity appropriate to the conditions of their writing. This appropriate reading must of course likewise be intelligent and discerning, rising to the masterful writing of Deśika and de Sales. It must also be a spiritual practice, an intellectual commitment allowing for a fruition that is spiritually transformative, beyond what ideas and words normally make happen.

To understand reading as a spiritual practice, I have found two pertinent books to be particularly useful: Paul Griffiths's *Religious Reading: The Place of Reading in the Practice of Religion*; and Pierre Hadot's *Philosophy as a Way of Life: Spiritual Exercises from Socrates to Foucault.*[128] I will discuss each of these in turn.

1. *Paul Griffiths*

In his *Religious Reading*, even while describing particular details of reading and book production in several religious traditions, Griffiths draws our attention to the worldview and habitus of faith proper to religious reading. Over against a consumerist (and rather too often narrowly and clinically conceived) mining of texts for information, religious reading has to do

> primarily with the establishment of certain relations between readers and the things they read, relations that are at once

> attitudinal, cognitive, and moral, and that therefore imply an ontology, an epistemology, and an ethic. . . . [Such reading] will, in every case, imply a distinctive set of relations between religious readers and their works.

Griffiths's appreciation of reading a classic religious text aptly mirrors our expectations regarding the *Essence* and the *Treatise*; to learn, we must surrender ourselves to the mysteries latent in our reading:

> The first and most basic element in these relations is that the work read is understood as a stable and vastly rich resource, one that yields meaning, suggestions [or imperatives] for action, matter for aesthetic wonder, and much else. It is a treasure-house, an ocean, a mine: the deeper religious readers dig, the more ardently they fish, the more single-mindedly they seek gold, the greater will be their reward. The basic metaphors here are those of discovery, uncovering, retrieval, opening up: religious readers read what is there to be read, and what is there to be read always precedes, exceeds, and in the end supersedes its readers.

Here too, the bond of text and reader is very strong, even as the reader is being reconstituted in relation to the text:

> The second, and almost equally important, constituent of the relations between religious readers and what they read is that readers are seen as intrinsically capable of reading and as morally required to read. Their capacity for retrieving the riches of the work by an act of reading is something intrinsic to them: they are essentially and necessarily readers, to the point where *homo lector* can be substituted for *homo sapiens* without loss and with considerable gain.[129]

As we have already seen with reference to the *Treatise* and the *Essence*, learning to be and act as a *homo lector*—obviously an identity dependent on but beyond *homo sapiens*—is not a neutral or cost-free activity; what Deśika might call competence *(adhikāra)* marks a combination of innate capacities with prolonged study and spiritual practice. It requires self-effacement before the text, patience, perseverance, and imagination; though a humble practice, it also engenders productive ways of thinking that change the reader who is inevitably drawn into the world of what she or he reads. Readers who are willing to take this risk are those who become competent to read the *Essence* and *Treatise* and, receiving their riches, are able to speak, act, and write with power after such reading.

Griffiths's "religious reading" does not necessarily have anything to do with interreligious reading. Although he provides numerous insights into Christian reading and Buddhist reading, he does not give any special attention to the dynamics of a double reading, when texts of both traditions are read together. But our project is, in my judgment, a natural extension of his insights. For reading opens a way into deeper interreligious understanding, when two classics, their traditions, and the intellectual/spiritual paths they promote are brought together for the sake of the attentive reader able to endure the demands of both traditions at once. This book seeks to exemplify the dynamic that Griffiths has in mind but to do so in the practice of an (inter)religious reading, one that demands vulnerability to both texts, a practice that is intensified by the spiritual power generated in reading them together repeatedly and that refuses to reduce either to a component of some later and settled "higher" viewpoint.

The religious reader who would engage the *Essence* and the *Treatise* has to see herself or himself as more than a neutral investigator examining the texts impartially, as if immune to their message; impartiality is a virtue, but only as preparatory to a more intense engagement. Against the grain of ordinary academic practice, these texts expect and invite a humbler, less self-confident reasoning, ever off balance, that draws the mind into a situation it cannot control and that illumines and ignites the heart. Each text has this power, and so too both together, as their worlds are opened for us, neither preempting the other. My ambition here is to write in accord with the power of both texts, in deference to both of them, for readers willing to read intelligently, religiously, and without complete certainty about where the reading will lead them.

2. *Pierre Hadot*

Hadot's *Philosophy as a Way of Life* confirms Griffiths's insight into the integral way of life demanded by religious reading, for Hadot is particularly alert to the importance of philosophy envisioned and enacted as a spiritual practice.[130] He expresses well the demands of this kind of learning as an interpretive, commentarial practice that defers to the wisdom of "old" learning:

> It was believed that the truth had been "given" in the master's texts, and that all that had to be done was to bring it to light and explicate it. Plotinus, for example, writes: "These statements are not new; they do not belong to the present time, but were made long ago, although not explicitly, and what we have said in this discussion has been an interpretation of them, relying on Plato's own writings for evidence that these views are ancient."

The implied exegetical philosophy works from a strong presupposition of faith with its doctrinal expectations: "Each philosophical or religious school or group believed itself to be in possession of a traditional truth, communicated from the beginning by the divinity to a few wise men. Each therefore laid claim to being the legitimate depository of the truth."[131] The depository is the text, and the teacher (most often as commentator) is the agent of the transmission not only of the texts but also of their proper reading to the next generation. In oral discourse and then in writing, the enduring truth of the tradition is made available for new students, new readers. Both the transmission and the reception are instances of spiritual practice. In this sense, at least, "philosophy" becomes a way of life. As Hadot's editor Arnold Davidson puts it:

> The theoretical discourse of the school to which he belongs is inwardly repeated and assimilated by the philosopher so that he can master his own inner discourse, so that his discourse will be ordered according to the fundamental choices and principles that were the starting point and basis for the theoretical discourse of his school.[132]

This is, in Hadot's own words, a "discourse that is actually spiritual exercise."[133] Whereas discourse *about* philosophy can be divided into various subdisciplines,

> philosophy itself—that is, the philosophical way of life—is no longer a theory divided into parts, but a unitary act, which consists in *living* logic, physics, and ethics. In this way, we no longer study logical theory—that is, the theory of speaking and thinking well—we simply think and speak well. We no longer engage in theory about the physical world, but we contemplate the cosmos. We no longer theorize about moral action, but we act in a correct and just way.[134]

By extension, I suggest, both the writing and reading of the *Treatise* and the *Essence* are of the nature of this direct and unitary reflection, reasoning and speaking that are intended for the sake of transforming human ways of living.[135]

We should not imagine ourselves as turning back the clock, nor should we lightly let go of the values that accrue to systematic study such as is generally practiced in academic circles. But for an adequate reading of the *Essence* and *Treatise*, we do well to experiment in practicing the close reading and attentive receptivity underlying this older model that Hadot places before us, even if such a return appears less productive of useful data while nonetheless demanding more of us. This reappropriated "exegetical thinking" is more likely to be adequate to what Deśika and de Sales have in mind. The subject matter of the *Essence* and the *Treatise*, loving surrender to God, makes fuller sense to readers whose reasoning is disciplined by tradition—each tradition, both traditions, the new tradition of double reading—and who are vulnerable to the imaginative and affective dimensions of what both our authors put before us so intensely and insistently. Such readers are less likely to write as if "from outside" the texts being read together. Indeed, though my own text might be assessed in terms of the coherence and logic of its arguments, a more appropriate measure is whether I have written out of a clear indebtedness to these traditions, by a reasoning that is a religious reading and a spiritual exercise and that is faithful to both the Śrīvaiṣṇava and Catholic Christian traditions, and recognizable to the Śrīvaiṣṇavas and Catholics who may pick up my book and seek their traditions in it.

Of course, things are never quite as simple as I have just suggested. As indicated in chapter 1, claims I propose regarding the nature of our reading practice must be nuanced in accord with three forms of reading. First, there is the bedrock value of a reading practiced within one's own religious tradition, as occurs when I read the *Treatise* and learn from Francis de Sales more of the truth and spirit of my Catholic tradition. In this case, what is learned will most often appear consonant with established and practiced dispositions.

Second, there is also at stake a reading practiced across religious boundaries, as when I, a Roman Catholic, read the *Essence*, a Hindu text, and learn it in accord with the reading traditions of Śrīvaiṣṇavism. The reader comes to this text out of a significantly different background and with differing ways of thinking and speaking of religious matters. Reading is still a learning process, but more is at stake in another way: Growing familiarity with a previously unfamiliar text draws the reader toward the ideas, images, emotions, and ways of practice of that text and its tradition. At this point, the reader may think twice and draw back at the prospect of a kind of belonging to the other tradition: I, a Catholic, can learn from Deśika's Śrīvaiṣṇava text, but there is no guarantee that I am ready to learn and appropriate *all* that he teaches me. If I stake out a common ground with the term "loving surrender," the reasonable and attentive reader may wonder or worry how far the analogy can be taken.

Third, there is the reading that crosses back and forth between two such texts, a process of interreligious learning that further unsettles the reader who, once sufficiently educated by the texts, will be neither here nor there or, perhaps, both here and there. This reading also places both texts and their communities in a situation neither author could have anticipated, the very prospect of which both would likely have disapproved. A delicate balance is required, since it would be easiest to resolve the difficulties by subordinating both texts to a manner of reasoning that objectifies and controls them both. But such a strategy might be merely a matter of giving free rein to the very reasoning of which the authors are skeptical, a detached observation immune to the spiritual effects of either tradition. Our goal, even in this novel interreligious situation, must be to honor the demands of tradition by subordinating reason to both texts and the learning processes they inculcate seeing where is old, new process leads us.

But all of this is still rather vague. If the reader is to be able to rise to the challenge of reading these texts religiously, authors must write in a way that educates and transforms readers who stay with their texts. In chapter 3, therefore, I reflect more closely on how Deśika and de Sales craft their writing and hence our reading; they are not magicians, and they must inscribe their texts in particular ways with the ideas, words, images, and persons of tradition, so that the promised power of transformation actually accelerates in the course of reading.

Chapter 3

Awakening

Reading and Learning on the Way to God

> Such is the devout soul in meditation. She passes from mystery to mystery, not at random, or only to solace herself in viewing the admirable beauty of those divine objects, but deliberately and of set purpose, to find out motives of love or of some heavenly affection; and having found them she draws them to her, she relishes them, she loads herself with them, and having brought them back and put them within her heart, she lays up what she sees most useful for her advancement, by at last making resolutions suitable to the time of temptation.
>
> De Sales, *Treatise*

> Drawing on such authoritative texts, devout practitioners can reflect clearly on the seven faults inherent in experiences of non-conscious, material reality: being puny, unstable, rooted in sorrow, mixed with sorrow, the cause of sorrow's rising, the root for wrong ideas about oneself, and contradiction to one's own innate bliss. These practitioners also reflect clearly on the faults inherent even in the experience of pure consciousness, insofar as this is accessible amidst material things—finally on that unique experience of the Lord that is contrary to all inferior experiences.
>
> Deśika, *Essence*

In chapter 2, I explored the role and limits of reasoning according to Deśika and de Sales, and how they dealt with the unreliability of our ideas and questions and the words in which they took form. Both were convinced of the deficiency of reasoning that has not benefited from the discipline of tradition, and yet too they were hopeful that properly educated discourse, grounded in tradition and purified of mistaken notions and bad habits, could in practice play a productive, transformative spiritual role. Putting reason back where it belongs is necessarily also a return of language to its grounding in scripture and tradition. Since Deśika and de Sales venture to draw upon this reconstituted reasoning and language, we would do well to reflect on their writing as well reasoned and well expressed, imbued with a lingering ambivalence about how we are to think and speak but also directed by faith that human ideas and words can become spiritually charged and effective. Loving surrender remains an extraordinary spiritual goal that cannot be reasonably accounted for or easily reduced to words. But the well-composed text can help readers to appropriate imaginatively and affectively even mysteries of God and graces that no words can reproduce.

We must now consider in some detail but still very selectively how Deśika and de Sales wrote so as to produce texts that aid readers (ourselves included, however we may differ from their original audience) in acquiring, page by page, a humbler, more vulnerable relationship with God, imagined and felt in a way that makes real and proximate the possibility of loving surrender.[1] Since a consideration of full array of such strategies would require a book in itself, I present just a few of the ways in which de Sales and Deśika make their texts more capable of educating and transforming their attentive readers.[2] I consider examples of their use of scripture and the efficacy of this use; their presentation of persons honored in tradition as models for imitation; and strategies for persuading readers to shift how they respond to texts, engaging them more intensely and personally. At the chapter's end, I extend our reflections on reading as a transformative spiritual practice by introducing Charles Altieri's appreciation of the priority of imaginative and affective transformation in fiction and drama.

Here too I choose to privilege ways in which the *Essence* and *Treatise* are complementary in style and image and affective intensification, rather than ways (should there be any) in which they might irreparably diverge. But we still do well to be alert to the distinctiveness of each text. The *Treatise* is an ample narrative of love from its primal beginnings in need and desire (book 1) to its ecstatic culmination in God (book 9), and concludes (books 10–12) with further instructions that primarily have to do with life after loving surrender. As de Sales sees it, there is continuity, in a single flow, from the simplest human desire to complete abandonment into the hands of God; such is the journey of Jesus Christ and of all who would follow his path. The text is composed with this continuity in mind, and the reader committed to the study of it reads through the subtleties of human experience, moving—being moved—toward making more honest choices about how to live in accord with her or his deepest identity before God.

The *Essence* also has a dramatic tone. As I discussed in chapter 2, Deśika introduces early in the *Essence* the parable of the child lost in the forest, then found and restored to his true identity. All that follows in the *Essence* is in a sense the process of retrieving our lost identity as we sift through our own identities in the clearer, sharper light of Deśika's ongoing analysis of loving surrender. Yet the *Essence* does not read like a narrative; rather, it is a complexly constructed, multidimensional analysis, the three holy mantras retold over and again with different concerns in mind. Through theology and psychology, ethics and pedagogy, and the sheer work of exegesis, Deśika intentionally circles back to the mantras and their basic truths and values, over and again from different angles. In the ever clearer light of the *Essence,* the larger, sweeping narrative of love told by de Sales is grounded in the realities of self and God clearly seen and uttered in the words of the mantras.

The *Essence* and *Treatise* therefore have to be read differently, and yet can be especially profitable when read together. Once noted, differences become interconnected and complementary in the mind and heart of readers, enhancing how we read either text by mindfulness of the other, our manner of good reading always placed next to yet another manner of good reading. Reading the *Treatise* and *Essence* together then is neither repetitious nor a dispersal of attention back and forth between merely different texts with merely different purposes: Both draw on the resources of tradition to create shifts in the ways individuals think about themselves. The melodic flow of the *Treatise* dramatizes the intense clarity of the *Essence,* which in turn interrogates the manner of our love.

But let us now see how this works out in these texts by the several examples that make up this chapter.

I. Scripture, Inscribed in the *Treatise* and *Essence*

Frequent citation of scripture is a striking feature of both the *Treatise* and the *Essence.* No chapter of the *Essence,* and hardly a chapter of the *Treatise,* is without quotations from scriptural sources. Both Deśika and de Sales write in deference to scripture and tradition and, as teachers, they see their own texts as vehicles by which to make those older, revered, and authoritative words known to new readers. De Sales draws on a wide range of Old Testament and New Testament texts; Deśika must handle a much wider variety of possible scriptural sources of various ranks and in the Sanskrit and Tamil languages. Even while exhibiting an orthodox reticence about citing Vedic and Upaniṣadic sources in the *Essence* as a text for a wide audience, he consistently draws on a rich variety of Sanskrit and Tamil holy texts. The regular and insistent introduction of multiple scriptural texts repeatedly places before readers potent words, images, states of mind and heart, and these in turn educate the reader and open her or him to the spiritual realities of which the texts speak. Scripture becomes the lens through which the reader hears and sees the world and begins to take to heart that more radical possibility, loving surrender.

1. *De Sales' Use of Scripture*

In his masterful study of de Sales' sources, Antanas Liuima catalogues the biblical texts cited by de Sales, and the list is impressive. The *Treatise* contains some six hundred direct biblical quotations. The Old Testament is quoted more than three hundred times, and the New Testament nearly as many. Notable is de Sales' preference for the Psalms and St. Paul's letters (both cited more than 110 times), the Song of Songs (cited more than 70 times), and the Gospels (more than 75 times). Many chapters, even short ones, have multiple citations that lend them cohesion and direction and give them their direction. If we include biblical allusions that do not form precise quotations—André Ravier identifies many of these as "near quotations"—and passages that more elementally echo biblical images and sentiments, the number of times the reader is directed to biblical ideas, images, and words is at least doubled. Even apart from the point and effect of any particular quotation, the sheer frequency of citations works to great effect, as this potent concatenation of words and images flows over the reader again and again, immersing her or him in the words and images fundamental to the Christian worldview.[3]

In his second volume, Liuima examines how de Sales uses the Bible in constructing examples, persuasive images, and support for arguments;[4] by richness of image and emotion, the resultant weave of argument, text, and image is quite often more potent and interesting than any of the arguments by themselves. Gathering from scripture an anthology of potent words and images, de Sales uses them in creative ways, even in place of other arguments that might have been added, so as to persuade the reader by appealing to her or his Catholic consciousness at a deeper level where images and emotions are so vividly encapsulated in and released from within biblical texts.[5] If the *Treatise* is a practical manual aimed at the transformation of mind and heart, the books of the Bible offer credence and nourishment in support of transformation:

> The soul penetrated by faith eagerly receives each word which Saint Francis de Sales utters. He stimulates the imagination and catches the attention by words and phrases taken entirely from Sacred Scripture. These in turn confer a tone of authenticity and certainty on his teaching.[6]

Through de Sales' work, the reader is increasingly drawn into the still richer world of biblical texts, a perspective that in turn enables that reader to articulate her or his own world differently, in accord with these ancient but fresh words and images.

Liuima also charts the Bible's influence on de Sales' manner of presentation.[7] De Sales often opts simply for the evident, literal meanings of cited words, without delving into the complications of original context. But then he allows those very words to play out their own effect in context, as the reader receives rhetorically effective figures of speech into her or his repertoire of ideas, words, images, and affective states, and these in turn disclose a wide range of imaginative possibilities.[8] Even fairly definite thematic arguments are enhanced and deepened by scripture and bear with them a richer set of images and moods that affect the reader on deeper, less noticed levels; even when de Sales is reinforcing relatively clear basic points, he uses scripture to bring his arguments to life, as a guide to ways of living.[9] De Sales' goal is not simply to teach people more about the Bible or to ensure that they will think correctly about it in conformity with Catholic doctrine, but rather that his readers will be shaped by the biblical worldview and begin to imagine living differently. Citing the Bible, which he takes to be composed of words charged with the power of the Spirit, thus aids de Sales in his work as a spiritual director who wants to engage the reader in the experience and practice of the dispositions and virtues so vividly portrayed in the Bible.[10]

But precisely because such words—with their concomitant images and affective states—are the vehicle of the Holy Spirit's inflaming power, they cannot be imagined the *only* vehicle of that Spirit's wider work in the world. However important the Bible may be, it cannot be absolutized as the exclusive means of divine communication. What is cited in the text should ideally overflow into every corner of ordinary life. In his preface, de Sales stresses the intensity with which the Holy Spirit acted upon the newborn Church, creating an oral tradition of living, powerful words even before there was a "New Testament":

> This heavenly spouse, when he thought good to begin the promulgation of his law, cast down upon the assembly of those disciples whom he had deputed for this work a shower of fiery tongues, sufficiently intimating thereby that the preaching of the gospel was destined entirely for the inflaming of hearts.[11]

In the ongoing history of the Church, this divine inspiration is channeled through spoken as well as written discourse:

> The Church is indeed adorned with an excellent variety of teachings, sermons, treatises, and pious books, all very beautiful and pleasant to the sight, by reason of the admirable mingling which the Sun of Justice makes of his divine wisdom with the tongues of his pastors, which are their feathers, and those pens which sometimes hold the place of tongues and form the rich plumage of this mystic dove.[12]

God teaches in nature, [The Spirit] uses countless means of inspiring. "St. Anthony, St. Francis, St. Anselm, and a thousand others, often received inspirations at the sight of creatures," de Sales writes. The vast variety of signs and events is evident in the spiritual histories of other notable Christians:

> St. Mary of Egypt was inspired by the sight of a picture of Our Lady; St. Anthony, by hearing the Gospel read at Mass; St. Augustine, by hearing the history of St. Anthony's life; the Duke of Gandia (Francis Borgia), by looking upon the dead empress; St. Pachomius, by seeing an example of charity; the Blessed Ignatius of Loyola, by reading the lives of the Saints; St. Cyprian (not the great Bishop of Carthage but a layman, yet a glorious martyr) was moved by hearing the devil confess his impotence against those that trust in God.[13]

Even the inevitable travails of life confirm what scripture teaches:

> The ordinary means is preaching, but sometimes those whom the word does not help are taught by tribulation, according to what

> the Prophet said: *Affliction will give understanding to hearing* [Isa. 28:19]; that is, those who do not amend by hearing the heavenly threats against the wicked, shall learn the truth by events and their effects, and by feeling affliction shall become wise.[14]

So too, devotion to God is evident in the practice of the Christian life built around the Word:

> When I was a youth at Paris, two scholars, one of whom was a heretic, passing the night in the Faubourg St. Jacques in debauchery, heard the Carthusians ring to Matins. The heretic asked the other why they rang. He explained to him with what devotion they celebrated the Divine Office in that holy monastery: "O God," he said, "how different is the practice of those religious from ours! They perform the office of angels, and we that of brute beasts." Desiring the day after to see by experience what he had learnt by his companion's relation, he found the fathers in their stalls, arranged like a row of marble statues in their niches, motionless except for the chanting of the Psalms, which they performed with a truly angelic attention and devotion, according to the custom of this holy Order. This poor youth, wholly ravished with admiration, was taken with the exceeding consolation which he found in seeing God so well worshipped amongst Catholics, and resolved, as he did afterwards, to put himself into the bosom of the Church, the true and only spouse of him who had visited him with his inspiration, in the infamous litter of abomination in which he had lain. Oh how happy are they who keep their hearts open to holy inspirations![15]

The salutary effect of this Word is also evident in a wide variety of simple, pious practices:

> For on this account we stand while the Gospel is read, as being prepared to obey the holy signification of God's will contained therein; hence we kiss the book at the place of the Gospel, in adoration of the sacred word which declares his heavenly will. Hence many men and women saints of old carried in their bosoms the Gospel written as an epithem [talisman] of love, as one reads about St. Cecilia, and St. Matthew's Gospel was actually

> found upon the heart of St. Barnabas after his death, written with his own hand. Wherefore in the ancient councils, in the midst of the whole assembly of Bishops, there was erected a high throne, and upon it was placed the book of the holy Gospels, which represented the person of our Savior, King, Doctor, Director, Spirit and sole Heart of the Councils, and of the whole Church, so much did they reverence the signification of God's will expressed in that divine book. Indeed that great mirror of the pastoral order, St. Charles, Archbishop of Milan, never studied the holy Scripture but on his knees and bareheaded, to testify with what respect we are to read and hear the signified will of God.[16]

It is clear that de Sales envisioned a broad and rich context for his frequent citation of the Bible; as its words appear everywhere in his book, so devotion to the Word should be evident everywhere in the Christian's life. There is no marked boundary between what is in the book and life in the world; reading, after all, is all about returning to ordinary life with new ideas, images, and sentiments.

a. Appropriating Scripture's Wisdom

De Sales is also concerned to advise his readers on how to hear and learn from the scriptures he keeps quoting to them. The wisdom of scripture also shapes how readers are to receive its truths; to understand this, it is useful to note several key passages in book 6 of the *Treatise* on the practice of meditation, itself a kind of religious reading and consequent deepening reflection.[17] In chapter 2 of that book, titled "On Meditation, The First Degree of Prayer or Mystical Theology," de Sales details the ways in which meditation differs from the more ordinary, distracted movements of the mind:

> Every meditation is a thought, but not every thought is meditation. Many times we have thoughts to which our spirit is carried without any design or aim, by way of simple musing, as we see common flies flying from one flower to another, without drawing anything from them. And however attentive this kind of thought may be, it cannot bear the name of meditation, but should simply be called *thought*.[18]

In words that echo the ambivalence toward reason we saw in the preceding chapter, he notes how study can go wrong, as the learning process is kept at arm's length:

> Sometimes we consider a thing attentively to learn its causes, its effects, its qualities, and this thought is named *study*; in it the mind acts as locusts do, which promiscuously fly upon flowers and leaves, to eat them and nourish themselves therewith.[19]

By contrast, proper meditation is a deeper and more discerning immersion in the mysteries of God known from scripture for the sake of engagement, consumption, transformation:

> But when we think of divine things, not to learn, but to make ourselves affectively drawn to them, this is called meditating, and the exercise is called meditation. In it our spirit, not as a fly for simple amusement, nor as a locust to eat and be filled, but as a sacred bee, moves over the flowers of holy mysteries, to extract from them the honey of divine love.[20]

Disciplined mental activity is not of itself enough, since it may fall short of the deeper appropriation achieved in steady meditation on scripture:

> Thus many persons are always dreaming, and engaged in unprofitable thoughts, almost without knowing what they are thinking about; and, which is noteworthy, they are attentive to these thoughts only inadvertently, and would wish not to have them; witness him who said: *My thoughts are dissipated, tormenting my heart* [Job 17:11]. Many also study, and by a most laborious occupation fill themselves with vanity, not being able to resist curiosity.[21]

Proper study is most prominently a patient savoring of the divine word:

> Meditation is nothing but the mystical rumination required for not being unclean [Lev. 11:3, 8; Deut. 14:3, 6], to which one of the devout shepherdesses who followed the sacred Sulamite woman invites us: for she assures us that the holy doctrine is as a

> precious wine, worthy not only to be drunk by pastors and doctors, but also to be diligently relished, and, so to speak, chewed and ruminated.[22]

Properly practiced, meditation engages the whole person and enables that person to imagine living differently:

> But there are a few who meditate to inflame their heart with holy heavenly love. In conclusion, thoughts and study may be upon any subject, but meditation, in our present sense, has reference only to those objects whose consideration tends to make us good and devout. Meditation then is nothing other than attentive thought, voluntarily reiterated or entertained in the mind, to excite the will to holy and salutary affections and resolutions.[23]

The devout, meditative soul moves like a bee across these scriptural treasures, drawing sustenance that is pleasing and nourishing:

> The devout soul passes from mystery to mystery, not at random, or only to solace herself in viewing the admirable beauty of those divine objects, but deliberately and of set purpose, to find out motives for love or some heavenly affection; and having found them she draws them to her, she relishes them, she loads herself with them, and having brought them back and put them within her heart, she lays up what she sees most useful for her advancement, by at last making resolutions suitable to the time of temptation.[24]

Meditation opens into direct encounter with God, who is experienced in a series of small, intimate touches. Scripture prepares us for this experience and gives us the words by which to understand what is happening, yet without piling up words between God and the soul:

> Thus in the Song of Songs the heavenly lover, as a mystical bee, settles, now on the eyes, now on the lips, on the cheeks, on the hair of her beloved, to draw thence the sweetness of a thousand passions of love, noting in particular whatever she finds best for this.[25] So that, inflamed with holy love, she speaks with him, she questions him, she listens to him, sighs, aspires, admires him, as he on his part fills her with delight, inspiring her, touching and

> opening her heart, and pouring into it brightness, lights and sweetnesses without end, but in so secret a manner that one may rightly say of this holy conversation of the soul with God, what the sacred text says of God's with Moses: that *Moses being alone upon the top of the mountain spoke to God, and God answered him* [Exod. 19:19–20, 23:11].[26]

When the "eye" is trained by scripture—to see by and through its texts—it is able to grow more intimate in its knowledge of God and go forward in contemplation, knowing God still more intimately. As the reader contemplates the perfections of God, scripture provides the mind's eye with its object of vision, for instance, some scene from the New Testament:

> And finally we at other times consider neither many nor only one of the divine perfections, but only some divine action or work, to which we are attentive; as for example the act of mercy by which God pardons sins, or the act of creation, or the resurrection of Lazarus, or the conversion of St. Paul: as a bridegroom who might not regard the eyes—but only the sweetness of the looks which his spouse casts upon him, nor take notice of her mouth—but only of the sweetness of the words uttered by it.

The Bible may provide even the "spontaneous" prayers by which the devout person speaks to God:

> And here, Theotimus, the soul makes a certain outburst of love, not only upon the actions she considers, but upon him from whom they proceed: *Thou art good; and in thy goodness teach me thy justifications* [Ps. 118:68]. *His throat* (that is, the word which comes from it) *is most sweet, and he is entirely desirable* [Song of Songs 5:16]. Ah! *How sweet are thy words* to my innermost self [literally, "my entrails"], *more than honey to my mouth* [Ps. 118:103]; or with St. Thomas: *My Lord and my God* [John 20:28] and with St. Magdalen: *Rabboni, Ah! my master!* [John 20:16].[27]

By the continuous and reverent study of scripture, one's consciousness infused with its holy words, the reader's own words, ideas, and eventually person are transformed, articulated differently, so as to see and express the world in a new way. Scripture is not simply an object of study; in humbly submitting to the Word, the reader becomes able to see God as scripture itself anticipates: *Moses being alone upon the top of the mountain spoke to God, and God answered him.* Though here too, de Sales tells us little of his own experience, it is possible to assume that the *Treatise* is written out of such experience, with such vision.

b. An Example: The Liquefaction of the Soul

The style and power of de Sales' scriptural writing can be illustrated with reference to a single remarkable chapter in book 6, "The Outflowing or Liquefaction of the Soul in God," in which biblically rooted imagery of liquids and melting—liquefaction—gives structure and direction to an entire meditation. Throughout book 6, de Sales has been exploring the dynamics of contemplation, particularly the soul's growing recollection as it ever more deeply takes repose in the Lord, discovering itself in self-abandonment to God. The image of mingling self in God comes to the fore, confirming the deep intimacy of the growing love between God and the soul. De Sales begins with a commonplace analogy:

> Moist and liquid things easily receive the figures and limits which may be given them, because they have no firmness or solidity which stops or limits them in themselves. Put liquid into a vessel, and you will see it remain bounded within the limits of the vessel, and according as this is round or square the liquid will be the same, having no other limit or shape than that of the vessel which contains it.[28]

But the soul is rarely soft and pliable; it most often seems hardened against divine action, and requires cutting, softening, even breaking. Citing Ezekiel, de Sales meditates on the hardness of the human heart and its need to be even forcibly transformed:[29]

> The soul is not that way by nature, for she has her proper shapes and limits: she takes her shape from her habits and inclinations, her limits from her will; and when she is fixed upon her own inclinations and wills, we say she is hard, that is, opinionated, obstinate. *I will take,* says God, *the stony heart out of your flesh* [Ezek. 36:26], that is, I will take away your obstinacy. To change the form of stones, iron, or wood, the axe, hammer and fire are required. We call that a heart of iron, or wood, or stone, which does not easily receive the divine impressions, but dwells in its

> own will, amidst the inclinations which accompany our depraved nature.[30]

By contrast, the soul ready for God melts easily, though not without cost:

> By contrast, a gentle, pliable and tractable heart is termed a melting and liquefied heart. *My heart,* said David, speaking in the person of our Savior upon the cross, *is become like wax melting in the midst of my bowels!* [Ps. 21:15][31]

Jesus himself dissolved into God:

> Our Savior's heart, the true oriental pearl, singularly unique and priceless, thrown into the midst of a sea of incomparable bitterness in the day of his passion, melted in itself, dissolved, liquefied, gave way and flowed out in pain, under the press of so many mortal anguishes; but *love, stronger than death* [Song of Songs 8:6] mollifies, softens, and melts hearts far more quickly than all the other passions.[32]

Deepening in love, the soul should likewise welcome this same fate, such as was prefigured in both the Song of Songs and Numbers:

> *My soul,* said the holy lover, *melted when he spoke* [Song of Songs 5:6]. And what does *melted* mean save that it was no longer contained within itself, but had flowed out towards its divine lover?[33] God ordered that Moses should speak *to the rock,* and that it should produce *waters* [Num. 20:8]; no marvel then if he himself melted the heart of his spouse when he spoke to her in his sweetness.[34]

While liquids naturally thicken and grow sluggish over time, love melts the beloved, who flows upon hearing God's intimate word:

> Love had made the beloved fluid and flowing, whence the spouse calls him *oil poured out* [Song of Songs 1:3]; and now she tells us that she herself is all *melted* with love. *My soul,* said she, *melted when he spoke* [Song of Songs 5:6].[35]

De Sales' reflection itself is a rapid flow of associations, a current of citation and insight whereby his words give way to and mix with the sacred and potent words of scripture. He cites the text, but he also reimagines what he himself wants to say, through the text. We need not imagine that while writing he would stop every now and then, sifting through his Bible to find passages mentioning "heart" and "melting." More likely, his prolonged meditation on the text intuitively brought this concatenation of images to the fore; his writing itself flows from that conformity to scripture and so too, ideally, draws the reader into the same scriptural learning, at first through de Sales' own words.

The resultant flood, again imagined through the words of the Song of Songs, is wine mixed with honey, lovers mingled in their embrace:

> The love of her spouse was in her heart and *breasts* as a strong new *wine* which cannot be contained in the *cask*, for it overflowed on every side; and, because the soul follows its love, after the spouse had said: *Thy breasts are better than wine, smelling sweet of the best ointments,* she adds: *Thy name is as oil poured out* [Song of Songs 1:1, 2]. And as the bridegroom had poured out his love and his soul into the heart of the bride, so the bride reciprocally pours her soul into the heart of the bridegroom.[36]

Honey melts in the honeycomb at the sun's warmth, and so too the soul, "going out of herself and passing the limits of her natural being," pursues the beloved who has spoken to her. For de Sales, these natural and spiritual events are innate, spontaneous:

> As we see a honeycomb touched with the sun's ardent rays go out of itself, and forsake its form, to flow out towards that side where the rays touch it, so the soul of this lover flowed out towards where the voice of her well-beloved was heard, going out of herself and passing the limits of her natural being, to follow Him that spoke unto her.[37]

This motion accelerates as the soul instinctively lets go of itself, and enters into God, melting like balm, like clouds transmuting into rain and mixing into earth:

> An extreme deep pleasure of the lover in the thing that is loved begets a certain spiritual powerlessness, which makes the soul feel no longer able to remain in itself. Wherefore, as melted balm that no longer has firmness or solidity, she lets herself pass and

> flow into what she loves: she does not spring out of herself as by a sudden leap, nor does she cling as by a joining and union, but gently glides as a fluid and liquid thing, into the divinity whom she loves. . . . [The soul] goes out by this sacred outflowing and holy liquefaction, and quits herself, not only to be united to the well-beloved, but to be entirely mingled with and steeped in him.[38]

This outpouring, an ecstasy, is a kind of self-annihilation in God to which Paul and Teresa give words:

> You see then clearly, Theotimus, that the outflowing of a soul into her God is nothing but a true ecstasy by which the soul is entirely outside the limits of her natural form of existence, being wholly mingled with, absorbed and engulfed in, her God. Hence it happens that such as attain to these holy excesses of heavenly love, afterwards, having come to themselves, find nothing on the earth that can content them. Living in an extreme annihilation of themselves, they remain much weakened in all that belongs to the senses, and have perpetually in their hearts the maxim of the Blessed Mother Teresa: *What is not God is to me nothing*. And it seems that such was the loving passion of that great friend of the well-beloved, who said: *I live, now not I; but Christ lives in me* [Gal. 2:20], and: *Our life is hid with Christ in God* [Col. 3:3].[39]

At the chapter's conclusion, de Sales begs his readers not to fear the dissolution that follows since what Paul had in mind is a process both mystical and natural, like drops of water merging in the ocean, starlight subsumed into sunlight:

> The soul that has flowed out into God dies not, for how can she die by being swallowed up in life? But she lives without living in herself because, as the stars without losing their light still do not shine in the presence of the sun, but the sun shines in them and they are hidden in the light of the sun, so the soul, without losing her life, lives no more when mingled with God, but God lives in her.[40]

All this anticipates book 9, where loving surrender in God appears as the end of all striving; meditating on the imagery of melting and merging prepares the reader intellectually and affectively for the great challenge that is to come some pages later.

De Sales' manner is gentle; he never admonishes the reader harshly for possible (or likely) timidity and mediocrity. The Bible, particularly the Psalms, the Song of Songs, and the letters of St. Paul, catalyze intensely the discourse of the *Treatise*, heating its words on love and union, describing, imagining, even producing the melting of heart that is here the larger theme of book 6 of the *Treatise*. Examples from nature, romantic love, the lives of saints, and the intimacy of the soul in God are disclosed through the insight of scripture as the natural, psychological, social, and spiritual realms are shown to be seamless in their connections. The most radical claim—loss of self entirely in God—is introduced gently, by allusions to drops of water, new wine that ages slowly, bees distilling their honey: What will appear most unnatural and improbable in terms of ordinary measures of human living is here suggested, urged on, as everywhere implicit in the world about us. In the same way, loving surrender to God arises in keeping the basic nature of things. At the chapter's end, de Sales hopes, the reader will be closer to the unsettled, fragile position of a Philip Neri and a Francis Xavier, saints who wanted nothing but immersion in God: hearts now tender, broken, redeemed, lost in bliss.

This example could be echoed in many other passages of the *Treatise*, since everywhere de Sales is seeking to tell us about the realities of God and human beings, through the living words of scripture that give the *Treatise* its own vitality. To read the *Treatise* is to enter many times over into that biblical world, not simply to accumulate texts, themes, and images, but through pondering to learn to see one's own world in accord with biblical insight and affect, and thus vulnerable to the transformative power of tradition. This is a practice, manner, and purpose de Sales very much shares with Deśika, to whom I now turn.

2. *Deśika's Use of Scripture*

Many of the values we have highlighted regarding de Sales apply also to Deśika.[41] He too quotes very frequently from scripture, with more than thirteen hundred explicit citations in the thirty-two chapters of the *Essence*.[42]

Like de Sales, Deśika selects texts he deems valuable for meditation and internalization by readers who thereby become increasingly conformed to the truths and affective states operative in the contexts from which passages are cited. Deśika quotes scripture with familiarity, some bravado, and yet discerningly so as to promote and give life to the themes he is discussing at any point in the *Essence*. To some extent, he is adducing texts in support of his ideas, warrants to show that his positions are correct and authentic. By writing the *Essence*, he is also weaving a new context in which the reader can learn scripture, as her or his memory is infused with unaccustomed words and images conducive to seeing the world differently. Deśika too appears the master of his scripture, deciding by his own intuition what to quote in or out of context, and which lists of texts to place near one another. He makes his choices from deep personal knowledge, as if the words he cites have become his own. But as with de Sales, here too there is circularity, since Deśika's own intentions and choices as teacher and author arise only from study that is richly imbued with scripture and its ways of understanding, imaging, and acting in the world.

His sources include a wide range of popular texts: the *Rāmāyaṇa* account of the loves and sufferings of Rāma, Sītā, Rāma's brother Lakṣmaṇa, and a host of other figures; the great war epic that is the *Mahābhārata* (and including the Bhagavad Gītā); a variety of traditional mythological accounts known as *purāṇas*; and, occasionally, more technical scholastic works such as the *Mīmāṃsā Sūtras* and *Laws of Manu*. It is very important that Deśika also quotes profusely from the Tamil hymns of the āḻvārs, which seems to bespeak his intent to emphasize that all of scripture, in both languages, speaks to the same reality of God.[43] The *Rāmāyaṇa* in particular provides for the reader an array of proper, exemplary models who come before the reader by way of Deśika's often brief quotation of their words. He also cites or alludes to the (written or oral) Sanskrit teachings of his predecessors Āḷavantār and Rāmānuja, the Tamil and *maṇipravāḷa* ("jewel-coral," Sanskrit-Tamil) works of other teachers, personal memories of what his teachers told him, and citations from anthologies of teachers' sayings, such as the *Itihāsa Samuccaya*.

To understand better how Deśika uses scripture to educate his readers, we turn again to *Essence* chapter 7, "On the Person Desirous of Liberation," which I introduced in chapter 2 to illustrate the dynamics of conversion. Deśika quotes scripture liberally here not only to describe but also to provoke so great a dissatisfaction with the world that the reader will want to free herself of it. Deśika does not savor just a few words as did de Sales, but here, as he often does elsewhere, simply offers for meditation a list of texts that capture the human dilemma:

> Having tasted things with little essence, I have let go of them. [*Tiruvāymoḻi* 3.2.6][44]

Seeing, hearing, touching, smelling, tasting, the pleasure of the five senses, plus that other, hard-to-fathom but still inferior joy: I have let go of them all. [*Tiruvāymoḻi* 4.9.10][45]

When He is gracious, what here cannot be obtained? Enough of mere *dharma*, worldly prosperity, and pleasure, such small things! If you take refuge at the infinite Brahma-tree, you will surely gain much fruit there. [*Viṣṇu Purāṇa* 1.17.91]

The fruits obtained by these weak-minded men are finite. [Bhagavad Gītā 7.23]

Having arrived in this impermanent and joyless world, participate in Me. [Bhagavad Gītā 9.33]

Having heard of kings who were mighty, heroic, possessed of great wealth—yet now gone, nothing left but old stories, the wise man never considers himself a possessor of sons and wives, houses and fields, possessions, and so on. [*Viṣṇu Purāṇa* 4.24.68c–69]

This world is entirely made of sorrow. [*Viṣṇu Purāṇa* 1.17.69]

Even in heaven there is no happiness, since for a person who is perishing, the fear of falling never ceases. [*Viṣṇu Purāṇa* 6.5.50]

Fools hanker after kingdoms, their minds captive to possessiveness; people like me are not intoxicated by the strong drink of egoism. [*Viṣṇu Purāṇa* 6.7.7]

From the mansion of Brahmā downwards, O great sage, these flaws exist; therefore the wise never desire to attain heaven. [*Itihāsa Samuccaya* 3.48]

Above the mansion of Brahmā is the supreme world of Viṣṇu, pure, eternal, light, known as "highest Brahman"; fools never go to that world, those obsessed with objects, tormented by vanity, covetousness, arrogance, anger, perfidy, and delusion; only good people go there, those without possessiveness and egotism,

> indifferent to dualities, their senses controlled, dedicated to yogic meditation. [*Mahābhārata, Āraṇya Parva* 217.37–39]
>
> O king, in that world are beautiful vehicles, movement as one pleases, assembly halls, varied gardens, and lotus pools full of clear water. [*Mahābhārata, Śānti Parva* 196.4]
>
> Compared with that world of the highest self, these are Niraya hells. [*Mahābhārata, Śānti Parva* 196.6][46]

This list reinforces over and again Deśika's view that this world is full of woe—a feeling the reader must acutely feel, if she or he is to become truly desirous of liberation. The reader is thus invited to appropriate scriptural ideas and images that call into question ordinary life in the world and on that basis to reverse ordinary standards about what is good and bad in human living. By meditation on such texts, the reader is to see anew her or his own world, and to live differently, now with a scripturally informed worldview. After the citations, Deśika sums up the benefit of internalizing scriptural wisdom:

> Using such textual authorities, devout practitioners can reflect clearly on the seven faults inherent in experiences of nonconscious, material reality: being puny, unstable, rooted in sorrow, mixed with sorrow, the cause of sorrow's rising, the root for wrong ideas about oneself, and contradiction to one's own innate bliss. These practitioners also reflect clearly on the faults inherent even in the experience of pure consciousness, insofar as this is accessible amidst material things—and finally on that unique experience of the Lord that is contrary to all inferior experiences.[47]

As much as possible, Deśika lets his sources, presumably read as his teachers had read them before him, impart the instruction.[48] As was true of the *Treatise*, the knowledge Deśika is transmitting is imparted specifically for the sake of transformation, and scripture is to be received in a spirit that allows its force to be effective in the life of the reader. The kind of illumination Deśika aspires to is best understood in light of the passages from *Essence* chapter 9 detailing the double "ascent" through the three yogas of action, knowledge, and devotion, and thereafter—or alternatively—from a higher devotion (*para bhakti*) to a higher knowledge (*parā jñāna*) and finally to supreme devotion (*parama bhakti*) that is direct vision tantamount to union with God. Recitation, study, and insight into scripture are key to this meditative process; indeed, it is in meditation that such texts arose, and to meditation they draw their readers.

Deśika also uses scripture to map out how one is to live after loving surrender to God. In *Essence* chapter 15, titled "How One Should Act after Taking Refuge," he offers instruction on the expectations for life after refuge, and here he uses scriptural citation amply to characterize that life. For example, he uses twenty-four quotations to illustrate the first instruction in the chapter:

> They should become people who do what must be done after [taking refuge], passing their time in ways fitting to their proper nature.[49]

Here are just a few of the quotations from the āḻvārs, those poet saints whose Tamil songs were revered as sacred scripture and equal in status to the Sanskrit Upaniṣads and Vedas:

> Reading, listening, reverencing, worshiping, offering worship, thus I made the time pass. [*Nāṉmukaṉ Tiruvantāti* 63]

> If by thinking upon words rich in His excellence, we got rid of the sorrows of our enveloping deeds—then what should we think upon next? [*Periya Tiruvantāti* 86]

> For all time, without stop, we should perform service without ceasing. [*Tiruvāymoḻi* 3.3.1]

> Every moment I count on my fingers the names of Tirumāl of Tirukkoṭiyūr. [*Periyaḻvār Tirumoḻi* 4.4.3]

> When I do not eat is not the day when I go hungry, but only the day when I do not say "Obeisance to Nārāyaṇa" or with the flowers of the Rg, Yajur, and Sāma Vedas approach your feet. [*Periyaḻvār Tirumoḻi* 5.1.6]

> I do not long for birth accompanied by wealth, which merely makes the body grow. . . . I pray only to be born as a bird in the Veṅkaṭa hills. [*Periya Tirumoḻi* 4.4.3]

The citations offer simple and striking examples of religious practice—study, meditation, service, prayer, and devotion to holy places—that any pious reader could imagine practicing. As potent revelatory texts, the passages show the way but also enable the reader to become that kind of devout, dedicated person. After the nineteen Tamil quotations, Deśika closes with six Sanskrit passages:

> I do not long for the lordly power of the Lord of creatures or the Lord of beasts;
> may I be a kadamba or kunda tree on the bank of the Yamunā River. [unidentified source][50]

> Take me as your servant;
> there is nothing improper in this.
> I will be satisfied, and Your purpose will flourish. [*Rāmāyaṇa, Ayodhyā Kāṇḍa* 31.22]

> Whether you are asleep or awake, I will render service to You. [*Rāmāyaṇa, Ayodhyā Kāṇḍa* 31.27]

> I am Your servant, Kākutstha [Rāma], even for one hundred years; let this happen for You where You wish, just tell me. [*Rāmāyaṇa, Sundara Kāṇḍa* 15.7]

> I long only to be a Vaiṣṇava in all my births. [*Jitante Stotram* 1.13]

> I will be ready, five times of the day, in accord with my ability,
> with auspicious flowers and scents I have picked on my own;
> I will worship Hari with devotion, and in that way make my days pass. [35–36 of the verses of Vaṅkipuṟattunampi][51]

Here too, at issue is single-minded devotion expressed in love for the whole of a life and even over multiple lifetimes, and such is the point of scripture as Deśika cites it. He chooses citations that exemplify the spirit underlying the details of the devout life, and evokes (simply by their words, for we are told nothing of the persons who speak in the first person in these quotations) the good example of persons who lived that exemplary life of dependence on the Lord. More detailed prescriptions regarding how to live remain implicit, as do the scenes in the *Rāmāyaṇa* and other texts from which such passages are chosen. For many, of course, the good example of outstanding members of the community in any case matters most in determining how best to live. And yet for those who will read attentively, to study the cited texts is to imbibe their spirit and to begin experiencing the world in accord with these sentiments handed down in the words of scripture.

a. "Five Things to Be Known": First, God's Nature

The fourth chapter of the Essence offers a still fuller example of Deśika's concise, telegraphic use of scripture as a resource for meditation, illumination, and change of life. This doctrinal chapter, which includes about eighty quotations, is dedicated to an exposition of "the five things to be known": the Lord, the self, the means of attainment, the goal of attainment, and hindrances to attainment. But it is also strikingly rich in quotations gathered in a dense concatenation—very different from the more intuitive flow of *Treatise* book 6.12, wherein de Sales worked imaginatively with a small set of richly symbolic texts. Let us look more closely at this part of the *Essence* to see how scriptural citation functions in the chapter.

The first and most important topic of the chapter is the proper nature of the Lord. In this regard Deśika lists seventy quotations in four subcategories: first, the proper form of God as knowledge and bliss, in eternal relationship with the Goddess Śrī (twenty-six quotations); second, Nārāyaṇa's lack of bad qualities and limitless treasury of good qualities (twenty-one quotations); third, Nārāyaṇa's divine auspicious form (thirteen quotations); fourth, the infinite manifestations of divine power that pervade the world (ten quotations). Under each category, quotations are cited either en masse—one after the other in a long list, with only the simple instruction, "meditating on these . . ."—or as supportive of some still narrower theme.

For example, here are quotations intended to illumine and make real the proper nature of Nārāyaṇa in his relationship with Śrī:

> [In Vaikuṇṭha, the world beyond,] the Lord of the universe is ever with Lakṣmī, half of Himself. [*Liṅga Purāṇa*]
>
> This Nārāyaṇa is always with Śrī. [*Harivaṃśa* 2.55.59]
>
> You are the divine Nārāyaṇa, the spouse of Śrī, You hold the wheel, You are omnipresent. [*Rāmāyaṇa, Yuddha Kāṇḍa* 120.13]

> The Lord has the *śrīvatsa* mark on His chest and Śrī is with Him eternally. [*Rāmāyaṇa, Yuddha Kāṇḍa* 114.15][52]

> Śrī, inseparable from Viṣṇu, . . . [*Viṣṇu Purāṇa* 1.18.17]

Against the background of the simple vision of Śrī (Lakṣmī) and Nārāyaṇa represented in these quotations, Deśika introduces five more from the *Rāmāyaṇa* that show the inseparability of Sītā (Lakṣmī) and Rāma (Nārāyaṇa embodied; also called Kākutstha and Rāghava in this section, and Govinda or Kṛṣṇa farther below). Interestingly, most of the cited words (all but the third of these five) are actually those of Rāma's brother, Lakṣmaṇa, though he is not mentioned by name.

> [Lakṣmaṇa] spoke this word to Kākutstha in the presence of Sītā [*Rāmāyaṇa, Āraṇya Kāṇḍa* 15.6]

> The illustrious Lakṣmaṇa steadfastly touched his brother's feet, and spoke thus to Sītā and to Rāghava who bore this great vow. [*Rāmāyaṇa, Ayodhyā Kāṇḍa* 31.2]

> This Sītā is capable of protecting this host of demonesses from Rāghava. [*Rāmāyaṇa, Sundara Kāṇḍa* 58.87][53]

> I will protect you Rāma, with Sītā [*Rāmāyaṇa, Sundara Kāṇḍa* 58.90]

> With Vaidehī [Sītā], you will enjoy yourself on the slopes of the hills; whether you are asleep or awake, I will do everything for you. [*Rāmāyaṇa, Ayodhyā Kāṇḍa* 31.27][54]

Lakṣmaṇa speaks to Rāma—with Sītā present; Sītā, like Rāma, is a protector even from Rāma; to guard or serve Rāma is of course also to guard and protect Sītā. By careful reflection on these words, the reader as it were takes on the persona of Lakṣmaṇa, and becomes ready to acknowledge through service the unity of Nārāyaṇa and Śrī that is dramatically declared in the quotations.

The next quotations—interestingly, all chosen from the works of revered teachers Āḷavantār (11–13) and Rāmānuja (14–17)—seem intended to smoothly draw in the tradition of teachers, and perhaps even to give the reader words for use in addressing the divine couple, Nārāyaṇa (Viṣṇu) and Śrī:

He is seated along with Her on the serpent named "Endless" (in its delight). [*Stotra Ratna* 39]

Your beloved is the highest male. [*Catuḥślokī* 1]

The Lord with Śrī, pleased by the service rendered by the eternal celestial beings who find their enjoyment in that service. [*Ātmasiddhi*, opening verse]

Obeisance to Viṣṇu, ocean of pure bliss, with Śrī. [*Vedānta Sāra*, opening verse]

The infinite beloved of Śrī, whose form is the unique abode of all eminent qualities. [*Vedānta Dīpa*, opening verse]

May my intention, taking the form of devotion, be ever set upon the highest, who is Brahman, foremost in the revelatory texts, resplendent, the abode of Śrī. [*Śrī Bhāṣya*, opening verse]

The Lord of Śrī, whose essential nature is opposed to all that is objectionable, unique abode of auspicious qualities, infinite knowledge and infinite bliss. [Bhagavad Gītā Commentary, opening verse]

Deśika closes this opening meditation with six more quotations, all in Tamil; these reinforce the inseparability of the divine couple, and the necessity and appropriateness of envisioning them together:

If You and the holy Lady abide here. [*Mutal Tiruvantāṭi* 86]

I see You and the Lady with shining bracelets, abiding together. [*Tiruvāymoḻi* 4.9.10]

You and the great, holy, lovely Lady. [*Tiruvāymoḻi* 6.9.3]

By your holy grace and the holy grace of the Lady in the flower. [*Tiruvāymoḻi* 9.2.1]

Your lotus Lady and Yourself. [*Tiruvāymoḻi* 9.2.3]

> [Śrī says,] "I cannot be apart from You [Nārāyaṇa] even for a moment." [*Tiruvāymoḻi* 6.10.10]

The final quotations, a Tamil and Sanskrit pair, provide a kind of summary, seeming to present Nārāyaṇa in transcendent glory, as if beyond any lesser distinctive features:

> You are knowledge and complete bliss. [*Periya Tirumoḻi* 3.8.1]

> You are the light that never goes out, beyond all limitations. [*Viṣṇu Purāṇa* 1.22.53][55]

Deśika thus invokes a magnificent final vision of light and bliss, as it were an eschatological glory that can be glimpsed only by over time prepared, by long prior meditation on the preceding texts about Śrī and Nārāyaṇa.

Taken together, all these citations provide, almost without further instruction, the substance of a rich, subtle, multidimensional contemplation of Nārāyaṇa with Śrī. The divine persons are not simply described; they are invoked and made present for the sake of the contemplation that leads toward loving surrender to them. Deśika, like de Sales, is the master of scripture, deciding which texts are to be cited, in accord with his own preferences. And yet too, in marshaling so many, with so little commentary, he also subdues his own voice and allows tradition to speak through these words revered long before him: Discover the power of the tradition you already know. On a practical level, he is making available a rich array of images and, inscribed in the texts, exemplary relationships—Nārāyaṇa with Śrī, Rāma with Sītā, Lakṣmaṇa with Rāma and Sītā—that turn a proper theological conceptualization of Nārāyaṇa into an imaginable and pleasurable site for meditation, as the divine couple is brought near through these very texts. Though the cited words themselves are insufficient to inform us of the situations in which they were spoken, we can assume that teachers would have little trouble providing the contexts as needed. But it seems wise also to assume that Deśika has also carefully chosen these particular words for citation, because they are eloquent and effective on their own, irrespective of what else might be said in the context of the cited words. Context, after all, can be distracting when focus is required.

But even after this long list, *Essence*'s chapter 4 is just near its beginning. Still recounting the reality of the Lord, Deśika goes on to speak next of the divine auspicious qualities (with twenty-one quotations), the divine forms (with thirteen quotations), and the all-pervasive powers of the Lord (with ten quotations). Here too, the citations fall somewhere between ample description and bare assertions that the Lord is of a certain nature, possessed of all imaginable supreme attributes. Space does not permit citation of all these quotations, and the citations that indicate the divine qualities must suffice. First, Deśika states and supports his thesis:

> The Lord is to be thought of as the opposite of all that is deficient;
> as has been said,
> That supreme goal, called Viṣṇu, is free of all imperfections.
> [*Viṣṇu Purāṇa* 1.22.53]
>
> He is greater than the great; in this Lord of the great and low,
> there is no such manner of pain at all. [*Viṣṇu Purāṇa* 6.5.85]

Deśika goes on to portray the Lord as possessed of all the qualities essential to the Person who is the goal of life and yet also the means, the one who makes it possible to reach that goal:

> Hear now of a man possessed [of all these qualities]. [*Rāmāyaṇa, Bāla Kāṇḍa* 1.7]
>
> [Rāma], endowed with all these qualities. [*Rāmāyaṇa, Ayodhyā Kāṇḍa* 2.48]
>
> He is possessed of all the best qualities. [*Rāmāyaṇa, Bāla Kāṇḍa* 1.20]
> Benevolence, compassion, erudition, integrity of character, control of the senses, control of the mind: these six qualities make resplendent Rāghava, the best of men. [*Rāmāyaṇa, Ayodhyā Kāṇḍa* 33.12]
>
> His qualities cannot be enumerated, even in tens of thousands of years, even by all the gods assembled together. [Mahābhārata, *Karṇa Parva* 83.15]
>
> It is because of a lack of arrows, not from a lack of space in the sky
> [that men cease shooting arrows].
> So too, we cease praising Govinda
> only because of our lack of understanding,
> not due to some lack in His qualities. [Unidentified]

It is striking that only a few specific qualities are mentioned, notably in the fourth quotation. Deśika is surely making the point that scripture speaks firmly in favor of the Lord's infinite qualities, but he is at the same time leaving it to the reader's imagination to produce her or his own list of the actual qualities, gleaned from still other familiar texts and perhaps from the reader's own mind.

In fact, after giving his full lists of citations regarding the Lord's form and powers, Deśika concludes his rich scriptural consideration of the Lord with a list of qualities, each implied in previously cited and yet still further scriptural passages:

> And so the consort of [Śrī] Lakṣmī is possessed of infinite knowledge and bliss, opposed to all that is imperfect and objectionable, and distinguished by countless auspicious qualities, such as wisdom and power. He has a celestial, transcendent form of auspicious nature, and has two realms of power which are His body. He has, for His play, the work of creating the world, and so forth. He is the goal, He is Brahman.[56]

The point of citation is practical, since scripture is practical: Know the tradition through its sacred texts, and in that way come ever nearer to the Lord.

b. The Self and Obstacles to Attaining God

Deśika's treatment of the remaining four topics—the self, the means, the goal, and the obstacles—is relatively brief. He identifies three kinds of self (the eternally free, the liberated, and those in bondage) and simply mentions key characteristics of self: It is atomic in size; has an essence possessed of knowledge, bliss, and purity; is entirely dependent on the Lord; and is destined for the perfect happiness of union with the Lord. Deśika offers no quotations regarding the means and goal of attainment; since these topics are amply considered elsewhere in the *Essence,* here Deśika is content to refer to the three mantras, themselves considered to be a distillation of all that scripture has to say.[57]

Regarding the hindrances to attainment, however, Deśika has more to say, and so, of the five truths to be known, two—the nature of the Lord and the obstacles to reaching the Lord—dominate the chapter.

Deśika first considers the attachment of the self to matter, and the restriction of its knowledge by infatuation with sense experience. In this context, he twice cites the āḻvār Śaṭakōpaṉ to emphasize how this sense infatuation is a terrible suffering:

> Lord Kṛṣṇa, dark jewel of the heaven-dwellers, ambrosia,
> I'm near to You yet not near to You,
> here now, in-between, in a body that binds and destroys my strength,
> You've bound me with the strong cord of my many deeds,
> covering over my sores,[58] You've shoved me outside. [*Tiruvāymoḻi* 5.1.5][59]

and,

> You created the worlds amidst the three waters, O cloud colored Lord, and
> I wander about in the body You gave me then;
> to destroy the diseases of the cruel day
> by destroying deeds all the way to their root—
> when will I reach You and become one with You? [*Tiruvāymoḻi* 3.2.1][60]

It is notable in both quotations that Śaṭakōpaṉ, who sees everything in God, places on the Lord the responsibility for their separation. Deśika neither denies nor emphasizes this nuance; he is content to enlist the saint to make that provocative point, leaving further interpretation up to the reader.[61]

Deśika next adds a series of quotations that highlight the nature of the obstacles blocking the way to the Lord and that also elicit an intense repugnance for the human condition as we experience it. Five quotations appear in a single dense paragraph, which I reproduce here:

> Even among those not caught [in the bodies of animals or in heretical sects,] there is an inclination to ignorance of what is true and undue familiarity with what is contrary [to finding the Lord], because of the delusion and distortion that arise through contact with primal matter, etc. As Śrī Rāmānuja says,
>
> > This (contact with matter) obscures the proper nature of the Lord; it generates contrary knowledge and also the idea that (other, illusory) objects are delightful. [*Śaraṇāgati Gadyam* 17][62]

Consequently, this [association] induces [the individual self] to disobey His commands, and to do what is not to be done, merely for the sake of petty pleasures. As the āḻvār asks,

> Is it right on Your part
> to excite my five senses and thus confound my soul
> by showing this sinner all kinds of petty pleasures? [*Tiruvāymoḻi* 6.9.9]

Thus the person is immersed in a series of transgressions. As it says,

> Sin committed over and again destroys wisdom,
> and the person whose wisdom is destroyed
> commits still further acts of a sinful kind. [*Mahābhārata, Udyoga Parva* 34.74]

Consequently, as it says,

> I ever throw them into asuric births. [Bhagavad Gītā 16.19]

And so the Lord makes the individual self wander again and again around the circle of womb, birth, old age, death, hell, etc. By means of the *rājasic* and *tāmasic* scriptures,[63] which are the means to petty pleasures, etc., the individual self is made to fall down at the feet of minor deities who themselves are wandering about, fettered with chains like his own. As it says,

> The *rājasic* worship spirits and demons, while others who are *tāmasic* worship the dead and elemental spirits. [Bhagavad Gītā 17.4][64]

People are thus foolishly satisfied with demeaning pleasures that induce disgust, like worms [delighting in filth].[65]

Again, Deśika defers to his texts, offering minimal interpretation and allowing them to disclose for readers the dire state of ordinary human existence. The reader who meditates on such texts and takes them to heart begins to see the world through them, and to feel the intensified states of which scripture speaks.[66]

Apparently to highlight the chapter's overarching tension between its two primary elements—the lengthy scriptural descriptions of the Lord and of the stubborn obstacles blocking the way to that Lord—Deśika finally cites Rāmānuja's *Śrī Bhāṣya* 1.4.1:[67]

> The root of this succession of undesirable results lies in transgression of the Lord's commands. The primary obstacle then is the Lord's punishment arising because of them. How can this punishment be removed? The author of the *Śrī Bhāṣya*, commenting on the succession of things to be overcome mentioned in the *Kaṭhavalli Upaniṣad*, has declared, "But the only way to win over the Lord is to take refuge with Him."[68]

Scripture shows the goal and enables us to come near to the Lord; and it shows us our own situation, and why our best efforts most often fail. There is nothing left, after all this learning, but to turn to the Lord.

De Sales and Deśika see their writings as the fruit and vehicle of scriptural and traditional words spoken and written in earlier generations, writing indebted to oral sources and ultimately to positive acts of divine speech. In the *Essence* and *Treatise*, the power of the ancient discourse is made newly present. Precisely by the abundance of quotations in their writing, sacred words become each author's own best words, whether this be done by de Sales' contemplation of just a few texts that draw the reader into the great divine plan of love and surrender, or Deśika's long lists of quotations that pinpoint, over and again, insights that deconstruct every model of life that competes with loving surrender. Such quotations give life and force to the *Essence* and *Treatise* and make older scriptural wisdom available to a wider audience that probably would not read the cited texts in their original contexts. They write in such a way that their own words enable the presence and power of the older, still necessary words. Readers, it seems, are being asked to learn to read in the same transparent and uncluttered way, whatever the cost.

II. Engaging the Reader: Person to Person

De Sales and Deśika value the use of scripture to educate and prepare the reader. The *Treatise* and *Essence*, and even the revered scriptural texts themselves, are instrumental to the larger purpose of disclosing and intensifying the reader's oncoming encounter with God. For similar reasons, both Deśika and de Sales recognize the importance of persons—encountered directly, recollected from tradition, received through texts—as inspirations whose intensely lived spiritual journeys and wise words give a personal face to the truths and values by which loving surrender becomes probable. Hence both writers find ways to promote such people in their texts. They realize that exemplary figures who live the ideals of the tradition are also spiritually interesting persons who are likely to capture the imaginations of readers and give them confidence that they can make similar choices. Although God need not be imagined as only a distant figure, such human persons become nearly essential to the divine plan, helping practitioners to see concretely how they should think, feel, speak, and act on the way to God. And yet, as we shall also see, each writer brings a distinctive perspective to bear on the matter; if de Sales is straightforward in placing before us inspiring lives that should awaken a reader's desire to emulate them, Deśika prefers, once again, to give us the words of such persons, as if those words simply bear within them the power to capture and transform the reader's own life.

1. *De Sales Makes It Personal: Learning by Example*

De Sales is very good at catching the attention of readers with intriguing and inspiring tales. He loves to tell stories and tells them very well. Topics range from the curiosities of nature and tales famed in the ancient world to the lives of saints and to anecdotes about heroic individuals, including even "ordinary" men and women who took to heart the message of love and surrender to God. Putting before us individuals who have made and lived the radical choices of which he speaks, he makes it easier for the reader to imitate them, living properly these same life choices.

a. Reports of Heroic Persons

Chapters 9–14 of book 7 of the *Treatise* provide us with a fine extended example in a series of accounts of people who died for love of God. At the end of chapter 8, which focuses on St. Paul's "exhortation to the ecstatic and superhuman life," de Sales offers an intense prayer that sets up the chapters to follow:

> I will die with him and burn in the flames of his love; one and the same fire shall consume this divine Creator and his poor creature. *My* Jesus *is* wholly *mine, and I am wholly his* [Song of Songs 2:16]: I will live and die upon his breast, *neither life nor death shall ever separate me from him* [Rom. 8:39–39]. Thus then is made the holy ecstasy of true love, when we live no longer according to human reason and inclinations, but above them, following the inspirations and instincts of the divine Savior of our souls.[69]

De Sales thereupon commences an extended reflection on death and love in chapter 9 of book 7 with a simple citation that stands as a kind of heading to the chapter: "Love is as strong as death" [Song of Songs 7:6], followed by this thesis: "Holy love is sometimes so violent that it actually causes a separation of the body and the soul, making lovers die a most happy death, better than a hundred lives."[70] By way of evidence, he then lists saints who were carried off by love: Simeon Stylites, whose body was consumed by heavenly fire after his self-oblation in love; Abbot Julian, who witnessed the immolation of Simeon; Homobonus of Cremona, who died while listening to the Gospel at Mass; and famed saints who died while speaking, teaching desire and love:

> Many saints, however, have departed this life not only in charity and with the habit of heavenly love, but even in the act and practice thereof. St. Augustine died in the exercise of holy contrition, which is not without love; St. Jerome exhorting his dear children to the love of God, of their neighbor, and of virtue; St. Ambrose in a rapture, *sweetly discoursing* with his Savior, immediately after he had received the holy Sacrament of the altar; St. Anthony of Padua after *reciting a hymn* to the glorious Virgin Mother, and while *speaking* in great joy with our Savior; St. Thomas Aquinas joining his hands, elevating his eyes towards heaven, raising his voice very high, and *pronouncing* by way of ejaculation with great fervor, these words of the *Song* (the last which he had expounded): *Come my beloved, let us go forth into the field, let us abide in the villages* [Song of Songs 7:11].[71]

His final examples model the act and words of efficacious prayer:

> The admirable St. Eusebia, surnamed the stranger, died on her knees and in fervent prayer; St. Peter Martyr, writing with his finger and in his own blood the confession of the faith for which he died, and uttering these words: Lord, *into thy hands I commend my spirit* [Ps. 30:6; Luke 23:26]; and the great Apostle of the Japanese, Francis Xavier, holding and kissing the image of the crucifix, and repeating at every kiss these ejaculations of his soul: "O Jesus! *God of my heart*!"[72]

In chapter 10 of book 7 de Sales enlists martyrs and other holy figures who died because of their love and deeds of love: John the Baptist, Peter and Paul, the bishops Stanislaus and Thomas of Canterbury, Catherine of Siena, Francis, Stanislaus Kostka, Charles, plus "hundreds more who died so young."[73]

In chapter 10, de Sales recounts at length the deaths of Francis of Assisi, Mary Magdalene, and Basil—fascinating accounts that cannot detain us here—but he begins with a more general yet still powerful scenario of love, death, and desire:

> The soul is powerfully drawn by the divine sweetness of her beloved, to correspond on her side with his sweet attractions; with force and to the best of her power, she springs out towards this longed-for beloved who attracts her. Not being able to draw her body after her, rather than stay with it in this miserable life, she quits it and gets clear; flying alone like a lovely dove, into the delicious bosom of her heavenly spouse. She throws herself upon her beloved, and her beloved draws and ravishes her to himself. And as the bridegroom *leaves father and mother to cleave to his dearly beloved* [Gen. 2:24], so this chaste bride forsakes the flesh to unite herself to her beloved.

As the reader might wonder about how this passionate moment works out in more ordinary lives, de Sales offers some analogies:

> Now this is the most violent effect of love in a soul, and one which requires first a great offstripping of all such affections as keep the heart attached either to the world or to the body. As fire, having little by little separated an essence from its mass, and wholly purified it, at length brings out the quintessence, even so holy love, having withdrawn man's heart from all humors, inclinations, and passions, as far as may be, does at length make the soul come out, to the end that by this *death, precious in the divine eyes* [Ps. 115:5], she may pass into eternal glory.[74]

Ideally, it seems, the reader is inspired by the stories of great lovers and, reflecting on the instances of natural fire and purification, sees that an experience that most people think to be impossibly rare—being consumed with love of God—is actually a natural way of living.[75]

Chapter 12 of book 7 recounts at length the memorable story of "a very illustrious and virtuous knight" who goes to Jerusalem to see the holy sites and is enraptured by his experiences. With great ardor he visits each and every holy place related to the life of Christ:

> He *ascends at last,* this devout pilgrim, to Mount Calvary, when he *sees in spirit* the cross laid upon the earth, and our Savior, stripped naked, thrown down and nailed hands and feet upon it, most cruelly. He *contemplates* then how they raise the cross and the Crucified into the air, and the blood which streams from all parts of this ruined divine body. He *regards* the poor sacred Virgin, quite transpierced with the sword of sorrow; then he *turns his eyes* on the crucified Savior, whose seven words he *hears with a matchless love,* and at last he *sees* him dying, then dead, then receiving the lance-stroke, and showing by the opening of the wound his divine heart, then taken down from the cross and carried to the sepulchre, whither he *follows* him, *shedding a sea of tears* on the places moistened with the blood of his Redeemer.

Along the way, he is so intensely taken up in devotion that he is overwhelmed:

> At last returning to Mount Olivet, where the mystery of the Ascension took place, and he *saw* there the last marks and vestiges of the feet of the Divine Savior, *prostrating himself* upon them, and *kissing* them a thousand thousand times, with sighs of an infinite love. He began to *draw* up to himself all the forces of his affections, as an archer draws the string of his bow when he wishes to shoot his arrow, then *rising,* his eyes and his hands turned to heaven: O Jesus! he said,
>
> > My sweet Jesus! I know no more where to seek and follow you on earth. Ah! Jesus, Jesus, my love, grant then to this heart that it may follow you and go follow you above.

This mysterious gentleman in each step models behavior the reader can follow; to a large extent, he might just as well be someone sitting in his room in Europe, practicing the visualizations and the application of the senses prescribed in the *Spiritual Exercises* of Ignatius Loyola, whose practices were well known to de Sales. But the sequel in de Sales' story is not the safe practice of standard prayers, for the gentleman dies:

> And with these ardent words, he at that very moment shot his soul into heaven, a sacred arrow which as an archer of God he directed into the white-center of his most blessed target.

His heart had "broken with excess and fervor of love," as a physician carefully verifies, as love separated soul from body.[76] The chapter closes with the story of yet another man who, unable to take food, died after being blessed with the consecrated host, and with the story of Clare of Montefalco, whose heart was pierced by love.

In chapters 13–14, de Sales closes this intense series of high-intensity examples by meditating on the death of Mary, mother of Jesus, whose love and death mirror his passing. She is attentive and courageous in her contemplation of her son's death, even as she "experienced the most ardent and painful attack of love that can be imagined: for although the attack was extreme, yet, at the same time, it was at once equally strong and gentle, mighty and tranquil, active and peaceful, consisting of a heat which was sharp but sweet."[77] Echoing the theory of the two portions of the soul—the inferior ("reason") and superior ("spirit")—explained earlier in the *Treatise*, de Sales explains how Mary, whose self was not divided with contrary desires, exemplifies perfect, integral love of God:

> But I say that in this celestial Mother all the affections were so well arranged and ordered, that divine love exercised in her its empire and domination most peaceably, without being troubled by the diversity of wills and appetites, or by the contradiction of the senses, because neither the repugnances of the natural appetite nor the movements of the senses ever went as far as sin, not even as far as venial sin; but, on the contrary, all was employed holily and faithfully in the service of holy love, for the exercise of the other virtues, which, for the most part, cannot be practiced save amid difficulties, oppositions and contradictions.

This good example, for which the disciplined reader may strive, is a foretaste of the abandonment that stands at the heart of the entire *Treatise*:

> The most holy Mother, having nothing in her which hindered the operation of the divine love of her Son, was united unto him in an incomparable union, by gentle ecstasies, peaceful and without travail, ecstasies in which the sentient powers ceased not to

> perform their actions, without in any way disturbing the union of the spirit, as again the perfect application of her spirit did not much divert her senses.[78]

Readers will not presume to compare themselves to Mary, but her example (here and throughout the *Treatise*) confirms that an unhindered love of the Son is possible, marking the only really satisfying conclusion to the human drama. The cumulative effect of chapters 9–14 of book 7 is to make the case for potentially life-transforming imitation.

Now all of this, we must recall, is a kind of commentary on "Love is as strong as death" (Song of Songs 8:6), the words opening chapter 9 of book 7. Obviously, this prolonged meditation is neither technical exegesis nor a systematic theology of life and death. Rather, it is the accumulation and intensification of that spiritual and material energy by which persons become willing and able to die for love. By the long series of examples, these chapters make the case that some humans have in fact died of love for God in the past and that such a dying is to be yearned for. The reader is invited to imagine herself in those scenes, seeing herself in the mirror of the holy person who dies of love, and perhaps too beginning to die in that way. The way is cleared, most immediately, for books 8 and 9, wherein the reader finds further encouragement and inspiration and even a growing sense of obligation to choose loving surrender to God.

Book 9 of the *Treatise* has a number of simpler stories, drawn perhaps from popular piety. De Sales tells us of a king's deaf lute player who plays simply to please the king, though he cannot hear his own music (chapter 9). He recounts a pious believer's dialogue with the baby Jesus carried by Mary, expressing amazement that this Lord of the universe lets himself be carried wherever his mother wishes to go (chapter 14). Particularly memorable is his account of a fevered child who entirely trusts her father, a physician (chapter 15). In her suffering, the girl explains to her friend her complete surrender of all concern to her father: "I will only wait to let him will to do what he judges expedient, and when he comes to me I will only look at him, testify my filial love for him, and show my perfect confidence." Even when her physician father asks if he may bleed her, her trust is total:

> My father, she responds, I am yours; I know not what to will for my cure; it is yours to will and do for me what seems good to you; it is enough for me to love and honor you with all my heart, as I do. So her arm is tied, and her father himself opens the vein. And while the blood flows, this loving daughter looks not at her arm

> nor at the spurting blood, but keeping her eyes fixed on her father's face, she says only, from time to time: My father loves me, and I, I am entirely his.[79]

After rehearsing in vivid detail her loving abandonment of herself into the hands of her father, de Sales puts his reader on the spot:

> Why do you trouble yourself with willing or not willing the events and accidents of this world, since you are ignorant of what you should wish, and since God will always will for you, without your putting yourself in trouble, all you could will for yourself? Await therefore with peace of mind the effects of the divine pleasure, and let his willing be sufficient for you, since it is always most good: for thus he commanded his well-beloved St. Catherine of Siena: "Think upon me, said he to her, and I will think for you."[80]

De Sales' delight in such stories in part has to do with his sense about how to hold the attention of a listener. It can also be traced to his view that Christianity itself is a very great story, that of God made human and of Jesus who is courageous enough to give himself entirely into God's hands. All Christian stories, such as de Sales tells and those of readers too, derive from that original story.[81]

b. Addressing the Reader: O, Theotimus

As we saw in his telling of the story of the sick girl, de Sales intensifies the challenge of his text by recurrent direct appeals to his readers. Identified as "Theotimus," the reader is directly addressed more than 150 times in the *Treatise*: "Theotimus to whom I speak is the human spirit desirous of making progress in holy love, which spirit is equally in women as in men."[82] In this way, de Sales seeks to make very clear that the truths he communicates and the heightened states leading to loving surrender are not merely information to be received, nor edifying reports about ancient figures, but possibilities that directly pertain to the reader's own life.

Here are just three examples of this more personal address to Theotimus. First, de Sales urges his Theotimus to embrace personally the words of St. Paul:

> But finally, I think that St. Paul makes the most forcible, pressing and admirable argument that ever was made, to urge us all to the

> ecstasy and rapture of life and activity. Hear, *Theotimus,* I beseech you; be attentive and weigh the force and efficacy of the ardent and heavenly words of this Apostle, ravished and transported with the love of his Master. . . . *The charity of Christ presses us,* says his holy Apostle, *judging this* [Phil. 2:8]. What does "judging this" mean? It means that our Savior's charity *presses us* then especially when we *judge,* consider, ponder, meditate, and attend to the resolution of this question which faith gives.

As a result, Christ enters deeply into Theotimus's own heart:

> Mark, my good *Theotimus,* how he proceeds, fixing and impressing his idea deeply on our hearts.[83]

Second, at the end of book 9, he points out to Theotimus his destiny, even the movement of God within his (and de Sales' own) soul:

> Then, Theotimus, the soul has reason to cry out: I have put off my garment, how shall I put them on again? I have washed my feet of all sorts of affections, how shall I soil them again? [Song of Songs 5:3] *Naked came I out of the hand of God, and naked shall I return there*: God gave me many desires and God hath taken them away: *blessed be his holy name* [Job 1:21]. Yes, Theotimus, the same God who made us desire virtues in our beginning, and who makes us practice them on every occasion, is the very one who takes from us our affection for virtues and all spiritual exercises, that with more tranquility, purity and simplicity, we should care for nothing but the divine Majesty's good pleasure.[84]

Third, and perhaps most extraordinarily, one reason the image of Jesus on the cross should command Theotimus's direct attention is that even as he dies, Jesus has Theotimus directly in mind:

> O *Theotimus, Theotimus,* this soul of Our Savior knew us all by name and by surname; but above all on the day of his Passion, when he offered his tears, his prayers, his blood and his life for all, he breathed in particular *for you* these thoughts of love: Ah! my eternal Father, I take to myself and charge myself with all poor *Theotimus*'s sins, to undergo torments and death that he may be freed from them, and that he may not perish but live. Let

> me die, so he may live. Let me be crucified, so he may be glorified. O sovereign love of the heart of Jesus, what heart can ever bless you with enough devotion![85]

De Sales' hope is that no one who can imagine this scenario—Christ dying on the cross thinking of *me*—will casually put aside the text and return to ordinary business with the same feelings and habits as before. The entirety of the *Treatise*, we are to realize with Theotimus, is about me, the reader, and how I live my life: So what choices shall I make?

De Sales thus perfects a strong, direct style; he has a light touch in his use of his erudition and sources, wanting in every way to make smoother and clearer his appeal to the reader. By the end of the *Treatise*, we have not only learned a great deal, but we have been disposed to see our lives differently, as the images and exemplars of tradition suddenly become options we can adopt in our own lives. Reading is all about who we can become.

2. *Deśika's Sparer, More Traditional Approach*

Deśika takes a very different approach in presenting to his readers those persons who exemplify the truths and practices of loving surrender. Like de Sales, he has a wide range of resources at his disposal, but he is spare in using them. He occasionally points to ordinary people or royalty,[86] but much more frequently he alludes to stories known in scripture and tradition. In his typical way, however, he is relatively spare in naming even well-known figures or telling us their stories. Perhaps he is confident that his readers know the stories. Perhaps he also believes that the foundation of good example lies in the right *speech* of teachers and saints, in the words they utter in passing down the wisdom they have received. And so it is for the most part to their words, and not their individual personalities or particular anecdotes, that Deśika refers his readers.

a. Hearing Great Persons of the Śrīvaiṣṇava Tradition

We have seen already that the *Essence* is rich in citations, and these invoke concisely the great stories of the tradition. Drawing most frequently on the *Rāmāyaṇa*, Deśika highlights the sentiments, deeds, and choices of Rāma and Sītā in their exile, her captivity, and his heroic efforts to win her back. He draws our attention to Lakṣmaṇa and Vibhīṣaṇa, for instance, since by word and intention they exemplify utter devotion to Rāma and Sītā. On the one hand, Lakṣmaṇa is ever by Rāma's side, engaged entirely in serving him along with Sītā. On the other hand, he also favors the words and sentiments of Vibhīṣaṇa, the good brother of the evil king Rāvana (kidnapper of Sītā). He is particularly interested in how Vibhīṣaṇa shows us the meaning of perfect faith when he leaves Laṅkā, his brother's domain, and throws himself upon the mercy of Rāma, thus becoming a quintessential instance of surrender. But even these most famous figures appear only by their words, often enough without mention of their names, and with little descriptive characterization of their virtue. In chapter 11 of the *Essence*, for instance, Sītā is reverently named "the lady," and her honest advice to the demonesses guarding her is simply quoted, reminding the reader that however wicked our lives and occupations, we can still take refuge with the Lord. Lakṣmaṇa, five of whose declarations I cited earlier in this chapter, is likewise never mentioned by name even as he is repeatedly quoted. Vibhīṣaṇa too is not named, even when his surrender to Rāma is praised and studied; he appears simply in his words. Deśika's chief concern is perhaps to remind readers of these figures they already know about from tradition, but then to focus entirely on giving them the living words that can change the reader's way of living, whatever the external circumstances.

The Śrīvaiṣṇava community in Śrīraṅgam (where Deśika wrote the *Essence*) was relatively small. Tradition seems to have been embodied primarily in familiar and beloved great teachers, past and present, known to exemplify the ideal of loving surrender, by their lives giving visible and verbal form to the tradition's truths and values. Deśika repeatedly expresses reverence for Śaṭakōpaṉ and other āḻvār poet saints who lived centuries before his time, and also for the great teachers who set the tradition on its course just a few generations before him. He is particularly attentive to how Āḷavantār (Yāmuna) and Rāmānuja authoritatively taught the core truth and value of loving surrender to God. And yet here too, even when he praises such teachers for the wisdom they embody and communicate, this praise is stated in general terms as if to comprehend a much wider array of such teachers, and to honor teachers simply through passing along the knowledge they had received from their teachers and then shared with their own students—as if to say, "Remember them, remember me and my treatise, by getting beyond our personalities and cherishing what we *said*."

Thus, a typical verse at the end of chapter 31 of the *Essence* is a tribute to the character and talents of the true teacher; Deśika's praise is both intense and self-effacing:

Lighting the bright lamp of wisdom in our minds,
they dispelled all darkness—
for such teachers even the marvelous Lord can see no recompense;
we praise them, we rejoice,
keeping their glory in mind, ever exalting them,
and so their renown grows greater—
but is all this not little in return
for all we've gained?[87]

Deśika certainly could have told stories of these great teachers—naming more of them—and recounted instances of their edifying devotion, since such stories had already been told in previous generations.[88] But analogous to the way he treated the great figures of scripture, he prefers to allude to what his readers already know of the great teacher that they might apply *their teaching* to their own personal situations.[89]

A passage at the beginning of chapter 17 clarifies the delicate balance between the person of the teacher and the words he communicates, giving us insight into the style of inspiration that Deśika envisions. In the passage, the great teacher Rāmānuja is on his deathbed. He instructs his disciples to remain committed to the life of service in the community and, insofar as possible, to his teaching and writing. As guidance to the service that lives before them, he offers this scaled set of duties:

1. Study the *Śrī Bhāṣya*; or if not, then
2. learn the songs of the ā̱lvārs (the Divya Prabandham); or if not, then
3. offer physical service in the holy places; or if not, then
4. meditate on the meaning of the Dvaya Mantra; or if not, then
5. serve another Śrīvaiṣṇava.[90]

Reading Rāmānuja's *Śrī Bhāṣya* commentary is presented as the most perfect way of honoring his memory as the great teacher who is still to be encountered in his writing. But the ensuing four options—perhaps increasingly realistic for the wider audience—are illuminating. If study of the very demanding *Śrī Bhāṣya* is not possible, that study may also be acceptably replaced by reflection on the pleasing richly varied vernacular songs of the ā̱lvārs; for what Rāmānuja said in technical terms, they said in the most attractive way.[91] But still more accessible nontextual options follow. One might offer to clean, cook, or do similar chores at the holy temples praised in the ā̱lvārs' hymns, or one might meditate on the Dvaya Mantra, which includes in its six words the entire teaching of the tradition.

Or, shifting to the most personal and interpersonal option, one might serve another Śrīvaiṣṇava. All of these are occasions of grace, and all of them honor Rāmānuja. Teachers communicate brilliantly in their books, but the books lead us back to even the simplest members of the community who enact all these ideals in serving and being served. Implicit is a message for the reader: You can study the *Essence* your entire life, but if you understand what I am saying, you can also find other good ways to serve the community and live out what I am talking about.

b. Shifting the Way We Read: From Prose to Poetry

Every chapter of the *Essence* begins with at least one Sanskrit verse and ends with at least a pair of Tamil and Sanskrit verses, and some chapters have still other verses interspersed with his prose exposition. The way that Deśika offsets his prose and the myriad embedded citations with verses of his own composition marks one of his most notable and pleasing literary strategies, a matter of style that is also pertinent to his larger purposes. He seems to delight in turning to verse, and does so with a flourish, showing his mastery of Tamil and Sanskrit styles; and by this practice he also makes his reader shift into a different way of engaging whatever theme is at hand. In part, he is simply composing in accord with an expected and admired South Indian tradition that highly favored poetry and song. Yet the verses also reinforce his themes and provide fresh and persuasive ways of drawing key conclusions. By bringing a variety of words and images to his own text, he reinforces the idea that the truth is always larger than any given expression of it; even the best ideas can be uttered, imagined, and enjoyed in other forms. By shifting to poetry, he wakes up his readers, asking them to shift to a different mode of reading and perhaps even to memorize these verses as an alternative way of receiving his text and its message.

This is not the place to study Deśika's verses with respect to Tamil and Sanskrit poetic tradition,[92] and instead I take up only a few instances illustrative of the role verse plays as a complement to prose and citation. Verse adds a new dimension to how the reader can engage the *Essence*, the wisdom of its tradition, and even the reading process itself. I take as our example the six verses concluding the prefatory *Lineage*.[93]

Each of these verses discloses and praises a dimension of the power of the teachers—specifically Nāthamuni, Āḷavantār, and Rāmānuja—and reimagines devotion to them. Speaking in the first person, Deśika acknowledges that his own salvation is inextricably intertwined with his devotion to that lineage of teachers, beginning with his own teachers:

> I take refuge with my teacher who graciously bestowed on me my life,[94]
> and in turn I reverence the lineage of his teachers, and after that
> by grace I place before me Rāmānuja,
> the flood that rose in Perumpūtūr, along with
> Periyanampi, Āḷavantār, Maṇakkālnampi and
> Uyyakoṇṭār who taught him the good path,
> Nāthamuni, Śaṭakōpaṉ, Senānāthaṉ, and
> the auspicious Lady Śrī of sweet ambrosia—
> and putting Him first,
> I take refuge at the holy feet of my Lord.[95]

What was already stated in the *Lineage*'s prose passages is now performed—and the reader can join in the recitation of the verse, enacting the praise that Deśika has been promoting; in this confession, he acts out the theme of the chapter, stating his own gratitude and devotion to the lineage. Proper and clear ideas are enriched with images—grace, the flood, the path, the ambrosia—and so too with the names of the great teachers. In verse, Deśika can also express more freely his own piety, his own refuge at the Lord's feet.

The first Sanskrit verse among the concluding six verses also draws attention to the lineage of teachers, the importance of learning from a teacher; it introduces the image of a divine river of compassion into which the author, his teachers, and his readers have plunged:

> To extract the stinging arrows of desire,
> I take delight in Nāthamuni and the other teachers too,
> each pure, each different, each glorified by the three Vedas;
> they channel everywhere the river of divine compassion
> of that Couple with whom refuge must be taken in full faith;
> they are foreign to the paths of envy, error, and deception,
> they are my teachers.[96]

Pure conduits of divine compassion, these teachers remove the affliction of desire and inculcate joy that is their own and yet divine as well, in the same great current. A second Sanskrit verse brings in another striking image, suggesting that their powerful teaching echoes the resounding cry of Nārāyaṇa—the white horse Hayagrīva—arising from within them; by its sheer power, opposing views are blown away with all the subtlety of a trumpet's blast:

In the lotus of the teacher's heart
with heart Hayagrīva enjoys his lion's throne,
sounding from there
the neighing echoes that knock low the pride of adversaries:
possessed of many good qualities,
clearing the good path,
blowing away like balls of fluff all those religious positions shaken
  by this wind
that gusts in the banners of victory fastened to palaces on all sides:
in triumph, the lineage of our teachers.[97]

The point, again, is simple: The teachers teach the truth and defeat expositors of wrong and incomplete views. Yet the images in the verse—lotus and heart, horse and lion, neighing and gusts of wind, fluff and banners and glorious palaces—one by one seize the attention of the reader; when meditated on, they instill a vivid picture of the clean triumph of these good and wise persons over their opponents.

As I noted in chapter 1, the final three verses of the *Lineage* portray the three great teachers honored by all Śrīvaiṣṇavas, linking them with right thinking, right word, and right deed. Rāmānuja is glorious and unstoppable, like an elephant crashing through the forest; Āḷavantār too is radiant, a conquering hero who affects how we learn; and Nāthamuni, first in the "modern" lineage of teachers who widened the path of spiritual learning by retrieving the Tamil hymns of the āḻvārs and making them accessible to a broad audience:

The sage Rāmānuja adorns the world by his renown,
he is a rare elephant against those reasoners who wreak great havoc
on the subtle path of the forest books,
he is the Lord who destroys the plantain pith of their arguments:
we have reflected on the sweet excellence of his teachings
and can no longer even *think* of doing evil.

After a long time, finally now, by our good fortune, our minds are
  focused;
lest we fall again and wander about amidst this body's deeds,

we stay at the feet of Āḷavantār of radiant, gracious excellence,
who came to rule,[98] who conquered all:
and now we *study* nothing improper.

For his two good, loving disciples—his trumpet and conch—at his feet
Nāthamuni poured forth the sweet melodies of the Tamil Veda;
he widened the ascetic path, set it afire:
we *fall in worship* at his feet every day and rise up again:
in all directions there is no one like us.[99]

In such verses, the wisdom and effectiveness of the teachers—plus others in their lineage, Deśika included—are praised, each with vivid natural and social images, and with tones of emotion that should, if vividly imagined by readers, fill their minds and thereby draw them to that lineage and its modern representatives, for learning and worship. Each presents and recommends a new practice: a mind cleared of all evil, study pursued far from erroneous words, and a life dedicated to regular worship. Though this praise of the teachers in a sense averts attention from the *Essence* to the masters themselves, Deśika's praise is uttered so eloquently that indirectly he is also enhancing the fame of his own text that so skillfully points beyond itself, but in such a lovely way.

c. A Lineage of Verses, A Lineage of Teachers

Of particular interest are the Tamil verses that conclude each of the thirty-two chapters.[100] These are in the *antāti* style, whereby the last word or words of one verse closely resemble or replicate the word or words beginning the next verse, imparting continuity without necessarily fixing a logical or thematic connection. Usually, the word or words ending the very last verse of such a set is found also to begin the very first verse—thus completing a great circle of verses. In employing *antāṭi*, Deśika draws on a style familiar in South India and often used by the āḻvārs. But he chooses to hide his usage in plain view, mentioning only at the end of chapter 32 that "these thirty-two (*antāti*) verses display Tamil in its three forms."[101] These verses and the one that ends the *Essence* bind the text together, linking its chapters by this "hidden" thread. Forming a self-contained unity—for the verses read nicely as a separate entity—they are a text within the text.

The two *antāti* verses in chapter 32 locate Deśika's own creative action with reference to his work that is now complete:

Knowledge gained from those gone before,
the removal of confusion,
selves gained in explaining the three mantras,
unique mercy for the humble:
for those appreciating excellence,
among those learned in the secret texts[102]
who teach how to gain a firm foundation,
of what value now are petty gains?
all these things I have made it possible to *hear*,[103]

Ambrosia for ears that *hear*,
a grace for those faultless and possessed of resplendent qualities,
joy in dwelling on the inner meanings of the incomparable four
  Vedas,[104] radiant, ambrosia for the ears—
these thirty-two verses displaying Tamil in its three forms,
auspicious [*tiru*] words.[105]

The word "auspicious" occurs in the first *antāti* verse in chapter 1, which mentions the goddess Tiru—Śrī—and so the great garland of verses makes its round:

Along with *Tiru*
a lustrous gem came to abide near the heart of Tirumāl, and
like that, we manage to touch His lotus feet;
lest we disappear into that flood of deeds
started even in the womb,
the learned ones, knowing the five subtle truths,
make this knowledge all we need.[106]

This verbal link binds together the whole *Essence*, and by catching the attention of the discerning reader who notices so subtle a feature of the text, enables that reader to reread the whole differently.

The verses are lovely but not ornamental, for they reinforce the gracious teachings of the tradition, with particular emphasis on the importance of the teachers themselves. We can see this by considering the three *antāti* verses that end chapters 10–12, which pertain to the act of taking refuge. From chapter 10:

Everyone suffering in this world in its confines,
from the brahmin to the mixed castes,

everyone withers away, having no one else:
that everyone might take refuge,
those who know and love our Beginning without End
Who grieves for us in His mighty compassion
have made Him known.

In their wisdom and love, they steer seekers away from inferior deities, and back toward the true God, according to the *antāti* verse ending chapter 11:

Those who love us *have made known* how to reach the Highest One
who aids us in our poverty and grief,
when we lacked even that ambivalent means,[107]
and so the idea of begging,
"End the grief of birth!" from yonder divinities just like us yet with
no real relationship to us—
such a bad idea—
is all *done away with.*

Appropriating to their own persons the truth of the ancient Veda, they make known the determination of the Lord to save his people, say the *antāti* verse of chapter 12:

"Let's be done with the burden" is the goal they set:
"The Lord is greatly compassionate,
He intends to get hold of us,
He protects the life of the person at His feet:
do not forget this truth,
He is the life-breath of our world":
thus our rulers speak,
wearing the Veda as their crown.

Such verses are informative in emphasizing the gracious teachers who have compassionately made known to those seeking relief from life's miseries the saving truths and saving path of escape. In the *antāti,* it is always the teachers who show the way, by their ideas, their words, and in the compassion and splendor that mark their person. Together such verses form a garland of praise for the teachers to be heard and recited by those grateful for their teaching. In a sense, this *antāti* garland might also be taken to stand in for the *Essence* as a whole; some readers could learn all that is needed simply from these thirty-three verses alone, and by following up on their exhortation seek the needed teacher. Even more: The succession of teachers reaching back to Nārāyaṇa with Śrī is itself replicated in the uninterrupted flow of these verses, a lineage of teachers and *antāṭi* noticed only by the discerning disciple who is able to read back from the end to the beginning. The tradition, the *Essence*, the *antāti* verses, and the lineage of teachers are all unbroken garlands—really, the same garland seen differently—without beginning or end.

We can also notice that the Sanskrit verse ending each chapter complements the *antāti* by adding a different kind of summation and putting a different seal upon the chapter. The Sanskrit verse often summarizes the chapter's content by a teasingly laconic enumeration that makes sense only to those who have studied the chapter already, as if to render its truth again in a (too) brief, pleasing form that can be memorized and even sung. If the Tamil verses highlight the role of the teacher, the Sanskrit verses accentuate the rarity of the good student who understands this subtle teaching.

Consider the Sanskrit verses paired with the *antāṭi* verses I have just cited. The Sanskrit verse that ends chapter 10 summarizes the deficiencies that make a person suitable for, desperate for, that act of refuge taught by the teachers in the *antāti* verse, which promises an efficacious teaching valuable for everyone. The Sanskrit verse ending chapter 11 summarizes the chapter, though by so bare an enumeration that it offers little assistance to those who have not read it already. It seems also to turn our attention to the accompanying Tamil verse that depicts the teachers and

Tamil and Sanskrit Verses Concluding *Essence* Chapter 10

Tamil (*antāti*) Verse	Sanskrit Verse
Everyone suffering in this world in its confines, from the brahmin to the mixed castes, everyone withers away, having no one else: that everyone might take refuge, those who know and love our Beginning without End who grieves [for us] in His mighty compassion have made Him known.	Lack of ability for devotion, etc., lack of sure knowledge, exclusion due to the instructive scriptures, inability to endure the passing of time: of necessity these four conditions arise, and good people, in accord with their innate competence for one or two or three or more of these, together or separate, obey the injunction to take refuge, just that, and with no hesitation take refuge with the Lord of Śrī for the sake of liberation.[a]

[a] *Essence*, chap. 10, 206–7/114.

the influence of their teaching. In chapter 12, the Sanskrit verse's image of the horse, chariot, and charioteer[108] illustrates the tripartite structure of reality (conscious selves, all insentient matter, the Lord), all of which orients us to the gracious Lord as destination and refuge. Here too, the Tamil verse praises the teachers who make a direct appeal to the reader. The Sanskrit verses may have been intended for a more expert audience than were the *antāṭi* verses, so that Deśika's chapter endings were crafted with two kinds of readers in mind: those who could master the teaching (in Sanskrit) and those who would benefit most from personal guidance (in Tamil). Or Deśika may have intended to instruct the same readers in two ways: in Sanskrit to appropriate and internalize the precise and subtle details of his exposition, and in Tamil to approach the teachers who would facilitate real learning.

The shift from prose to verse purposely complicates and enriches the work of reading, introducing images and emotions that stimulate readers to look beyond the *Essence*, into their own memories and imaginations, for vivid representations of what the verses propose. The verses summarize and stand in for the prose portion of the chapters; they can be memorized and recited, and in that recitation the religious reader appropriates and affirms what has been taught.[109] And just as the verses point to the great teachers of the tradition, so the reader is led through the *Essence* and beyond it, to the necessary living encounter, a more intimate encounter with those teachers, a wisdom beyond the text.

Tamil and Sanskrit Verses Concluding *Essence* Chapter 11

Those who love us have made known how to reach the Highest One who aids us in our poverty and grief, when we lacked even that ambivalent means, and so the idea of begging, "End the grief of birth!" from yonder divinities just like us yet with no real relationship to us— such a bad idea— is all done away with.	This yoga is proclaimed by the instructions of the Lord: it has *five* or *six* limbs and is to be performed *once*: by *two* limbs it is shown that there is no pleasure in transgression, by *one*, that there is no other means, by *one*, that we must be certain within ourselves regarding our burden, and by *the last*, we desire to reach the goal; with these, knowledge of reality and so a realization of our dependence even regarding refuge and its subsidiary helps and all the rest.[a]

[a] *Essence*, chap. 11, 226/125–26.

Tamil and Sanskrit Verses Concluding *Essence* Chapter 12

"Let's be done with the burden" is the goal they set: "The Lord is greatly compassionate, He intends to get hold of us, He protects the life of the person at His feet: do not forget this truth, He is the life-breath of our world:" thus our rulers speak, wearing the Veda as their crown.	The horse, chariot, charioteer in sequence, shown in "the final part of the three Vedas," three realities arranged with respect to their various appropriate activities; all three are causes, two are agents, but just one is dependent on Himself alone; whosoever's burden is accepted by the Lord, he has no burden for himself, no effort.[a]

[a] *Essence*, chap. 12, 241/134–35.

If de Sales appeals to exemplary saints and ordinary heroes, and to his "Theotimus," Deśika personalizes the reading practice by getting his reader to make the words her own, and this ownership makes progress toward loving surrender possible. Both authors compel the attentive reader to reflect more deeply on what she is learning as she reads and to notice more carefully where—and to whom—that reading, honestly appropriated, is leading her.

III. Reading More Intensely to Discover a Destiny

I have explored just a few of the elements of style and strategy that make the *Treatise* and *Essence* the literary classics they are, instructive, persuasive, and emotionally forceful. Though the authors have distinctive styles, cite different scriptures in accord with different traditions, bring disparate methods of interpretation to bear, and put different kinds of role models before us, de Sales and Deśika have remarkably consonant goals as they push toward the ideal of loving surrender. That differences in manner of writing can still be recognized as converging in this way gives added force to our double reading, coloring our appreciation of each text as we shift back and forth from one to the other. De Sales' text is all of a piece, a great, rising exposition of the history of love and our journey toward immersion in God, beyond human words. Deśika's text is distinguished by the variety of approaches he takes to illumine the three mantras from different angles: philosophical and theological discourses; argumentative and lyrical expositions; minutely exegetical, psychological, and ethical reflections; and final instructions on how to read and how to teach.

Throughout the *Essence*, Deśika insists that his text is a secondary teaching aid, the occasion for preliminary learning that is filled out with a teacher. Indeed, its value lies precisely in the indication that even the best of texts is only preparatory for more transformative encounters. The *Treatise* is but a witness to the divine action and work of the Holy Spirit, ever at work in the church and world. De Sales too hopes that divine power will be operative in his words, giving to them a spiritual substance that he himself cannot impart.

Each author fashions a distinctive vantage point for contemplating the world, in comprehension of the larger panorama (in the *Treatise*) or the finely drawn intimate detail (in the *Essence*). De Sales seems at times more passionate and Deśika more instructive. De Sales seeks to inflame the hearts of his readers and draw them into the larger divine drama of love, whereas Deśika brings light to the mind and heart in an effort to free his readers from needless, mistaken bondage. Their approaches entail matters of style that are no less noteworthy than differences in content and doctrine, as de Sales and Deśika educate their readers and change how they view their lives and make choices. Read together, the *Essence* and the *Treatise* cooperate in providing the engaged reader a more complex set of imaginative and affective resources, articulated in terms of the language and images of two traditions. By close reading, we are trained in a double set of complex skills, afforded a richer register of affective possibilities. And, of course, Deśika and de Sales write from and for their larger communities. They draw upon the richly varied treasures of scripture, tradition, the lives and utterances of revered persons of the past; they make their own texts sites and exemplars where tradition comes alive for new readers, by words that enable the meditation that leads to loving surrender to God. Their hope is that readers will draw upon the deep, traditional learning that awakens the imagination and intensifies desire for the sake of loving surrender, in community.

1. The Particulars of Rapture: *Advice from Charles Altieri*

At stake then is a transformative process grounded in receiving and appropriating texts written with that process in mind. Like all careful teaching, effective writing—words and images, narratives, persons, direct appeals and admonitions—realizes its effect slowly in small and incremental achievements that are to be measured line by line and page by page and are not to be completed by way of shortcut. In reflecting upon this transformative learning we must necessarily pay more attention to how reading affects us, and in doing so, we take up questions familiar to the field of literary criticism—and most particularly, it seems, from discussions of how we learn from reading fiction. To shed further light on the literary dimension of our project, I turn to Charles Altieri, a careful interpreter and theorist with special interest in the aesthetic and moral implications of literature (novels, dramas, poetry) for philosophical and ethical reflection. He has ably explored how authors shape their writing so as to produce affective change in their readers, so that readers not only identify themselves with characters portrayed in the books they read but also find in their reading resources an altered response to their own life situations. Altieri does not discuss religious texts, and I do not suggest that religious texts are exactly like works of fiction; rather, I suggest that Altieri's insights can be usefully extended to illumine the affective and performative force of the *Treatise* and the *Essence*.

At the beginning of his 1990 *Canon and Consequences*, Altieri reminds us that the great texts are more than vehicles of information or conveyors of reasons for behavior. A text becomes normative (and canonical) because over time it remains capable of helping readers to reimagine their own life choices in accord with imaginative and affective energies that are deeper and more enduring than overt reasons that might be given to justify behavior. Such texts help us to expand and enrich our set of imaginative and affective resources; accordingly, the proper way to think about our reading of literature is to see that we are educated by it to react differently in our own specific situation. "By reading *through* [the text]," Altieri writes, "we can gain a rich grammar for interpreting particular experiences or projecting self-images that have significant resonance in how we make decisions in the present."[110] In the current context we can extend Altieri's insight: *Through* texts such as the *Essence* and *Treatise*, we learn not simply to enter upon the (past or ideal) religious worlds inscribed in those texts, but by their words, images, exemplars, and prose and poetic forms we learn also to reread our own daily lives so as to make room for new choices, such as recognizing loving surrender as a life choice that is viable in our own situations.

Later in the same volume Altieri returns to the notion of "reading through" and captures something of the humbler commentarial disposition I have favored in this book: "We better fit the ideals about reading developed by those writers whom we take the time to read if we imagine ourselves as *reading through the text*. By submitting ourselves to [the text's] provisional authority as an integrated work, we can hope to construct the best possible case for the text as a window on possible values in [our own] experience."[111] This application of what we read to our lives is not simply a determination of rational alternatives or obedience to directives announced in the text. Rather, attentive reading works productively because it draws us into encounter with the great texts, "forcing us to extend our imaginations; and it keeps authority within an imaginative dialogue with great minds, rather than placing it in some contemporary interpretive practice."[112] Reading-through, extending our imaginations, participating in dialogues with great minds: By this same model, we can also appreciate better the potential of our reading of the *Essence* and *Treatise* to open for us a new window on our lives beyond and after reading.

In *The Particulars of Rapture* (2003), Altieri further studies the production of emotion in acts of reflective and imaginative reading that do not reduce texts to information about a possibly more interesting alternative to the "real world."[113] We learn to reverse the expected relationship between text and context, reading and social interests:

> And dwelling on immanent values may help us try modes of responsiveness to a range of art works that *emphasize how history enters art rather than how art can be placed in historical contexts.* Analogously, I can hope that these arguments offer a way of seeing how art works can serve social interests without depending on the thematic allegorizing that now seems necessary for taking art as a serious human practice.[114]

It seems to me that this submission to the text and reconsideration of our world in light of it brings to the fore values of particular benefit in reading *religious* texts, and Altieri's words can just as well direct our religious reading. "Stressing the affect," he writes, "emphasizes modes of caring about the self and the world. It also creates opportunities for experiencing states like intensity, involvedness, and plasticity while encouraging us to reflect on who we become as we experience such states."[115] These subjective states become ends in themselves which together redefine the way of being of the reader:

> These states are the experiences of how *intensity* modifies subjectivity, the experience of an *involvedness* within which we feel our personal boundaries expanding to engage other lives on

> the most intimate possible levels, and the experience of the psyche's *plasticity* as it adapts itself to various competing imaginative demands.[116]

Altieri offers examples of these states from poetic and dramatic works where the power of literature on its readers is evident, once we look to the affective dimensions of the reader's real-life choices, and not simply to that reader's stated reasons for revised programs of action. Literature enables us to imagine and feel differently, more intensely, with respect to the ways of life that stand before us. I suggest that likewise the *Essence* and *Treatise* can be helpfully conceived as generating the same conditions, the transformation of the reader into a person able to make more radical choices. Deśika and de Sales draw the reader into fresh relationships with the exemplars and contemporary representatives of tradition and challenge the reader to adapt differently to a "new" world now reconfigured around loving surrender as life's central ideal. To surrender lovingly, or even to envision becoming the kind of person who can act that way, requires the reader to enter a religious space wherein our awareness is intensified, our relationships modified, and our experiences re-formed in light of the insights and affective states we cultivate in reading.

In the fourth chapter of *The Particulars of Rapture,* titled "Why Manner Matters," Altieri explores the complex presentation of the human situation in fiction, poetry, drama, visual art, and other modes and the consequent, desired complexification of the reader's response. In examining the values-in-practice that emerge as people are moved by what they read and then respond differently in the ongoing situations of their lives, Altieri shifts primary emphasis from belief—and the assumption that affects and actions are primarily expressive of belief and the reasons enunciated to fit beliefs—to a new modality of allowing expressions to "matter for what they do rather than for what they reveal."[117] Though novels and plays do portray people as acting in accord with plausible reasons, they show how people reread their own situations imaginatively and affectively and reshape even familiar tasks settled within familiar relationships. By modeling the imaginative and affective dimensions of possible choices, works of literature provide paradigms for the reader's own life; it is not that the reader now lives inside the world of the novel or drama and responds to its situation in a kind of fiction, but rather that by the reading she or he is able to imagine, feel, and choose differently. Similarly, the *Essence* and *Treatise* do not invest us with fourteenth- or seventeenth-century sensibilities or give us temporary residence in ancient stories; rather, they affect how we assess the truths and values of our current situation and come to see loving surrender as a real option.

But this imaginative and affective change requires introspection and adjustment in our self-awareness, something more than appreciating the behavior of the characters in a novel or play. It also "requires modifying substantially how we envision our roles as interpreters." When a literary work stimulates our imagination, its basic role

> is simply to keep salient details vital and to project means of composing these details into overall attitudes that carry expressive significance. Imagination, in other words, is the aspect of our mental life responsible for registering vividness and synthesizing the particular energies producing that vividness. Imagination is our way of opening ourselves to being affected.[118]

"Being open" and "being affected" are practical ideals very much at the core of writing undertaken by Deśika and de Sales, ideals achieved precisely through the kind of writing practices we have examined in this chapter, strategies that educate us, deepen our attention, and awaken our imaginations.

According to Altieri, it is helpful to conceive the dynamic involved as a shift from an "adjectival" to an "adverbial" manner of glossing changes in the relationships among meaning, action, and affect:

> When we consider emotions adverbially we consider them as *direct modifications of activities by the subject.* For what becomes vivid is not our idea about the emotion but our sense of what goes into expressing the emotion. . . . The expression has force because of the qualities it exhibits as features of the forming of an attitude.[119]

Acutely attuned to the possibilities of living differently, reoriented to the very particular and very local realities of life for God as de Sales and Deśika understand such a dedication of life, we come to see and feel how loving surrender might indeed reshape what we are and how we behave in our everyday lives:

> Manner matters because it puts the emphasis on *concrete vividness as the locus of significance for the activity.* Consequently, when we register the emotion adverbially we adjust how

> we project identities—about our own emotions or about agents whom we observe. We are responding not to how beliefs shape a person's world but to *who the person becomes* as he or she manifests the working out of attitudes in relation to that world.[120]

The discourses leading to loving surrender, replete with examples of people who attest to and enact the ideal of loving surrender, similarly model how after our reading we can continue to go about our ordinary business, yet with a different adverbial force coloring how we act and understand what we do.

Altieri draws a conclusion that nicely catches the deeper power of the *Essence* and *Treatise* as texts providing a place where readers change in the modality of their actions, even if older reasons, beliefs, and various specific practices rightly remain in play. We learn to "project ourselves imaginatively into what creates the vividness [of this writing] and gives it the possible power to modify its environment,"[121] and in so doing, we are adjusting *ourselves* and not simply our explanations of reality and assessments of right behavior:

> The expression [of literature] asks of us not that we offer an interpretation of it but that we adjust to its specificity. If we seek only explanations for actions, we tend to ignore everything that might give such particular expressions distinctive vividness and force. Analogously, if we treat fictions only in terms of belief we miss the range of motives and qualities that might be expressed in how the fiction is presented. . . . [An adverbial approach] helps us emphasize what [fictionality] involves for the subject. And then we have a clear rationale for treating the entire work not as a construal but as a presentation directly engaging real emotions in fictional worlds.[122]

Here too, we ought not leap too eagerly from literary to religious discourse; Altieri makes no such move, and religious traditions are loath to see their great texts as (mere) literary accomplishments. But if prudently employed, Altieri's wisdom remains operative with respect to religious texts. Close reading compels us to adjust to the specificities written boldly into the *Essence* and *Treatise*—Christ on the cross, the devout person dying for love, refuge at the Lord's feet —and then also to yield to the "vividness and force" of such images as commanding our lives too. All of this is possible, as we learn to read both texts, individually and together.

De Sales and Deśika have single-mindedly composed the particular and distinctive trajectories of their own texts, their own themes written in their own styles. But with respect to the transformation of the reader who dares to engage each and then both texts, the differences harmonize rather than diverge. De Sales gives us the intellectual and emotional resources by which it becomes imaginable to enter into intimate colloquy with Christ, an intimacy that culminates, ideally, in loving surrender into God's hands. Deśika likewise educates his readers that they—we—might well imagine loving surrender at the feet of Nārāyaṇa with Śrī. By the time we have read these texts thoroughly, what may have begun simply as an act of inquisitive or strictly intellectual inquiry ideally becomes irreversibly complicated with manifold images, stories, verses, and recollections of the older teachings presented to us in both texts. The *Essence* and the *Treatise* leave us with our freedom, and also with still more intensely felt options about our future. As readers, we thereby begin to take very seriously the supreme value that both texts propose to us, loving surrender to God.

It is on this basis, again, in a kind of refracted authenticity, that this book is best assessed, not for any originality that may occur in the course of my writing, but more simply with respect to the vivid presence of the *Essence* and *Treatise* that I so abundantly cite. Ideally, *Beyond Compare* turns out to be the kind of exercise in religious learning that enriches its readers with the wealth of the two traditions on which I am drawing, a writing that draws its power simply from its steadfast attention to two spiritual classics. Ideally, readers will be able to think, read, imagine, and desire a little differently, because in the act of reading they will have appropriated fresh modes of experience, ways of practice that extend from reading into living. And then I shall have succeeded where it counts most.

2. *The Complex Text and the Complex Reader*

The preceding pages had been written with both the *Essence* and *Treatise* in mind, and most immediately with respect to the intended effects of each text on its expected Christian or Hindu audience. The point of such writing is to draw readers more deeply into their own traditions. Neither author sought in these texts to contribute to a wider missionary effort, as if to win over an audience of nonbelievers or skeptics. Writing for the sake of the conversion and transformation of their own communities is not a simple or casual task, but it is at least plausibly focused on retrieving and intensifying truths and values to which expected readers are already at least nominally committed. In the reading, what is already known is reconsidered and deepened; whatever is learned or retrieved anew is comprehended in a way that harmonizes with truths and values already in place.

We must complicate this situation too by allowing for the added dynamics at play in reading across religious boundaries and in performing a double reading of both texts together. When a reader from one tradition reads a text from the other tradition, it can inform, educate, and inspire that reader, even if he or she never appropriates that tradition or understands the text as readers born and raised in that tradition might. The attentive "outside reader" learns from the reading and is infused with images, memories, and dispositions affecting how he or she will think, feel, and act. Wherever we start our reading, as we progress in it, the saints and teachers even of that other, previously unfamiliar tradition come to life for us and become nearby teachers and role models. Even if I, a Catholic, remain intellectually and affectively committed to my own Catholic tradition, reading Deśika affords me insights, desires, and impulses to action that cannot be neutralized or conveniently left aside simply because I am a Catholic. If I actually learn from my reading, then going forward and coming to terms with the new ideas, images, affective energies, and persons to be encountered and imitated will be easier than retreating into a religious world where the other barely exists, as if I might forget all that I have read. Similarly, the devout Śrīvaiṣṇava can learn from reading the *Treatise*, and there is no reason why she or he cannot profit deeply, as a Śrīvaiṣṇava, from appropriating the riches of the Catholic tradition inscribed by de Sales in his text. For her, too, there is no going back once learning has occurred.

And then there is the third dynamic, the creative, unsettling, and still more intense experience of the reader who with equanimity keeps reading *both* the *Essence* and the *Treatise*. This reader reads, learns, remembers, is exercised by both texts, and in her or his mind learns to weave both texts into a more ample new Text interwoven of the two. As we read both texts, together they instruct us in ways that cannot be neatly sorted out. We are inundated with new words, quotations, images, and exemplars, received now in new combinations that jostle and unsettle one another. We learn the rhythms of both scriptural traditions and begin to remember and imagine possibilities in accord with both. Persons known to us from one or the other tradition are now members of a new community arising from our reading, populated with multiple exemplars and stories. De Sales' inspiring recollections of Mary the mother of Jesus, Paul, and both Francis of Assisi and Francis Xavier are now placed alongside Deśika's pointed evocations of Sītā, Lakṣmaṇa, and Vibhīṣaṇa; the teachers of the Catholic and Śrīvaiṣṇava traditions are no less revered, but they are read newly, in light of each other. What is necessarily new to both traditions begins to be familiar to us, whereas the familiar is problematized in light of the unexpected possibilities that are now ours—not because we have decided to implement such a plan, or because we have devised a theory by which this result is to be effected, but because, in reading the *Essence* and the *Treatise* together, we find open before us paths that neither tradition can fully anticipate nor account for in terms of its distinctive narrative and doctrines. Our more intense rational and literary patterns are unsettled, shaken, the margins transgressed with the new words, images, desires of the other text and other reading project that now stands powerfully nearby in our memories and awareness. In knowing more, too much, we find ourselves to have surrendered exclusive allegiance to one tradition and to have become implicated in both, in accord with a new dynamic we will keep adjusting over time.

Where this might really lead us is the topic of chapter 4, as loving surrender finally becomes the explicit theme.

Chapter 4

Loving Surrender

Insight, Drama, and Ecstasy

> I have been wandering about this world from time without beginning, doing what does not please You, my God. From this day forward, I must do what pleases You, and I must cease what displeases You. But my hands are empty, I cannot attain You, my God; *I see that You alone are the way. You must be my way!* Hereafter, in the removal of what does not please You or in the attainment of what pleases You—can anything be a burden to me?
>
> Deśika, *Essence*

> But mark, I pray you, Theotimus, that even as our Savior, after he had made his prayer of resignation in the garden of Olives, and after he was taken, left himself to be handled and dragged about at the will of them that crucified him, by an admirable surrender made of his body and life into their hands, so did he resign up his soul and will by a most perfect indifference into his Eternal Father's hands. For when he cries out: *My God, my God, why have You forsaken me?* this was to let us understand the reality of the anguish and bitternesses of his soul, and not to detract from the state of most holy indifference in which he was. This he showed very soon afterwards, concluding all his life and his passion with those incomparable words: *Father, into Your hands I commend my spirit.*
>
> De Sales, *Treatise*

Everything up to now has been preparatory for the subject matter taken up in this chapter, for here we finally encounter the major theme of each text: loving surrender as abandonment into the hands of the God of our Lord Jesus Christ and as acknowledging one's helplessness and taking refuge at the feet of the divine couple, Nārāyaṇa with Śrī. In light of the preceding chapters' reflections on Deśika's and de Sales' conception of their reasoning and writing (chapter 2) and several key strategies of that writing (chapter 3), we can now examine how they present the rationale, value, and practice of loving surrender to help readers become people who can detach themselves even from the religious resources that have benefited them along the way—as devout practitioners, respected members of society, persons with every intellectual and spiritual resource at hand, even as literate readers—and actually make the choice for loving surrender. Though Deśika and de Sales dealt with very different communities and likely readers, both idealize the person who has nothing, who has lost everything other than God. Rather than simply report on it, both the *Essence* and the *Treatise* seek to catalyze and enhance this dependent yet free way of life. Let us see then how they describe and promote loving surrender, and put their discerning readers in the liminal situation where loving surrender is now a real option.

I. The Theological Presuppositions of Self-Abandonment

Although spiritual insight and practice are the authors' main concern, de Sales and Deśika are also alert to the rational and theological underpinnings of loving surrender as a radical yet intelligible religious goal. So it is important to understand something about the intellectual context for loving surrender that is presupposed in the *Treatise* and *Essence*. Both authors see keenly the enormity of the obstacles to self-improvement and self-liberation, and both feel the weight of the work that would be required were humans to see it as their own task to make themselves into new beings. Accordingly, they agree that the displacement of personal agency and responsibility, leading to loving surrender into God's hands, is the easier and better way even for humans capable of other worthy choices. But for this to work, proper dispositions regarding grace and human freedom must first be in place.

1. *De Sales: Freely Choosing to Let God Be All in All*

De Sales' early crisis regarding predestination—if grace and salvation are matters of God's sovereign and mysterious freedom, we cannot take it for granted that we ourselves are saved, and we cannot really change our situation in God's eyes[1]—is not a theme of the *Treatise*, but it may be presumed to influence his representation of love as the highest and truly liberative human act and experience, and his desire to balance divine grace with human agency in love experienced and chosen. We find in the *Treatise* a persistent concern to maintain human freedom even in the face of divine sovereignty, while yet also awarding supreme value to total surrender of the will to God. De Sales is concerned to avoid both a quietism in which humans simply wait upon God, and a scenario of struggle and self-valorization in which loving surrender might be just one more achievement of the righteous person. He was not directly a participant in what would grow, in the subsequent century, into a heated controversy over pure love as passivity before God, but his complex views seem to cut across the range of positions taken in the controversy. Among those who appealed to de Sales' writing in support of their views, for example, were Quietists Jeanne-Marie Bouvier de la Motte Guyon (1648–1717) and François de Salignac de La Mothe-Fénelon (1651–1715) and anti-Quietist Jacques-Bénigne Bossuet (1627–1704).[2]

Several passages in the *Treatise* illumine de Sales' desire for a balance of human and divine action. In discussing the dynamics of repentance and change of life in chapter 12 of book 2, for instance, de Sales reflects on how God attracts sinners to himself not by force but "by enticements, sweet attractions, and holy inspirations—which, in a word, are the cords of Adam, and of humanity, that is, proportionate and adapted to the human heart, to which liberty is natural." He explains the gentle power operative in the interaction of grace with human freedom:

> Grace is so gracious, and so graciously seizes our hearts to draw them, that she no ways offends the liberty of our will; she touches powerfully but yet so delicately the springs of our spirit that our free will suffers no violence from it. Grace has powers not to overpower but to entice the heart; she has a holy violence that does not violate our liberty but makes it full of love; she acts strongly, yet so sweetly that our will is not overwhelmed by so powerful an action; she presses us but does not oppress our liberty; so that under the very action of her power, we can consent to or resist her movements as it pleases us. But what is as admirable as it is true is that when our will follows this attraction and consents to the divine movement, she follows as freely as she

> resists freely when she does resist, although the consent to grace depends much more on grace than on the will, while the resistance to grace depends upon the will only. So sweet is God's hand in the handling of our hearts.[3]

Some pages later, de Sales further nuances this delicate balancing of divine initiative, holy inspiration, and delight, all respectful of the freedom of the person seeking God, a freedom necessary for this person caught between inspiration and temptation:

> Our Savior draws hearts by the delights he gives them, which make them find heavenly doctrine sweet and agreeable. But until this sweetness has engaged and fastened the will by its beloved bonds to draw it to the perfect acquiescence and consent of faith, just as God does not fail to exercise his greatness upon us by his holy inspirations, so too our enemy does not cease to practice his malice by temptations.[4]

Finally de Sales praises the patience and trust with which Abraham surrenders himself and his son Isaac serenely into the hands of God at the time of the terrible sacrifice, even as Abraham also struggles, in his lower self, to endure the terrible burden placed upon him.[5] De Sales elaborates this meditation as a threefold address, to Jesus, his own self, and finally the reader. He wonders with Jesus regarding the time when humans will respond fully to the love shown them:

> O Savior Jesus, when shall it then be, that having sacrificed to you all that we have, we shall also immolate for you all that we are? When shall we offer to you as a holocaust our free will, the only child of our spirit? When shall we extend and tie it upon the funeral pile of your cross, of your thorns, of your lance, that as a little lamb, it may be a grateful victim of your good pleasure, to die and to burn with the fire and by the sword of your holy love?

He asks himself the same question:

> O free will of my heart, how good a thing is it for you to be bound and extended upon the cross of your divine Savior! How desirable a thing it is to die to yourself, to burn forever a holocaust to the Lord!

The reader, Theotimus, is urged to make a free choice for loving surrender:

> Theotimus, our free will is never so free as when it is a slave to the will of God, nor ever so much a serf as when it serves our own will. It never has so much life as when it dies to itself, nor ever so much death, as when it lives to itself. We have freedom to do good or evil; yet to make choice of evil, is not to use, but to abuse our freedom. Let us renounce this miserable liberty, and let us forever subject our free will to the rule of heavenly love: let us become slaves of love, whose serfs are more happy than kings. . . . Let us sacrifice our free will, and make it die to itself that it may live to God![6]

Much of the *Treatise* is dedicated to balancing freedom with a loving surrender of freedom, necessity with a deep spiritual pleasure that respects human freedom. As a theologian, de Sales describes in glowing terms the destiny he urges upon this reader: Loving surrender is the grace for which we are destined, and abnegation of the will is the most satisfying free choice we can make.

2. Deśika: From Devotion to Human Readiness

Deśika's concern has directly to do with the supremacy and sufficiency of divine grace in bringing about human liberation, again in relation to the requirement that humans participate and choose. As we saw in chapters 1 and 2, Deśika is forever balancing the simplicity of loving surrender with elaborate practices required by orthodoxy. In chapter 2, I presented several passages from chapter 9 of the *Essence* that indicate a hierarchy of active devotion and loving surrender in which both ways are respected, even if the latter is superior. Here it suffices to note several of Deśika's subsequent clarifications. In chapter 11, titled "The Classification of Subsidiary Aids," Deśika lists five behaviors that he considers essential to gaining refuge: "choosing what is suitable to pleasing the Lord," "rejecting what is not suitable to pleasing him," "a realization of one's pitifulness and need," "great faith" (confidence in the power of taking refuge), and "choosing a protector." Whereas the core aids—"a realization of one's pitifulness" and "great faith"—suggest the necessary chemistry of human weakness and divine initiative, the other three point to the necessary human contribution. "Choosing" and "rejecting" entail those preparatory moral considerations for which humans are responsible, and "choosing a protector" most pertinently indicates the human decision to ask for help, a human admission of dire need that is taken to be the prerequisite occasion—pretext—for divine action.

In the ethical portion of the *Essence*, chapters 13–19, Deśika defends a fine balance between refuge as knowledge (a simple recognition of God and self) and refuge as inclusive of the expectation that the devotee will act in a certain way. Ever the defender of tradition, even when Deśika asserts the superiority of refuge, he does so without dismissing the more active path of devotion, and without giving the impression that human agency is irrelevant to the workings of divine grace. Insight, choice, and action are required; knowledge, desire, and loving surrender are in fact intertwined, just as grace and freedom are intertwined.

The whole issue is debated most technically, even juridically, in chapter 24.[7] In this long chapter, Deśika sorts through the subtle relationships among traditional practice, the act of taking refuge, and the core conviction that God alone is the means to salvation. If these elements are misunderstood, as if one is to be honored and the others dismissed, Deśika fears, the community will decline into quietism and abandon the requirements of orthodoxy, or on the contrary opt for a dismal reinsertion of ritual activities *in place of* total dependence on God. The modern editor Ramadesikacaryar offers a succinct summation of the relevant clarifications Deśika offers regarding simple refuge in relation to active devotion:[8]

1. Deśika explains the claim that faith and prayer [which look to divine action] are the core of taking refuge, when it is also asserted that the surrender of the burden of self-protection [which appears to be a human action] is the core [471–74];
2. He refutes erroneous or misleading and incomplete views: that realizing that one belongs entirely [to the Lord] is the means [474–76], and that there is no use in commanding the taking of refuge (in the *Carama Śloka* [476–77]);
3. He explains why the injunction to take refuge is not contrary to the Lord's nature [477];[9]
4. He criticizes the views a. that devotion cannot be the means since only taking refuge is [479–80], b. that taking refuge is not the means, since devotion is the means [480–81], c. that the injunction that one should take refuge is superfluous [481–83], and d. that pursuing the path of devotional activities is contrary to the self's proper nature [483–90];

5. He confirms the right view, that refuge is more excellent than devotion [490–92];
6. He explains the meaning of the requirement that the person taking refuge *must* come near to the Lord [501–508].

While we cannot here delve into the details of these claims, it is important to notice that Deśika's presentation is technical, even juridical. There is nothing comparable to Deśika's chapter 24 in de Sales' *Treatise*. These points from the *Essence* read very differently from de Sales' passionate appeals to inspiring examples of souls given over to love. Though a church leader, de Sales does not worry his audience with the theological and canonical implications of abandonment; Deśika very much wants his readers to value traditional obligations and acts of devotion even in light of loving surrender's greater value. The truth of an all-powerful and merciful Lord is of course of foremost importance, but the salvific act may not happen if one neglects the divine expectation that the person in need will offer some pretext—a word, an act—that signals the moment when God will act.

The Tamil verse at the end of the chapter catches in verse the mysterious coming together of divine sovereign initiative and human action (as pretext):

> That the Highest Being can choose anyone is explained in the Veda,
> but it is on some pretext
> that He chooses from among those burdened with karma;
> and so, pondering in every way the good path that has been explained,
> we carry on
> by the compassion of the Lord who carries the world.[10]

The person seeking God therefore proceeds with a kind of carefree determination, alert to every opportunity to approach God, while also remembering that God will come at the mysterious time of his choosing.

Both Deśika and de Sales, each in his own way, have the insight and theological skill to put forward a position that is not merely a compromise, but an integral harmony of grace and freedom: divine grace is all, and as such it makes possible total self-giving into the mystery of God. They agree in their ambition to emphasize human responsibility and the importance of human action even in the face of that grace of God that always comes first. Both also want to explain things in a way that prompts readers to consider most seriously choosing to engage in the act of loving surrender.

Their shared concern notwithstanding, Deśika and de Sales devised distinctive expositions of freedom and responsibility on the basis of which they could develop their cases for surrender; as readers committed to both texts, we will do well to notice and appreciate how their approaches exercise us in two different ways. De Sales narrates the path of love from primal desire all the way to the spiritual love for God that eventuates in total self-abandonment into God's hands. The *Treatise* moves with increasing fervor and intensity toward the climactic book 9 and the idealization of the once-for-all death of Jesus on the cross, the denuded self entirely dependent on God, lost and yet in bliss. Deśika, true to his quest for the utter clarity that transforms ways of living, explains the taking of refuge by a most precise exegesis of the Dvaya Mantra ("I approach for refuge the feet of Nārāyaṇa with Śrī, obeisance to Nārāyaṇa with Śrī"), words that make clear and effective the truth that God alone is the way and goal of all human aspiration. In his typically crystalline and precise manner, Deśika seeks to clear the mind of misunderstandings that stand as obstacles to divine grace, and on that basis to make it possible that the words of the mantra become the reader's own personal announcement of loving surrender to God. As readers of both texts, we are stretched in different yet complementary ways that cooperate in drawing us toward the desired conclusion, loving surrender into the hands of God. Individually and then together, Deśika and de Sales challenge us to leave behind life as ordinarily and safely conceived to do something greater.[11]

Let us examine their distinctive presentations more closely. We begin with Deśika's reading of the Dvaya Mantra.

II. Deśika's Exegesis of the Dvaya Mantra

To help readers grasp the content and manner of Deśika's case for loving surrender, in the following pages I simply analyze his exegesis of the Dvaya Mantra, the words of which stand at the core of the entire *Essence* as a work of performative mystical theology: "I approach for refuge the feet of Nārāyaṇa with Śrī; obeisance to Nārāyaṇa with Śrī."[12] Our goal is to see how Deśika understands the mantra and interprets it in making the case for refuge. Although dwelling on the details of the exegesis of a single mantra may seem rather restrictive and lacking a parallel with de Sales (who only much less formally focuses on a few mantra-like words), so close a reading will aid us in understanding the density of this mantra as a most simple utterance that nonetheless also accounts for the entirety of the spiritual life as understood by Śrīvaiṣṇavas.[13]

The Dvaya ("Double") Mantra is a mantra of two moments or "clauses"—"I approach for refuge the feet of Nārāyaṇa with Śrī" and "Obeisance to Nārāyaṇa with Śrī." "Dvaya"—two, double, a pair—may be taken as referring to the two clauses of the mantra, or as indicating its double content: The Lord is *the means* to the Lord as *the goal* or even, perhaps, the eternal couple, Nārāyaṇa with Śrī.

Deśika is one with his predecessors in recognizing the importance of this mantra. For instance, Rāmānuja's "Song of Surrender" is usually understood as that revered teacher's dramatic prayer of taking refuge, his loving surrender to the Lord. Since Rāmānuja mentions the Dvaya Mantra several times in the "Song of Surrender," it may be understood as a fulsome reflection on the Dvaya Mantra and as a dramatic enactment of it, just as the Dvaya Mantra is a kind of distillation of the much longer work by Rāmānuja.[14] At the very beginning of the "Song of Surrender," the speaker takes refuge with Śrī:

> She possesses proper form, forms, qualities, glory, lordly power, generous disposition, and a host of innumerable auspicious qualities, unsurpassed and flawless, such as are appropriate and pleasing to the Lord Nārāyaṇa; She is the Lady, Śrī, Goddess; She is never apart from Him; She is flawless, divine queen of the God of gods, Mother of the entire world, our Mother, refuge of those who have no refuge: *I who have no other refuge take Her as my refuge.*[15]

She responds, giving permission and her blessing; then, even more at length, the devotee also seeks refuge with Nārāyaṇa, his confession seeming to climax in the Dvaya Mantra:

> You are the refuge of the whole world without exception and without consideration of any further qualifications; You dispel the distress of those who offer obeisance to You; You are an ocean of pure affection for those who depend on You, You know always the true nature and condition of all created beings, You are ever engaged in the control and ordering of all beings without excep-

> tion—the moving and the stationary, You are the one for whom all conscious and non-conscious beings exist, the support of the whole Universe, the Lord of the Universe, my Lord; all Your desires come true, Your will is ever accomplished, You are different from all else, You are the kalpaka tree[16] of those in want, friend in need of those in distress, consort of Śrī, You are Nārāyaṇa, refuge of those without refuge: *I who have no other refuge come for refuge to your lotus feet.* Here the Dvaya Mantra.[17]

The Dvaya Mantra both validates and is validated by Rāmānuja's prayer in the revered "Song of Surrender." The reader presumably knows of the interplay of the mantra and the "Song," and comes to the mantra with expectations heightened by the connection with Rāmānuja's devotion.

Deśika's word-by-word exegesis in chapter 28 of the *Essence* is prefaced by introductory comments that highlight core presuppositions. The opening Sanskrit verse praises the mantra as expository of life's goal and the way to it:

> Once heard, it discloses that what had to be done has been done;
> repeated, it indicates a person whose goal has been accomplished;
> after this world's gloom, it arrives like dawn:
> such is this mantra of refuge with the consort of the Lady in the lotus.[18]

Given the sacredness of the transmission of the tradition, it is not surprising that praise of this "king of mantras" is intertwined with praise for the teacher, the transmitter of the truth of the mantra. Deśika cites a long passage from the *Satyakī Tantra*:

> Let a person come to understand this king of mantras
> after saluting the teacher;
> the teacher alone is the highest Brahman, the teacher alone the highest way,
> the teacher alone the greatest wisdom, the teacher alone the refuge,
> the teacher alone the greatest desire, the teacher alone the greatest wealth;
> when you have been taught by the teacher,
> that teacher will be all the more revered.—
> This mantra requires no favorable circumstances, no auspicious star,

no dwelling at a holy place, no preparatory rites, no regular
recitation, etc.

The *Satyakī Tantra* text then describes how properly to learn and treasure the mantra:

> After first reverencing the teacher with three full-length prostrations,
> after grasping his feet and with proper courtesy putting them upon one's own head,
> a person should next take hold of this king of mantras,
> like someone who has no wealth and so desires treasure;
> holding onto this king of mantras, let that person come to Me for refuge;
> with this mantra alone should a person give his self over to Me.
> Giving himself over to Me, he becomes one who has done all he had to do.[19]

Tradition solidly supports the mantra, but, Deśika adds, we must personally have great faith in its efficacy:

> It is well known from the scriptures that even a single utterance of the mantra, preceded by knowledge of the whole of its meaning, saves a person of faith. Rāmānuja distinguished the potency of this mantra from that of other mantras when he said,
>
> > Since you have uttered the Dvaya Mantra, whatever may be the manner of that utterance,
> > solely by My compassion
> > you will have entirely eradicated all obstacles
> > to exclusive and single-minded higher devotion, higher knowledge, and supreme devotion for My lotus feet.[20]
>
> This mantra, uttered even once illumines fully the object of refuge, the way of refuge, and its fruit, in accord with the power that arises in praising the holy name; as it says,
>
> > The person who without compulsion praises this name
> > is immediately freed from all sins—
> > as if from beasts fearing a lion, [*Viṣṇu Purāṇa* 6.8.19]
>
> and,
>
> > Hari, the power of Your name in removing sins
> > cannot be countered even by the sins
> > committed by the eater of dog flesh. [*Viṣṇu Smṛti* 109][21]

The teacher personifies the tradition by his transmission of its truths, and the Dvaya Mantra is the intense condensation of that tradition, encapsulating what has been passed down from the beginning to the time of the current reader, practitioner of the mantra. Together, mantra and teacher embody tradition and ensure its life and continuity over generations. Since tradition, not detached reason, is the chief criterion, Deśika insists on deep reverence, and in this light steers the student/practitioner away from irreverent questions about what is, after all, secret (*rahasya*), indeed most secret (*rahasyatama*):

> It is not proper to seek reasons for most secret things of this kind. One should accept scripture and have faith, as it says in the *Mahābhārata* and elsewhere. Consider texts such as this,
>
> O Goddess, reason is of no use regarding matters hidden among the gods;
> Whoever desires what is beneficial should act like the deaf and blind. [*Mahābhārata, Ānuśāsana Parva* 206.60][22]

As we saw in chapter 2, Deśika fears an undisciplined reasoning that can wander in many directions for many purposes, for it may deviate from the teachings and customs of the tradition. The person who approaches the mantra with strictly rational criteria in mind will lack the attitudes of mind and heart required to understand and benefit from the mantra. Accordingly, it is better to depend on a proper teacher for a proper understanding of the mantra, and thus to reflect on it within an integral religious context. Or, as here, we can learn from the twenty-eighth chapter of the *Essence*, a teaching of the mantra composed by a teacher steeped in the tradition.

1. *The First Clause: I approach for refuge the feet of Nārāyaṇa with Śrī*

The first clause of the mantra combines words of surrender with layers of theological meaning. In the following pages, I trace Deśika's exegesis of the Dvaya Mantra to see how he builds the case for total surrender, rendering the mantra's words as clear and powerful as possible. I do this by a kind of thought experiment, first postulating a simplified version of the mantra and the taking of refuge and then elaborating the increasing sophisticated understanding of God and the spiritual life inscribed in the mantra.[23]

a. I approach Nārāyaṇa: *Nārāyaṇam prapadye*

For a simple expression of loving surrender, we can begin simply with the grammatical subject and verb of the mantra's first clause, *I approach Nārāyaṇa.*

Deśika first has us recall the exegesis of *Nārāyaṇa* in chapter 27.[24] That exegesis included reflection on the meanings of *nara* + *ayana* as expressive of the Lord's role as foundation (*ayana*) for all beings (*nara, nāra*) and, conversely, of the Lord's choice of his own resting place, foundation, among living beings. In that chapter Deśika also recounts the 108 characteristics proper to a deity who deserves to be called *Nārāyaṇa.*[25] In chapter 28, Deśika lists just twelve qualities that are pertinent to the representation in the Dvaya Mantra of Nārāyaṇa as the place of safe refuge: maternal tenderness, lordship, good disposition, accessibility, omniscience, omnipotence, success in having one's intentions come true, supreme compassion, gratitude in recognition of what has been done, steadfastness, perfection in every aspect, and superlative generosity.[26] In this shortened form as *I approach Nārāyaṇa,* the mantra might be taken as combining a proper and respectful theology of Nārāyaṇa with taking refuge as an appropriate act of loving surrender.

b. I approach Nārāyaṇa with Śrī: *Śrīman-Nārāyaṇam prapadye*

But the Dvaya Mantra is ever more interesting because it is much more than the brief prayer I have just offered; it offers and expects a fuller, theologically informed reading. A further complication (deserving fuller attention in another context) lies in the fact that a crucial modifier is added to *Nārāyaṇa*: He is *Śrīman*, with Śrī. *I approach Nārāyaṇa with Śrī.*

Like the word *Nārāyaṇa, Śrī* is a word with both general and specific meanings. On the one hand, Śrī is the Goddess, the divine person to whom one goes for aid and encouragement; she is the one by whose grace one is able to come near the Lord efficaciously. As Deśika insists here, it is with her as well as with Nārāyaṇa that one actually takes refuge. On the other, *Śrī* is a word with more expansive conceptual meanings, and Deśika lists six roots and verbal forms in relation to which her name can be derived, and over several pages elaborates each with ample quotations:

> *śrīyate*—She is taken refuge with: "She is taken refuge with by those who seek their personal uplift." [727/427]

> *śrayate*—She takes refuge: "She takes refuge with the Lord of all, for the sake of uplifting the people (who have taken refuge with Her)." [727/427]
>
> *śṛṇoti*—She hears: "When we, devout yet sinful, take refuge with Her, begging, 'Grant us access to the feet of the Lord of all,' She hears our anguished cry." [731/430–31]
>
> *śrāvayati*—She makes heard: "She then makes the Lord of all hear our petition, thus calming our anguish." [731/430–31]
>
> *śṛṇāti*—She removes: "She removes karma and other obstacles thwarting those who are (otherwise) competent for this means (taking refuge)." [733/431]
>
> *śrīṇati*—She ripens: "By Her qualities of compassion, etc., She ripens the qualities of those taking refuge, all the way to fruition in service." [733/432]

All six root meanings are applied to Śrī; they reflect her divine activity, and her relationship to the person and work of Nārāyaṇa; to invoke Śrī is to address this particular person and to evoke her entire array of blessed qualities.

In theory, Nārāyaṇa is entirely capable of rendering surrender efficacious, and it might be taken as superfluous, or simply reverential, to pray to Śrī in this context. Yet in Deśika's view, the Dvaya Mantra announces that Nārāyaṇa is always with Śrī, and she is afforded a full partnership in the protection of those who take refuge. The *with* [the *mat* in *Śrīmat*] requires delicate nuance, lest it seem that Śrī is merely linked to Nārāyaṇa in a momentary relationship that can be balanced by times when he is "without Śrī." After some technical discussion why the conjunctive *with* need not be interpreted as indicating two separate beings connected optionally or only for the moment, Deśika adds a comment that illumines the entire mantra:

> In the present instance, even if there are authoritative texts pointing to an eternal relationship [of Nārāyaṇa and Śrī] in the context of the means and of the result, their eternal relationship should also be illumined by the mantra itself. Accordingly, in both its first and second clauses the *with* indicates that [Śrī and Nārāyaṇa] cannot bear to be apart.[27]

Deśika cites multiple texts to illustrate the importance of the divine relationship, alluding yet again to Lakṣmaṇa, who loyally follows his brother Rāma into the forest vowing to serve not only Rāma but also Sītā, and to Śaṭakōpaṉ's act of loving surrender to Nārāyaṇa with Śrī:

> As it says,
>
> > The illustrious [Lakṣmaṇa] steadfastly touched his brother's feet [and then spoke to Sītā with Rāghava]. [*Rāmāyaṇa, Ayodhyā Kāṇḍa* 31.2]
>
> and
>
> > You [Rāma], with Vaidehī [Sītā], will enjoy yourself on the slopes of the hills; whether you are asleep or awake, I will do every thing for you. [*Rāmāyaṇa, Ayodhyā Kāṇḍa* 31.37]
>
> Nammāḻvār says,
>
> > "I cannot be away even for a moment," says the Lady in the lotus who dwells on Your chest. [*Tiruvāymoḻi* 6.10.10]
> >
> > The holy lady with her splendid bracelets and You abide together. [*Tiruvāymoḻi* 4.9.10]
> >
> > Neither here nor there did I see anything other than the Lord of Śrī. [*Tiruvāymoḻi* 7.9.11]
>
> [In such texts,] he is meditating on the eternal connection expressed in *Śrīmat* with reference to both the means and the result.[28]

Deśika then sums up what is possible for those who take most seriously the role of Śrī:

> This meditation offers reason for sinners to take refuge—if they reflect upon it without second thoughts.[29]

It is of great practical significance that Śrī is the mediator of divine salvation, since her continuing presence should encourage the doubtful with respect to both the goal and the way of liberation.

c. I approach the feet of Nārāyaṇa with Śrī: *Śrīmannārāyaṇa-caraṇau prapadye*

The mantra becomes still more complex if we say, *I approach the feet of Nārāyaṇa with Śrī*. What is the difference between approaching Nārāyaṇa with Śrī and approaching the *feet* (*caraṇau*) of Nārāyaṇa with Śrī? Certainly, there is a long tradition among the Tamil saints of devotion to the Lord's feet and of humble submission and service at those feet. But Deśika stresses that mention of the divine feet shows that the transcendent, perfect Nārāyaṇa, always accompanied by Śrī, is possessed of an eternal perfect material form.

> *Feet* stands in for the entire eternal and auspicious divine form. The most important things to be known are that the Lord of Śrī is higher than everything, and that He has an eternal form. As it says,
>
> O Pauṣkara, whoever is certain in his heart
> that the Lord's form is eternal
> and that He is superior to all—
> may the Lord come to such a person. [*Pauṣkara Saṃhitā*]
>
> Therefore, when we think of *Nārāyaṇa with Śrī* we should meditate on His transcendence joined with His accessibility, His eternal form in the context of His *feet*.[30]

Moreover, these feet are an adequate object of meditation for those incapable of more subtle reflection:

> For those who do not clearly understand the qualities previously implied [*Nārāyaṇa*] or the proper form of the divine self, it suffices to know this auspicious divine form. It is made entirely of pure-matter; knowing it ends the constriction of knowledge; it suggests both His transcendence and His accessibility.[31]

That refuge occurs at the Lord's feet marks the concrete and material immediacy of Nārāyaṇa with Śrī, the object of refuge: Not only is Nārāyaṇa with Śrī perfect in every way, but he is also accessible, the one at whose feet we can always take refuge. His form is attractive even to the senses, the most appropriate imaginable object for the meditation leading to taking refuge at those feet.

d. For refuge I approach the feet of Nārāyaṇa with Śrī: *Śrīmannārāyaṇa-caraṇau śaraṇam prapadye*

But we can move to still another level of complexity, from *I approach the feet of Nārāyaṇa with Śrī* to *For refuge I approach the feet of Nārāyaṇa with Śrī*. Mention of the word *refuge* may seem doubly redundant, nestled as it is between *feet*—the special place of refuge—and *I approach*, the verb indicative of the act of approach, the movement of taking refuge. But Deśika reads *refuge* in deliberate juxtaposition to *feet*: the accessible Lord himself is the refuge, and the human action of taking refuge is secondary: What matters are the Lord, the Lord's feet, the refuge—all one reality. The word *feet* is thus further specified by *refuge*, as if to say, "the Lord's feet, that is to say, the refuge." Deśika explains why only the Lord with Śrī is the "means," a fact marked by *refuge* in juxtaposition to *the feet of Nārāyaṇa with Śrī*:

> One may ask: if the Lord of all, who is worshipped in accord with all the scriptures and available to all competent persons, is the means to the result, why further specify this means [by adding *refuge*]? We respond: putting the Lord, distinguished by His innate compassion and other qualities, [explicitly] in the place of other means makes clear the nature of taking refuge.

But isn't the act of taking refuge the means to liberation? Both devotion and taking refuge lead to liberation, but the point here is to emphasize total dependence on the Lord, not partial dependence on the Lord and partial dependence on one's own action:

> After stipulating that the act of taking refuge can be subsidiary to meditation as a means,[32] subsequently, in order to gain the same result without that means and instead solely by taking refuge, [the person seeking refuge] has to depend on the Lord's distinctive nature, His innate compassion, and so forth. For the person who has nothing, the Lord takes the place of other means.

This is a logic of desperation about self tolerable only through confidence in the Lord:

> When a person who has nothing is unable to bear the burden enjoined as means to the desired result, he has the Lord take the place of other means when he says, "Be for me the means, protector!" That is, "If, instead of my bearing the burden of other means on my head, You bear my burden, then the task of bestowing everything desired is a burden to be borne by You who are both compassionate and capable."[33]

Were we to divide the prayer thus far into two sections, the best reading would not be "For refuge I approach / the feet of Nārāyaṇa with Śrī," but rather something like "I approach / the refuge, the feet of Nārāyaṇa with Śrī," thus reinforcing the connection of *refuge* to *Nārāyaṇa with Śrī.*

e. I APPROACH: *PRAPADYE*

The true refuge is therefore not the human act of taking refuge, but rather the "act" of enduring divine presence. But if the Lord is the refuge and if the human act of approach does not of itself give the person the desired refuge, the human act of *prapadye—I approach*—still requires explanation. For Deśika, *I approach* must be taken to indicate not so much a human movement or activity but rather the faith indicated by the action of coming near. Deśika makes space for the verb's cognitive dimension:

> As for *pra-padye*, the root *pad* expresses movement [*gati*] and has meanings of both "going" and "understanding."[34] Here it indicates the latter, the specific, desired understanding, the faith that is the firm conviction, "He will protect me [*Ahirbudhnya Saṃhitā* 37.29]."[35]

The prefix *pra* intensifies understanding, marking the powerful insight that is faith:

> This faith is essential among the subsidiaries of taking refuge. Putting it out in front here makes clear the means to be accomplished with its subsidiary components. How? We reply: The prefix *pra* indicates abundance, in the form of abundant faith. This abundant faith arises when one meditates on the mediator [*Śrī*], the relation [*mat*], the qualities [of *Nārāyaṇa*], and so forth, as found respectively in the words *Śrīmat* and *Nārāyaṇa*. Doing so ends all the doubts arising due to the abundance of one's transgressions and other such factors.[36]

After quotations that stress the importance of great faith, Deśika highlights its relevance to taking refuge:

> If this great faith exists, doubt never arises during subsequent reflection. Therefore, in order that afterwards doubt should not

> arise, at the very moment of taking refuge great faith is the key subsidiary to the action of approaching the Lord for the sake of refuge.[37]

In conclusion:

> When we indicate great faith—"I have made a firm resolution regarding the means"—it is a prayer that is a choice of the means, confirmed by authoritative texts such as these:
>
> When that which a person most desires can be accomplished
> by no one else,
> then asking, with great faith, that He alone be that means
> is itself the surrender, the taking of refuge.[38]
>
> As it says,
>
> "Taking refuge" is what is meant in the prayer,
> You alone be for me my means, [*Ahirbudhnya Saṃhitā* 37.29]
>
> and so too,
>
> Be my means. [*Viṣṇu Purāṇa* 3.7.33][39]

This interpretation shifts attention from human activity to a human recognition of the divine person's absolute priority: Nārāyaṇa is the means, the refuge, easily accessible and energetic in doing all that needs to be done. To take refuge is the act of faith that makes way for the Lord's sure action.[40]

We have thus traced by its logical development Deśika's interpretation of the first clause of the mantra, "For refuge I approach the feet of Nārāyaṇa with Śrī." Our "reconstruction" of this most theological of mantras indicates that there is inscribed in it a sequence of increasingly weighty theological claims pressed upon the reader who takes seriously the mantra's subtle complexity. In utterance, of course, the mantra simply flows without any need to separate out stages of meanings as we have done. Yet a person who is studious as well as devout recollects the meanings latent in the mantra; for such a person, simple utterance is also a comprehension and statement of all that the Dvaya Mantra implies, in each of its words.

2. *The Second Clause: Obeisance to Nārāyaṇa with Śrī*

The second clause of the Dvaya Mantra builds on the first and is less complicated, so we can review Deśika's exegesis more quickly.

a. With Śrī: *Śrīmate*

With Śrī reaffirms that the praise and obeisance offered to Nārāyaṇa in the second clause are also entirely for Śrī:

> When we speak of the object of attainment as endowed with both realms of earthly and heavenly glory, we also mean this: being the One on whom everything depends and thus too recipient of the oblation of self, and thus too being the One to whom all consequent service is due—all this pertains to this unique divine Couple, who together form the primary object of attainment. In order to show all this, *with Śrī* is employed here.[41]

Never does one pray to Nārāyaṇa, without also praying to Śrī; she is the mediator and surety, for all those seeking to surrender lovingly at the feet of the Lord, and the longed-for ultimate union is always union with Śrī as well.

b. For Nārāyaṇa: *Nārāyaṇa-āya*

Nārāyaṇa [in *Nārāyaṇa -āya*] in this second clause, already explained at length in the context of the Tiru Mantra and in the first clause of this mantra, also reaffirms core truths:

> In this context, *Nārāyaṇa* with its specification [*with Śrī*] has the primary purpose of indicating His characteristics, in accord with textual authorities: He is Lord, and so forth,[42] as is fitting to His being the goal; as Lord, He is an object of enjoyment that is unsurpassable in all modes, distinguished by endless realms of glory and good qualities.[43]

All this serves to illumine the divine nature and, most important, the divine relationship with those who come near the Lord:

> Even if the Lord's name is already implied as correlative to and specified by *with Śrī*, [explicitly adding] *Nārāyaṇa* serves to confirm the perfectly full experience of His relationships,[44] qualities, and glories, an experience that brings about the distinctive pleasure that inspires every kind of service.[45]

Deśika shows the full force of the dative case—the -āya in *Nārāyaṇāya*—by citing a Sanskrit verse on the freedom and bliss experienced when one recognizes that the Lord, and not one's own activity, is the means to salvation:

> Giving up as unattainable the notion of being saved by oneself
> or anyone else,
> dismissing the idea of existing either for oneself or anyone else
> because this person exists only for that Person—
> then, averse to all other enjoyments and freed of impurity,
> the person who has taken refuge savors his own enjoyment
> as complete, yet too as dependent on the Lord's enjoyment.[46]

Even after the now-accomplished act of taking refuge, says Deśika, we continue to realize our deep, innate dependence on the Lord: To be is to be for-God.

c. Obeisance: *namaḥ*

After refuge as before refuge, we still worship and give ourselves over completely to Nārāyaṇa with Śrī; this is the first meaning of *namaḥ* as "obeisance."[47] But in accord with tradition, Deśika also observes that *namaḥ* can be parsed to mean "not mine" (*namaḥ* as *na mama*). The reader should mentally supply an additional word, such as [*na mama*] *bhaveyam,* "May I *not be* 'my own.'"

> To *namaḥ* one must add some verbal formation, such as, "*May I* not *be* my own," "*May I* not *be* for myself."[48] Accordingly, "May nothing be mine" is a prayer to end all that is undesirable, by ending the sense of "mine" with respect to every object.[49]

Thus this second clause encodes a series of increasingly specific and radical confessions:

> Obeisance to Nārāyaṇa.
> Obeisance to Nārāyaṇa with Śrī
> May I exist for Nārāyaṇa with Śrī, not for myself.

The determination to take refuge enacted in accord with the words of the first clause thus recurs in the second clause as an expression of worship, again addressed to Nārāyaṇa with Śrī. After refuge, we live a radically new life, no longer for ourselves but in and for Nārāyaṇa with Śrī.

3. *The Whole Dvaya Mantra*

Deśika notes that both clauses may appear to be prayers expressive of the same desired result, that Nārāyaṇa with Śrī take the place of all other means and results. So why two clauses? He claims that there is no redundancy. When one begs the Lord to take the place of all other means and to be one's highest goal, one may still thereafter want to highlight some specific aspect of that divine reality. In the second clause one prays, "May I not be my own means—let Nārāyaṇa and Śrī be everything for me," and this prayer stresses that they are also the goal:

> I make this surrender of the burden of protecting my self, so that You, who stand in the place of other means for me who has nothing, may [at the same time] give me this unique result [that is, nothing but Yourself]. Thus, the surrender of the burden is connected with this specific prayer.[50]

Later, Deśika adds that loving surrender results precisely in that union and perpetual dependence expressed in the second clause, *Obeisance to Nārāyaṇa with Śrī*.[51] He drives this point home with more quotations that emphasize loving surrender:

> When I offer myself to Nārāyaṇa with Śrī, as it says,
> Right now, I am offered—by myself. [*Stotra Ratna* 52]
> Then the burden of protection and the result of self-protection
> belong to the Lord.
> As it also says,[52]
> What is surrendered is what needs protection . . . , [*Ahirbudhnya Saṃhitā* 52.36][53]
> and
> I am Your burden. [*Stotra Ratna* 60][54]

In this reading, *namaḥ* marks the definitive cancellation of the self-centeredness that might recur even during and after the act of loving surrender:

> *Namaḥ* indicates that the person now has no connection to self, nor to anything that belongs to self, nor to the protection of self and the results of that protection. The point is to enjoin a relationship to this [divine] Other and to prohibit having anything

> to do with self. This is the result accruing to both the dative [in *Nārāyaṇa-āya*] and to *namaḥ*. In the offering,[55] *namaḥ* [as "not-mine"] indicates the prohibition of agency and other factors that would be independent of this [divine] other.[56]

Deśika adds that even the ordinary sense of *namaḥ* as obeisance still includes a denial of self and choice for the Lord. By the end of one's recitation of the Dvaya Mantra, the devout person has lovingly surrendered everything to God and gained, as the result of this act of self-giving, union with the Lord. There is nothing else.

I close this exegesis of the Dvaya Mantra with a brief reference to chapter 12, where Deśika reflects again on the act of loving surrender. The preceding chapters in the *Essence* have led up to this actual enunciation of the mantra's words in the event of taking refuge, the reader's own embrace of this ideal act as her or his own. Deśika reflects on refuge as a declaration of complete self-surrender:

> This is how the person should undertake the specific meditation. In accord with the words,
>
> Let him give himself over to Me. [Satyakī Tantra]
>
> I do not belong to myself. Accordingly, the Lord, who is free and to whom all belongs, offers protection even as His own personal goal. I am entirely dependent, I exist for His sake, fit for no one else, dependent on no one else. In accord with the words,
>
> Even my self is not mine, [Mahābhārata, *Śānti Parva* 25.19]
>
> I do not belong to myself. I am not fit even to say that anything belongs to me unconditionally.[57]

After more quotations, Deśika closely connects this act of refuge—and the requisite choosing of Nārāyaṇa as protector—to the Dvaya Mantra:

> Thus, in the first clause of the Dvaya Mantra that deals with the means of taking refuge, surrender to the Lord of responsibility for one's own protection is accompanied by the thought that one exists entirely for Him. All this is to be understood in relation to the verb *I approach* in its proximity with the word *refuge*. This thought, preceded by great faith, prompts one to choose a protector.[58]

Surrender is an instantaneous event, a recognition and affirmation occurring all at once, no matter how many years of preparation lay before it. What might be analyzed and reflected on at length is condensed in the Dvaya Mantra. Deśika compares surrender to the shooting of an arrow. Just as many small actions lead up to a single shot of a single arrow, so realization, though preceded by the five subsidiary aids, occurs all at once in the utterance of the Dvaya Mantra:

> This enactment, with its five subsidiary aids, is the laying down of the burden of protecting oneself, an act which is the origin of giving up both one's own proper form and also the results of one's action. This is accompanied by the utterance of the Dvaya Mantra, preceded by meditation on choosing what is suitable and acts of reverence for the succession of teachers, and so forth. And in turn, this too is preceded by giving up the idea of being a doer, giving up the idea of "mine," giving up the result, and giving up all means to obtaining that result.[59]

Taking refuge is a heartfelt and intense act, as Deśika indicates by repeating the words of his esteemed teacher Naṭātur Ammāḷ:

> I have been wandering about this world from time without beginning, doing what does not please You, my God. From this day forward, I must do what pleases You, and I must cease what displeases You. But my hands are empty, I cannot attain You, my God; I see that You alone are the way. You must be my way! Hereafter, in the removal of what does not please you or in the attainment of what pleases you—could anything be a burden to me?[60]

Though not as passionate or dramatic as Naṭātur Ammāḷ's heartfelt words, the spare, utterly simple Dvaya Mantra is nonetheless brilliantly expressive of this core attitude and act of the Śrīvaiṣṇava tradition. It offers a theological basis for loving surrender to God, the psychological reassurance that gives one confidence in the value of loving surrender, the words to speak in the very act of surrendering; if all the preceding are understood, it is also the "spark" igniting this radical change in life.

Deśika's exegesis of the Dvaya Mantra and its use is meticulous and highly refined. He clearly does not aspire to a simple appeal to the heart, nor do we find much of the uplifting rhetoric so evident in the *Treatise*. Rather, Deśika seeks ever greater precision, for an utterly clear assessment of the human condition, the disposition of the divine person(s) toward the human, and the simple, clear response a human being can speak in acknowledging how things are and how we are to be. But this clarification is explosively transformative of heart, mind, and spirit. In Deśika's clear light, what can and should be done becomes transparent and nearly irresistible to the attentive reader, now as her or his own possibility. If we take seriously the mantra's inner logic and adhere to the logic it encodes, everything becomes clear, and no obstacle blocks the choice to utter the mantra. Understanding and analysis give way to a more primary performative utterance, when by the Dvaya Mantra we do actually take refuge: "I approach for refuge the feet of Nārāyaṇa with Śrī; obeisance to Nārāyaṇa with Śrī."

III. De Sales on Love and Loving Surrender

De Sales of course introduces the substance and way of loving surrender rather differently than Deśika. To understand the dynamic movement of De Sales' *Treatise* toward loving surrender, we need to trace out several more dimensions of his teaching on love and affective union with God. This teaching begins with theoretical presuppositions and foundations and culminates, in book 9, in an intense and passionate articulation of love's destiny.

1. The Foundations of Love

In book 1 of the *Treatise,* de Sales describes love's place in the human self, in relation to human will, and with respect to the journey toward fulfillment. First, "love in general" is "deep pleasure" (*complaisance*), an innate tendency toward the good and pleasure in it that lies at the source of even our earliest, simplest orientation to what pleases us:

> The will has so great a *sympathy* with the good that as soon as she perceives it she turns towards it to *take delight* therein as in her *most agreeable object.* She is so closely aligned with it that her nature cannot be explained except by the relation she has thereto, just as one cannot show the nature of what is good except by the affinity it has with the will. . . . The will, *perceiving and feeling the good* by the mediation of the *understanding* which proposes it, then feels at the same time a sudden *delight* and *deep pleasure* in this encounter, which *sweetly yet powerfully moves*

> and inclines her towards *this pleasing object* in order to unite herself with it, and makes her search out the most appropriate means.[61]

The cycle of this instinctive pleasure and its satisfaction marks a kind of love that opens into the larger reality of love properly named as such. Deep pleasure begins the work of love, yet because its destiny is God, it is completed beyond itself:

> Deep pleasure is the awakener of the heart, but love is its action; deep pleasure makes it get up, but love makes it walk. The heart spreads its wings by deep pleasure but love is its flight. Love then, to speak distinctly and precisely, is no other thing than the movement, effusion and advancement of the heart towards good.[62]

Though the affinity "which causes love does not always consist in resemblance, but in the proportion, relation or correspondence between the lover and the thing loved,"[63] this initial love deepens into a more intimate unity:

> But when this mutual correspondence is joined with resemblance, love is without doubt engendered much more powerfully; since resemblance is the true image of unity, when two like things are united by a proportion to the same end, this seems to be unity rather than union.[64]

But this is a kind of radiance that grows ever brighter and more intense, like the sun in its daily course, until a conclusion in union:

> Moreover, Theotimus, the deep pleasure and movement or effusion of the will upon the thing beloved is properly speaking love. Yet this is in such a way that the deep pleasure is but the beginning of love, and the movement or effusion of the heart which ensues is the true essential love. So the one and the other may truly be named love, but in a different sense: just as the dawning of day may be termed day, so this first deep pleasure of the heart in the thing loved may be called love because it is the first feeling of love. But just as the true heart of the day is measured from the ending of dawn till sunset, so the true essence of love consists in the movement and effusion of the heart which immediately follows deep pleasure and ends in union.[65]

Like marital love, this growing desire is a satisfaction that claims the whole person:

> But to what kind of union does it tend? Did you not note, Theotimus, that the sacred spouse expressed her desire of being united to her spouse by the kiss, and that the kiss represents the spiritual union which is caused by the reciprocal communication of souls? It is indeed the man who loves, but he loves by his will, and therefore the end of his love is of the nature of his will: but his will is spiritual, and this is why the union which love aims at is spiritual also, and so much the more because the heart, which is the seat and source of love, would not only not be perfected by union with corporal things, but would be degraded.[66]

The person trusting this love reaches beyond their natural capacity, hovering in a liminal zone between angels and humans:

> Those then who, touched with intellectual and divine pleasures, let their hearts be ravished by feelings arising there, are truly *outside themselves,* that is, above the condition of their nature, but by a blessed and desirable out-going, by which entering into a more noble and eminent estate, they are as much angels by the operation of their soul as human by the substance of their nature, and are to be called either human angels or angelic humans.[67]

Perhaps to explain this dynamism that cannot be accounted for by a rational or consciously defined plan but nevertheless offers a true human fulfillment, de Sales points to "a certain eminence or supreme point of the reason and spiritual faculty, which is not guided by the light of argument or reasoning, but by a simple view of the understanding and a simple movement of the will, by which the spirit bends and submits to the truth and the will of God."[68] Here there is a kind of darkness wherein touch and desire succeed even as vision and understanding falter. But this is an "knowing unknowing" that is more deeply satisfying than what might have been gained through an active comprehension:

> Sight in the supreme part of the soul is in some sort obscured and veiled by the renunciations and resignations which the soul makes, not desiring so much to behold and see the beauty of the truth and the truth of the goodness presented to her, but rather to

> embrace and adore the same, so that the soul would almost wish to shut her eyes as soon as she begins to see the dignity of God's will, to the end that not occupying herself further in considering it, she may more powerfully and perfectly accept it, and by an absolute deep pleasure unite herself to it without limit, and submit herself thereto.[69]

This mingling of embrace and adoration previews the emotionally charged climax of book 9, which presents radical and unrestricted surrender to God as the final state of self, a terrible suffering that is also the beginning of the bliss of union. In de Sales' mind, this is the sure course of the soul's gravitational pull toward God: Our deepest instinct guides us beyond ourselves to God.

2. A Note on Deep Pleasure (Complaisance)

Because the concept of deep pleasure is so central to understanding the dynamic of loving surrender in the *Treatise*, a brief detour into book 5, chapter 2, will help us understand deep pleasure better.[70] De Sales uses the language of sensual desire and its satisfaction to explain deep desire as an apprehension of the good:

> O God! How happy the soul is who takes pleasure in knowing and fully knowing that God is God, and that his goodness is an infinite goodness! For this heavenly spouse, by this gate of deep pleasure, enters into the soul and sups with us and we with him. We feed ourselves with his sweetness by the pleasure which we take therein, and satiate our heart in the divine perfections by the contentment we take in them: and this repast is a supper by reason of the repose which follows it, since deep pleasure makes us sweetly rest in the sweetness of the good which delights us, and with which we feed our heart.[71]

The Song of Songs provides words and images for this most pleasing arrival of God in the soul, when God and self find mutual delight in their exchanges with each other:

> *Let my beloved come into his garden,* said the sacred spouse, *and eat the fruit of his apple-trees* [Song of Songs 5:1]. Now the heavenly spouse comes into his garden when he comes into the devout

> soul; seeing that his delight is *to be with the children of men* [Prov. 8:31], where can he better lodge than in the land of the spirit, which he made to his image and likeness? He himself plants in this garden the loving deep pleasure which we take in his goodness, and on which we feed, just as his goodness takes its pleasure and feeds on our deep pleasure; so that, again, our deep pleasure is augmented in perceiving that God is pleased to see us pleased in him.[72]

As this mutual delight grows, the instinct for union with God becomes ever more particular and tangible:

> The soul which contemplates the infinite treasures of divine perfections in her well-beloved finds herself so very happy and rich; as a result, in deep pleasure love makes her mistress of all the good and contentment of this beloved spouse. Even as a baby makes little movements towards his mother's breasts, and dances with joy to see them uncovered, and as the mother on her part presents them to him again with a love ever more urgent, even so the devout soul feels the thrills and movements of an incomparable joy through the pleasure she takes in beholding the treasures of the perfections of the king of her holy love, and especially when she sees that he himself shows them to her by love, and that among them that perfection of his infinite love shines excellently.[73]

This realization is as intimate as a scent we breathe:

> Ah! the soul which by love holds her Savior in the arms of her affections, how deliciously does she smell the perfumes of the infinite perfections which are found in him, with what deep pleasure does she say in herself: *behold how the scent of my God is as the sweet smell of a flowery garden, ah! how precious are his breasts, spreading sovereign perfumes* [Song of Songs 1: 3–4].[74]

Faith in the value and reliability of this instinctive deep pleasure is key to the exposition de Sales makes central to the whole *Treatise*. Obedience to the pull of this pleasure draws its adherents to a deeper divine intimacy. Even when, later on, the vocabulary becomes that of obedience and abandonment, this deepest instinct for God remains at the heart of things.

3. *Deep Pleasure, Conformity, and Obedience*

In its purest and most intense forms, this pleasure reduces to a single point, a pleasure that is increasingly God's pleasure as the self reaches beyond itself into the God it desires. It then becomes a more intense union with God that is also a kind of submission. This subtle transition, so easily misunderstood as merely a kind of negation or violence, is key to books 8 ("The love of conformity, by which we unite our will to the will of God, signified to us by his commandments, counsels and inspirations") and 9 ("The love of submission, whereby our will is united to God's good pleasure").

In chapter 1 of book 8, de Sales begins his reflection on this conformity to God: Since the soul, even in its deepest satisfaction, finds itself only by going outside itself, increasingly it cares about the divine pleasure alone:

> As good ground that has received the seed renders it back in its season *a hundredfold* [Luke 8:8], so the heart which has taken deep pleasure in God cannot hinder itself from wishing to offer deep pleasure to God in return. For no one pleases us whom we do not desire to please in return.[75]

He offers a curious image for this assimilation to God by way of deep pleasure:

> They say there is a little land animal in the Indies, which finds such pleasure with fishes and in the sea, that by often swimming with them it becomes a fish, and instead of an animal of the land becomes entirely an animal of the sea. So by often delighting in God we become conformed to God, and our will is transformed into that of the Divine Majesty, by the deep pleasure which it takes therein.[76]

The heart, bearing the scent of love, yearns for God and blossoms upon its approach to God: "Our heart, together with the pleasure which it takes in the thing beloved, draws unto itself the quality thereof, for delight opens the heart, as sorrow closes it."[77] This divine-human mingling is a kind of divinization:

> In sum, the pleasure which we take in a thing has a certain communicative power which produces in the lover's heart the

> qualities of the thing which pleases. And hence it is that a holy deep pleasure *transforms us into God whom we love*. The greater that deep pleasure, so much more perfect is the transformation: thus the saints that loved ardently were speedily and perfectly transformed, love transporting and translating the manners and dispositions from the one heart into the other.[78]

Or, more simply and accessibly: "Whosoever truly takes pleasure in God desires faithfully to please God, and in order to please him, desires to conform himself to him."[79]

On this basis, de Sales links the logic of desire and deep pleasure to growing conformity, such as can conclude only in surrender of the will to God. In chapter 2 of book 8,[80] deep pleasure is transformed into this increasingly full conformity to God, who with increasing intensity illumines the self as the sun renders a mirror dazzling in its brightness:

> Deep pleasure then draws into us the traits of the divine perfections according as we are capable of receiving them. Just as a mirror receives the sun's image, not according to the excellence and amplitude of that great and admirable luminary, but in proportion to the capacity and measure of its glass, so too we thus become conformed to God.[81]

Quite distinct from extrinsic submission to the will of another, obedience marks an increasingly pure and single-minded devotion to the divine will as the self is drawn into harmony with God and God's world:

> We take delight in considering how God is not only the first beginning but also the last end, author, preserver, and Lord of all things, for which reason we desire that all things be subject to him by a sovereign obedience. We see God's will to be sovereignly perfect, right, just and equitable; and upon this consideration our desire is that it be the rule and sovereign law of all things, and that it be observed, kept and obeyed by all other wills.

Such an obedience is never a matter of fear or even of duty, but even so, its demand is all the greater, since it is now a matter of choice: "The love of benevolence moves us to render all obedience and submission to God by choice and inclination, yea by a sweet violence of love, in consideration of the sovereign goodness, justice and rectitude of his divine will."[82] Ultimately, conformity and intimacy, obedience and love, can no longer be sorted out:

> Even so is our heart conformed to God's, when by holy benevolence we throw all our affections into the hands of the divine will, to be turned and directed as it chooses, to be molded and formed according to its good pleasure. And in this point consists the most profound obedience of love, which has no need to be spurred by threats or rewards, nor by any law or any commandment; for it anticipates all this, submitting itself to God solely for the most perfect goodness which is in God, whereby he deserves that all wills should be obedient, subject and submissive to him, conforming and uniting themselves for ever, in everything, and everywhere, to his divine intentions.[83]

Although this might, in other contexts, seem a monstrous loss of autonomy and integrity in the presence of an overwhelming Other, de Sales insists that this unification is best described in terms of benevolence, pleasure, and a perfect good.

In the subsequent chapters in *Treatise* book 8, de Sales focuses ever more closely on conformity to God's will, each chapter further specifying the way to a union that is both obedient and pleasurable. In chapter 5 and thereafter, de Sales emphasizes fidelity to Catholic tradition as a foundation for the more subtle forms of surrender and union. The exercise of duty and obedience in the church makes us ready for a higher conformity to God, and the basic commandments and further demands of the counsels (regarding monastic life, poverty, chastity, stability, obedience, etc.) signal conformity to God's will. Conversely, violations of the commandments and disregard for the counsels signal a person who strays from God by preferring the way of autonomous reason, independence from tradition, and the achievement of personal goals. We shall return to this "ethical" description in chapter 5.

In chapters 11–13 of book 8, de Sales adduces from tradition many instances of this more perfect obedience: Paul, Moses, the ascetic Simeon Stylites, the medieval saints Francis and Dominic, all famed for their willingness to submit to and find their satisfaction in obedience to divine inspiration. Turning again to nature, he observes that just as sunflowers instinctively turn toward the sun,

> in the same way all the elect turn the flower of their heart, which is obedience to the commandments, towards the divine will, but souls entirely taken with holy love not only look towards this divine goodness by obedience to the commandments, but also *by the union of all their affections,* following this heavenly sun in his round, in all that he commands, counsels and inspires, without any reserve or exception.

Or the soul is trained and disciplined in the Lord's ways:

> Whence they can say with the sacred Psalmist: *You have held me by my right hand; and by your will you have led me, and with your glory you have received me. I am become as a beast before you: and I am always with you* [Ps. 73:23b–24a, 22b–23a]. For as a well-broken horse is easily, gently and properly managed by his rider, in any way that is required, so the loving soul is so pliable to God's will that he does with her what he wishes.[84]

This loving, obedient intimacy with God is akin to Deśika's obeisance in its complete surrender of the will; for both authors, what pleases God becomes indistinguishable from the soul's own pleasure.

4. *The Role of the Indifferent Heart*

Book 9 constitutes the thematic and rhetorical climax of the *Treatise.* Again de Sales urges submission, but it is now to be cultivated in "indifference." A first resignation "prefers God's will before all things," even though a person may still love other things as well. But this yields in turn to a second resignation, an indifference that "loves nothing except for the love of God's will, so that nothing can stir the indifferent heart, in the presence of the will of God."[85] As a thirsty person greedily drinks water from any available cup, in the same way the spiritually thirsty person cares only for God's will, whatever God may will at this moment. This soul is pliant, as if having no will at all but to adhere to the divine will:

> The indifferent heart is like a ball of wax in the hands of its God, receiving with equal readiness all the impressions of the eternal good pleasure; it is a heart without choice, equally disposed for everything, having no other object of its will than the will of its

> God, and placing its affection not upon the things that God wills, but upon the will of God who wills them.

Increasingly attentive, this person chooses only the divine will itself:

> Wherefore, when God's will is in various things, [the human will] chooses, at whatever cost, that in which it appears most. . . . In conclusion, God's will is the sovereign object of the indifferent soul; wherever she sees it, she runs there after the *odor* of its *perfumes* [Song of Songs 1:3], directing her course ever thither where it most appears, without considering anything else.

All calculations of personal benefit are cast aside:

> She is conducted by the divine will, as by a beloved bond; whichever it goes, she follows it. She would prize hell with God's will over heaven without it; nay she would even prefer hell before heaven if she perceived only a little more of God's good-pleasure in this rather than that, so that if, by supposition of an impossible thing, she should know that her damnation would be more agreeable to God than her salvation, she would quit her salvation and run to her damnation.[86]

This indifference, though laced with seemingly impossible prospects—such as damnation, for God's sake—and calculated without reference to ordinary pleasure, is surely not bland. De Sales draws on a vivid range of images to trace the intensification of indifference, as the person who seeks God chooses, with increasing passion, to submit to whatever God may give:

> Let us come, next, to ourselves in particular, and behold the multitude of interior and exterior goods, as also the very great number of interior and exterior pains, which the Divine Providence has prepared for us, according to his most holy justice and mercy: and, *as if opening the arms of our consent*, let us *most lovingly embrace* all this, acquiescing to his most holy will.

He continues with a brief meditation on words from the Our Father prayer, paring it down to the essential divine purpose:

> Let us sing unto him as it were a hymn of eternal acquiescence: *Your will be done on earth as it is in heaven* [Matt. 6:10]. Yes, Lord, *your will be done on earth,*—where we have no pleasure which is not mixed with some pain, no roses without thorns, no day without following night, no spring without preceding winter; *on earth,* O Lord! where consolations are rare, and toils innumerable. Yet, O God! *your will be done,* not only in carrying out your commandments, counsels and inspirations, which are things to be done by us, but also in suffering the afflictions and pains which have to be borne by us; so that *your will* may do by us, for us, in us, and with us, all that it pleases.[87]

But this acquiescence opens the way for a greater accumulation of suffering, which is not attenuated by an understanding of its meaning or value, for it overwhelms reason and obscures even hope:

> But what in this case augments our trouble is that even the spirit and highest point of reason cannot give any alleviation at all; for this poor superior portion of reason is beset round about with the suggestions of the enemy; she is herself all upset, and is fully engaged in keeping guard, lest she might be surprised by some consent to sin. As a result, she can make no sally to disengage the inferior part of her spirit. Although she has not lost heart, yet she is so desperately set upon, that although she is free from fault yet is she not free from pain. That her affliction may be complete, she is deprived of the general consolation which we ordinarily have through all the other calamities of this life, namely, the hope that they will not be of long continuance, and we will see their end.[88]

Finding itself deprived of love, the soul clings to the faith that resides in that high point of the soul whence mind and words fall back, but even that faith grows dark as the self no longer knows even itself.

> The heart in these spiritual afflictions falls into a certain inability of thinking of their end, and consequently of being eased by hope. Faith indeed which resides in the supreme point of the soul assures us that this trouble will have an end, and that some day we shall enjoy repose: but the loudness of the shouts and outcries which the enemy makes in the rest of the soul, in the inferior

> reason, will scarcely permit the advice and remonstrances of faith to be heard; and there remains in the imagination only this sorrowful foreboding: *Alas! joy I shall never have.*[89]

In chapter 12 de Sales turns to the final, most intense and intimate stages of union with God, ultimately a kind of death. Like Peter at the time of his dreamlike liberation from prison in *Acts*, the soul moves toward freedom, but it knows not and sees not where or how this liberation can occur:

> For although she has the power to believe, to trust, and to love her God, and in reality does so, yet she has not the strength to see properly whether she believes, trusts, and cherishes her God, because her distress so engages her, and so desperately overwhelms her, that she cannot return to herself to see what is going on there. And hence she thinks that she has no faith, nor hope, nor charity, but only the shadows and fruitless impressions of those virtues, which she feels almost without feeling them, and as if foreign and unfamiliar to her soul.[90]

This desolation is sheer anguish: "Alas! Theotimus, how the poor heart is afflicted when, as it were abandoned by love, she seeks it everywhere, but seems not to find it."[91] Such a person is dead even while alive:

> But what is the soul to do that finds herself in this case? Theotimus, she no longer knows how to behave amidst so much affliction; nor has she any power save to let her will die in the hands of God's will, in imitation of her sweet Jesus, who arriving at the height of the pains of the cross which his Father had ordained, and not being able any further to resist the extremity of his torments, did as the hart does, which when it is run out of breath and oppressed by the hounds, yields itself into the huntsman's hands, its eyes filled with tears, utters its last cries.[92]

De Sales keeps before his mind's eye Jesus, who even in agony still could utter the words of self-surrender that guide the person who enters upon this loving surrender to God:

> Thus did our Divine Savior, near unto his death, give up his last breath *with a loud voice* and abundance of tears: Alas! said he, *O*

> *my Father, into your hands I commit my spirit* [Luke 23:46]—a word, Theotimus, which was his very last, and the one by which the well-beloved Son gave the sovereign testimony of his love towards his Father.[93]

In a still deeper act of imitation, he appeals to his readers to surrender to this Jesus:

> When therefore all fails us, when our troubles have come to their extremity, this word, this disposition, this rendering up of our soul into our Savior's hands, can never fail us. The Son commended his spirit to his Father in this his last and incomparable anguish, and we, when the convulsions of spiritual pains shall bereave us of every other kind of solace and means of resistance, let us commend our spirit into the hands of this eternal Son who is our true Father, and *bowing the head* [John 19:30] of our acquiescence in his good pleasure, let us make over our whole will unto him.[94]

As the soul dies, it

> neither wills nor cares to desire any thing at all, but gives itself over totally and without reserve to the good pleasure of the Divine Providence, so mingling and saturating itself with this good pleasure, that itself is seen no more, but is *all hidden with Jesus Christ in God* [Col. 3:3], where it lives, not it, but *the will of God lives in it* [Gal. 2:20].[95]

At that extreme point, such a person has, by free choice, become bereft even of will itself:

> The heart that is embarked upon this good divine pleasure ought to have no other will than that of permitting itself to be conducted by the divine will. And then the heart does not as before say: *Your will be done, not mine* [Luke 22:42]: for there is now no will to be renounced; but it utters these words: *Lord, I commend my will into your hands,* as if it had its will not at its own disposition, but at the disposition of the Divine Providence.[96]

But because he is abandoned to God, this person, like the one who has taken refuge, no longer suffers any anxiety:

> He never troubles himself as to how he shall conform his will to his mother's, for he perceives not his own, nor does he think he has any, leaving all the care to his mother, to go, to do, and to will, whatever she judges profitable for him.[97]

Though this loss of self may seem a desperate fate, de Sales insists that what is gained is a good, sweet freedom in the Lord:

> To bless and thank God in all the events that his providence ordains, is in truth a most holy exercise; while we leave to God the care of willing and doing in us, on us, and with us, what pleases him, without attending to what passes, although fully feeling it, then we can divert our heart, and apply our attention to the divine goodness and sweetness, blessing it not in the effects or events it ordains, but in itself and in its own excellence; in this case we will certainly practice a far more eminent exercise.[98]

The waiting itself counts as the simplest act of the will:

> It seems to me the soul which is in this indifference, and which wills nothing, but lets God will what pleases him, should be said to have its will in a simple and general state of waiting: this waiting is not a doing or acting, but only remaining prepared for some event. And, if you take notice, this waiting of the soul is indeed voluntary, and yet it is not an action, but a simple disposition to receive whatsoever shall happen; and as soon as the events come and are received, the waiting changes into consent or acquiescence, but, before they happen, the soul is truly in a state of simple waiting, indifferent to all that it shall please the divine will to ordain.[99]

Here too the starkest example is Jesus, who "left himself to be handled and dragged about at the will of them that crucified him, by an admirable surrender made of his body and life into their hands." In this way, "by a most perfect indifference" he surrendered "his soul and will into his Eternal Father's hands."[100] But his cry of forsakenness is not his last word:

> For though he cries out: *My God, my God, why have You forsaken me?* [Matt. 27:46] yet this was to let us understand the reality of the anguish and bitterness of his soul, and not to

> violate the most holy indifference in which he was. This he showed very soon afterwards, concluding his whole life and his passion with those incomparable words: *Father, into Your hands I commend my spirit* [Luke 23:24].[101]

De Sales is captivated by these last words that form a kind of "Salesian mantra," and I will return to them shortly.

The meditation on the dying Jesus as mirror of the soul intensifies in chapter 16 of book 9 in vividly physical detail:

> Love did all this, Theotimus, and it is love too which enters into a soul to make it happily die to itself and live to God, and deprives it of all human desires, and of that self-esteem which is not less attached to the spirit than the skin to the flesh, and strips her at length of her best beloved affections, such as those which she had for spiritual consolations, exercises of piety and the perfection of virtues, which seemed to be the very life of the soul.[102]

Albeit terrifying, this experience is also a bridge over to new life:

> Even so are we to strip ourselves of all affections little and great, as also to make a frequent examination of our hearts to discover whether it be ready to divest itself, as Isaiah did, of all its garments: then we must take up again, at proper times, the affections suitable to the service of charity, to the end that we may die with Our Savior naked upon the cross, and rise again with him in the new man. *Love is strong as death* [Song of Songs 8:6] in making us quit all; it is as magnificent as the Resurrection, in adorning us with honor and glory.[103]

At this point, the long and winding story of love has climaxed in union, a union as sorrowful as the cross and as glorious as the resurrection that follows it. Ideally, the person who follows this path—beginning it by reading attentively the words of scripture in de Sales' words—finds herself or himself at least on the edge of this radical transformation, if not already irreversibly entered upon it.

How to recollect this final state and pray in accord with it? There is one additional point to be made.

5. *De Sales' Mantra?*

Now that we have read de Sales after reading Deśika, we can ask, if only for the sake of clarification: At the apex of his spiritual theology, does de Sales imagine some utterance with mantra-like concision, depth of meaning, and efficacious power? Although his grand narrative of desire and submission is in style and affect very different from Deśika's crystal-clear analysis of the Dvaya Mantra, after Deśika we reread de Sales with a new eye and, I suggest, gain new insight into scriptural words I have already cited: *Into your hands I commend my spirit.* Let us review his wider citation of them.

De Sales first uses the words in book 7 of the *Treatise* when recalling St. Peter Martyr: "St. Peter Martyr, writing with his finger and in his own blood the confession of the faith for which he died, and uttering these words: *Lord, into your hands I commend my spirit.*"[104] Then, at the end of a longer account of how St. Basil converted a Jewish physician, de Sales describes how at his death Basil uttered words of loving surrender that deeply touched the physician:

> St. Basil rose courageously out of his bed, went to the Church and baptized him with all his family, then returning to his chamber and to his bed, having engaged himself a good space with our Savior in prayer, he holily exhorted the assistants to serve God with their whole heart, and finally, seeing the angels approach, and pronouncing with an extreme delight these words: *O God I recommend unto you my soul, and restore it into your hands*; he died. But when the poor converted physician saw him thus pass away, he embraced him, and melted into tears over him. "O great Basil," he said, "if indeed you had willed it, you would no more have died today than yesterday." Who does not see that this death was wholly of love?[105]

The words of scripture, remembered and passed down through the generations, here become Basil's own words, at his moment of death—and as he utters them, they remain potent, deeply touching the physician's heart: These words "wholly of love" are recommended to the reader in this way.

In book 9, de Sales returns several times to the loving surrender that Jesus consummates on the cross. These are words to take within the heart and to repeat in imitation of Christ and assimilation to him; Jesus' words become our own words:

> And so the heart that is embarked upon the divine good pleasure, ought to have no other will than that of permitting itself to be conducted by the divine will. And then the heart does not as before say: *Your will be done, not mine* [Luke 22:42]. For there is now no will to be renounced; but it utters these words: *Lord I commend my will into your hands,* as though it did not have its will at its own disposition, but at the disposition of the Divine Providence.[106]

Jesus several times speaks powerfully from the cross but, as we saw earlier, his final words of loving surrender into God's hands are the most potent, as he concluded "his whole life and his passion with those incomparable words: *Father, into Your hands I commend my spirit.*"[107]

If we take seriously the logic and power of de Sales' exposition, and see how much is thus contained in just a few words, we do well to call these words a mantra. In their brevity and simplicity, easily remembered and easily spoken, this prayer begs for repetition, and inscribes loving surrender in mind and imagination, making possible deeper insight and the beginnings of the radical transition, abandonment into the hands of God. Although nothing of doctrinal substance has changed by rereading the words of Jesus after Deśika's Dvaya Mantra, we will have nonetheless learned from Deśika how to find in a few simple biblical words the truth and power of the entire Catholic tradition, now remembered, recited, even ignited.

IV. Loving Surrender—Intensified

We cannot but notice similarities between Deśika's ideal of refuge as rooted in a "great faith" that requires and then endures the loss of everything but God, and de Sales' ideal of loving surrender as a complete identification with God's will, God's intentions, God's holy desire. In both cases, everything exists for God, in dependence on God. What is necessarily the case can also be chosen freely in joy, a choice for the most intense object of human desire, God. Our authors share the presumption that we usually fail to live in accord with who we really are, clinging instead to false identities that do not satisfy and cannot be maintained. But even if we are lost and fallen, both authors insist that we are not ruined. By instruction and surer knowledge we can change our habits and patterns of desire; we can begin to acknowledge our fundamental orientation to God, and on that basis embark on deeper, more radical changes in life. Both Deśika and de Sales believe that with obstacles removed, clarity of vision grows, and in that light, love grows purer and more intense, and is all the more likely to flourish. Neither author recommends an entirely passive expectation of divine grace; neither would tolerate the notion that grace exists only on a vague horizon, never making any difference in a present moment. Grace does arrive on its own schedule—for both authors, somewhere just beyond our last, desperate effort—and yet we must still prepare the way through reflection on scripture, an inventory of our store of images and affective states, and the imitation of lovers who have preceded us. What matters ultimately is the gift, but persuasive teaching and writing, exemplified in the *Essence* and *Treatise*, remain instrumental in making us capable of receiving that grace intelligently and with passion. Readers who keep reading should eventually be on the verge of committing themselves to loving surrender.

What is true within the narratives of the *Essence* and the *Treatise* can therefore become true for readers too, if we remember and appropriate the words and images and exemplars of our reading and reconfigure our own situations in light of this newly compelling possibility of loving surrender. If we have been disciplined in our reading and persistent in reflection on our reading, this concerted reading practice enables us to interpret our own situation differently, now with more radical choices at hand. In this process, ideas and words may—improbably, in the interreligious situation—retrieve something of that deeper and older intensity Deśika attributes to the words of Rāmānuja and other great teachers, and de Sales to the mystical theologians of ancient times. Engaged and drawn in beyond our current capacities, we become better readers, religious scholars, and members of communities both learned and holy. Or so Deśika and de Sales would hope.

As I have insisted from the beginning of this book, although these two reading experiences do not require each other, once both are read in proximity this doubled intensity deeply affects the reader twice over, such that each text intensifies and magnifies the other rather than diluting its impact. It is hard to imagine giving up one of these texts for the sake of the other once we have begun reading them and can see what is possible in the double reading.

It is not that the texts themselves ever become truly irresistible; Deśika and de Sales remain aware of the inevitable limitations of the power of reasons and words, even religious words rooted in scripture and tradition. They do not claim to be in a position to ensure that their readers will choose loving surrender, as if their own words were so powerful as to make readers respond predictably. Meditation, prayer, and worship were still necessary, forming a more practical context in which the reading might have its chance to change hearts and minds. Today's reader is even less predictable, knowing multiple traditions from diverse vantage points, and with little authoritative constraint. Particularly in a pluralistic context, this reader is of course at liberty to read selectively, and to consume either text for purposes extraneous to its author's intentions. The reader faced with the prospect of reading about loving surrender has to decide whether to do so as a spiritual exercise (prompted by Pierre Hadot) and as a committed religious reading (as Paul Griffiths recommends).[108]

So too, de Sales' and Deśika's ambivalence toward reasoning and language, which I examined in chapter 2, remains a factor even as they are describing the final stages and insights of loving surrender. More is needed than their words: only those willing to enter within the tradition to learn from it would surely be changed by even a classic of that tradition. Beyond the text is the teacher, and deeper than the text is a fundamental longing already instilled in the heart by God. Authors and their texts at their best serve as occasions for more vital encounters, after and beyond them, in the reader's world. After we read, we need to find the life of the text, its possibility of loving surrender, back in the places where we live. And yet reading is still, very often, the best place to begin, whatever else might be done later; and reading two such texts can indeed occasion unpredictable and irreversible learning.

In using "loving surrender" as the guiding motif of this double reading, I have favored resemblance, in both style and content, between Deśika's and de Sales' views of loving surrender as a response appropriate to the divine person(s) as possessed of various perfections, compassion, eagerness to save, and a determination to bring about salvation. And yet, this resemblance regarding the person who surrenders in love, the act itself, and the recipient, does not preclude elements that distinguish the traditions. Differences may become more and not less sharply accentuated and well defined, because we are now receiving both texts as integral wholes, reasons, images, and all, and with greater attention to where all these resources lead. Analogies between the two texts, in content and style, do not translate into pure similarity, as if loving surrender might reduce to a single approach leading to a single conclusion.[109]

But it still seems the case that the differences we discover with respect to the *Treatise* and the *Essence* are complementary, encouraging us to read both texts together, for they work well together. Deśika's text, at its most powerful, is like a laser piercing and dispelling darkness, illumining everything in the sharpest detail, so that when ordinary ways of living are exposed, they can be experienced as intolerable, in need of an alternative, the recalculation of life that leads to loving surrender. De Sales' text is a great river, dams broken, every manner of love flowing into God; swept along by de Sales, we are likewise drawn to the brink of that surrender. With the *Essence*, the reader's mind may be so fully illumined that it becomes very difficult not to see differently and act in accord with that seeing. De Sales' deep trust in personal experience prompts him to appeal more directly to the heart, aiming to inflame his reader with new desires that will carry him beyond self and into God. The safety and assurance of Deśika's portrayal of refuge is less frightening than the death envisioned and exemplified at the heart of the Christian tradition, and yet de Sales' narrative, gentler and more pleasing, may be less likely to entirely clear the mind and open the way to real change.

Here too, our insights can be further sorted out in accord with the identity of the reader. Both Deśika and de Sales write with a persuasive power that can deeply affect readers in their own traditions, reminding them that loving surrender is a time-honored value, of an urgency relevant even at the current moment. Deśika shows Śrīvaiṣṇavas why taking refuge with Nārāyaṇa and Śrī is a most valuable idea most faithful to their tradition, while de Sales enables Christians to see again how Christ's loving surrender marks the utmost measure of love any Christian might dare. Were the *Treatise* and *Essence* to help us in becoming simply better Christians or better Śrīvaiṣṇavas, we will have profited greatly from reading these texts. And were the reader who is neither a Christian nor a Śrīvaiṣṇava to feel encouraged to seek out this possibility in her or his own tradition, that would be the proper way in which to generalize the practical dimension of this book.

But there is more. Because there are basic resonances that we can expect in these theistic theological contexts in which divine action, human freedom, and the highest destinies are at stake, and because the reasoned, aesthetic, and pedagogical dimensions of the *Essence* and *Treatise* affect *any* attentive reader, these texts can also make powerful sense to new readers who learn their way into a previously unfamiliar tradition of loving surrender. As we saw in chapter 3, new scriptural quotations, though unfamiliar at first, can certainly make sense to the reader who comes belatedly, later in life, to this reading. The images still flood the mind. And the inspiring examples, lives heroically tested and expended, and balance of text and truths beyond the text all gain force in the mind and heart of the attentive reader who is disposed to take seriously scripture, religious images and exemplars, and intensifications of desire. None of this can be so specific as to exclude any reader entirely.

There is no reason that a Śrīvaiṣṇava cannot be deeply affected by the passionate intensity of de Sales' narrative of deep pleasure, conformity, and abandonment. Nor is there any reason that a Catholic cannot find herself deeply appreciative of the image of Nārāyaṇa and Śrī as refuge and goal, even to the extent that she utters the Dvaya Mantra as her own spiritual utterance, closely consonant with, if not identical to, the Śrīvaiṣṇava appropriation of the mantra. What *should* be done by a Śrīvaiṣṇava or Catholic in this situation is another question—shall I surrender in this way or not? The fact that there are now choices is what matters.

And finally, again, there is the phenomenon cultivated in these pages, the reading back and forth between the two texts. This double reading remains unsettling even at this point where loving surrender is the object of our consideration. It unsettles us by its sheer abundance; such a reading dramatically expands intellectual and affective possibilities, as the reasons, images, and affective states proposed and promoted in each text enter into a most agile interplay with those of the other text; there are always more options available to us than we can manage to appropriate and reflect upon. But this complex reading also disorients us; even at this deepest point where practice matters most, the most powerful images of loving surrender offered by a tradition are shadowed as well as illumined by similarly potent images from the other tradition. This should deflate pride in the (largely unwarranted) conviction readers might have had that only their own tradition appreciates loving surrender or the supporting understandings of reason and language, religious imagination and emotion. Without the rhetoric of exclusivism and pluralism and without the comforts enjoyed by those who know only their own tradition or (seemingly) no tradition at all, the reader, bereft of such securities, finds older habits and comforts no longer possible. Now unsettled by both texts, she or he comes closer to the precipice of a real act of loving surrender.

Of course some religious communities may see this double reading as trespass on forbidden ground, precisely because loving surrender is at stake. Approval is readily granted when the attentive reader goes deeper into her or his own tradition, or simply gathers information about another tradition to enhance her place in her home tradition. But this approval turns to discomfort, puzzlement, even disapproval as a reader becomes seriously attentive to the words, images, affects, and practices of another tradition. Perhaps this lack of ease is appropriate. As surrender shows itself to be an attractive possibility both here and there, the *Essence* and *Treatise* may be identified as suddenly more dangerous texts, precisely because when read properly they show themselves still potent, still able to touch and transform their readers, even in the age of pluralism.

We notice that both Deśika and de Sales speak of a loving divine person, and both present us with features and dispositions that might be attributed to God in the Christian tradition and also to Nārāyaṇa and Śrī in the Śrīvaiṣṇava tradition. Neither author tolerates a vaguely conceived end point known as "God." Deśika may be thought of as speaking for de Sales too when in his exegesis of "I approach for refuge the feet of Nārāyaṇa with Śrī" he argues that the way is the goal: the divine persons themselves are the means and end point of human liberation. Even if de Sales and Deśika cannot be said to agree entirely on what God is like, we can conclude that loving surrender in both cases presupposes a divine recipient and refuge with most of the same characteristic features, including compassion, proximity, and the willingness and intention to protect. Who Deśika and de Sales are speaking about may in many ways seem to be the same person understood in accord with the same ideas and affective states and in evocation of the same goals.

But when faced with the prospect of identifying and assessing this divine person, some readers might also draw back because they are deeply rooted in their own traditions; they might deny to the other tradition the proper name and full reality of God and hence the efficacy of loving surrender to people within that tradition. This exclusion might occur not so much out of religious chauvinism or narrow-mindedness, but as the fruit of lives lived deeply within a single tradition. They might simply find it impossible to imagine loving surrender to a God known by that other name and form. That a Christian or Śrīvaiṣṇava would choose to read and think no further is entirely understandable. If there is no outside higher viewpoint from which he might adjudicate differences and decide where loving surrender really belongs and really leaves him, he has to decide "from within" his readings and double readings how to understand the destination of loving surrender, in God, at the feet of Nārāyaṇa with Śrī.[110] But at least we have something to ponder, a vast wealth of new learning that can be remembered in these prayers that can so easily be placed together.

The Two Mantras in Harmony

I approach for refuge the feet of Nārāyaṇa with Śrī; obeisance to Nārāyaṇa with Śrī.	Father, into Your hands I commit my spirit.

Originally, I had thought that this book might end with these two prayers. But neither de Sales nor Deśika is finished, even at the moment of loving surrender. Neither thinks that life ends with the taking of refuge, and so there is the awkward matter of what to do afterward. If we venture to read and write about such things, we too must face the question of ethics, life after our reading, and recognition of loving surrender as a choice we can at least imagine to be ours. What follows as we think our way through the implications of this kind of double reading is the subject of my final chapter.

Chapter 5

As We Become Ourselves

On the Ethics of Loving Surrender and of Persistence in Reading

One of the qualifications for taking refuge is grief before taking refuge. If a person has no grief before taking refuge, he will be lacking a necessary qualification for performing it since, by the principle "No cause, no effect," his means will be ineffective. Similarly, when he reflects upon himself after taking refuge, if then he still grieves owing to tepidity regarding the words of his protector, then, by the principle "No effect, no cause," it follows that his performance of the means must have been incomplete.

Deśika, *Essence*

We cannot long remain in this nakedness, despoiled of all kinds of affections. Wherefore, following the advice of the holy Apostle, as soon as we have put off the garments of the old Adam, we are to put on the habits of the new man, that is to say of Jesus Christ, for having renounced all—yes, even affection for virtues, neither desiring of these nor of other things a larger portion than God's will intends—we must put on again diverse affections, perhaps the very same which we have renounced and resigned.

De Sales, *Treatise*

Manner matters because it puts the emphasis on concrete vividness as the locus of significance for the activity. Consequently, when we register the emotion adverbially we adjust how we project identities—about our own emotions or about agents whom we observe. We are responding not to how beliefs shape

> the person's world but to who the person becomes as he or she manifests the working out of attitudes in relation to that world.
>
> Charles Altieri, *The Particulars of Rapture*

I. Life after Loving Surrender to God

After their intense reflections on loving surrender, Deśika and de Sales see before them the task of ethics or, more specifically, the need for a profile of the lives of religious persons who live in fidelity to the ideal of loving surrender.[1] Much of *Essence* chapters 13–19 is about the new moral and spiritual practice of the person who has taken refuge; much of *Treatise* books 10–12 focuses on how love undergirds, integrates, and infuses all the virtues of the person who has loved with the same abandon as Jesus. And we also can ask: If the believer, reader, writer, has taken to heart the message and implications of loving surrender taught by the *Treatise* and *Essence*, then how is this person to live, bereft of prior certainties but also more richly educated in two traditions, denying neither even if committed most fully to one of them? This is a matter of concern to both authors, neither of whom is naïve about the ways in which even the finest of ideals needs to be moderated by the wisdom of tradition in the face of the less-than-ideal realities of human life. Let us consider in turn how Deśika and de Sales portray the wholeness of life after loving surrender and the fragmentation of life lived otherwise.

1. Deśika on Life after Refuge

In *Essence* chapters 13–19, Deśika sketches the behavior of those who have taken refuge. Theirs is a new life entirely free from grief and anxiety—because all is in God's hands—yet still disciplined regarding what he sees as necessary and presupposed societal expectations (such as caste) that govern the lives even of people living in accord with God's will. Old structures pertain, but with new foundations and purposes.

Chapters 13–15 establish the framework and boundaries. In chapter 13 Deśika focuses on the person who has taken refuge,[2] just as he previously focused on the discontent (chapter 7) and desperate helplessness (chapter 10) of the person seeking the way of refuge. If the journey along the path was governed by the Dvaya Mantra, the ethical guide for the one who has traveled the path and gained refuge is the Carama Śloka: *Hav-*

ing completely given up all modes of righteousness, to Me alone come for refuge. From all sins I will make you free. Do not grieve.

The person who has surrendered responsibility to the Lord is free from further duties:

> Beginning immediately after taking refuge, the person established in this distinctive means no longer has any connection with anything that has to be done regarding the expected results. By performing just once the part he had to do, he is done.

Because the Lord is now the primary actor on behalf of such a person, she or he can live without anxiety or grief:

> The Lord of all, who is independent, whose intentions come true, and who gives the result, is the one who has said, *Do not grieve.* So [the person taking refuge] should examine his situation: having surrendered his burden he is now a person without any burden. The Lord of all, who has agreed to be the objective means and accordingly has said, *To Me alone come for refuge,* is also the one who has decided to give the result, saying, *From all sins I will make you free.*

A result of taking this promise seriously is a radical rearrangement of priorities, with consequent relief and deep joy:

> When he sees the Lord who is trusted, capable, and the means, [the person taking refuge] no longer has doubts regarding the accomplishment of the goal, and is freed of any burden. All other means are uprooted, and other goals disappear without a trace, and he is like a person with nothing who has received a great treasure without effort, and he rejoices at the prospect of the supreme goal of life he is now to obtain.[3]

Such joy cannot be mandated, but Deśika can highlight its normative value for the person who has taken refuge:

> One of the qualifications for taking refuge is grief before taking refuge. If a person has no grief before taking refuge, he will be lacking a necessary qualification for performing it since, by the

> principle "No cause, no effect," his means will be ineffective. Similarly, when he reflects upon himself after taking refuge, if then he still grieves owing to tepidity regarding the words of his protector, then, by the principle "No effect, no cause," it follows that his performance of the means had been incomplete, and so we know that its fruit will be delayed, since he still needs to complete the means. The person who was previously full of grief and who is now free from grief in accord with the prohibition, *Do not grieve,* is the one to known to have taken refuge properly.

As Deśika aptly suggests in chapter 11, the person who has taken refuge is like a person who has transferred responsibility for her or his worldly affairs over to a reliable friend—and thereafter sleeps peacefully at night, free from care about the future.[4]

Living without grief is the new affective state urged upon the reader, a sure consequence of proper understanding acted out in taking refuge. By choosing to make grief and joy the affective states by which to assess real change, Deśika moves our consideration onto the subtle terrain of how people feel, and the consonant manner of their action. Persons who have surrendered to the Lord are exemplary, but recognizing them as such requires discernment, since no settled external marks signify the change that has taken place: Where, in whom, is there manifest the joy that arises upon taking refuge with Nārāyaṇa and Śrī? Though this discernment is not independent of doctrine or of notice of the dispositions that led up to the moment of loving surrender, we still have to be able to discern how a person integrates right thought and word with the more subtle conditions of a liberated imagination, richer affect, and a joy that has banished anxiety about the future and guilt about the past. Successful discernment in this situation requires that mature persons encounter other mature persons for mutual recognition.

For the sake of this discernment of right persons and right ways of acting, *Essence* chapter 14 lists signs indicative of the deep settledness arising with respect to the truth of reality (*tattva*), the means (*upāya*), and the final goal (*puruṣārtha*). For brevity's sake, I offer a summary chart (table 5.1). Humility in the face of the truth, fearless behavior, single-mindedness in one's goal: The stated qualities present to us the person who is tranquil and even-tempered regardless of what is happening, because she or he knows that only God, Nārāyaṇa with Śrī, is the means and the goal.

Chapter 15 provides instruction in accord with a long list of categories further distinguished by nearly seventy accompanying quotations.[5]

Table 5.1 The Truth, Means, and Goal in *Essence* Chapter 14

tattva (truth)	*upāya* (means)	*puruṣārtha* (goal)
knowing the self, detached serenity with respect to bodily flaws and criticisms by others	knowing that only the Lord is one's resource, protector	feeling no anxiety regarding the body and karmic debts
compassion toward those who criticize	no longer fearing death but welcoming it as pleasing	
remembrance of the help given by those who criticize	clarity in dependence on the protector	no joy or sorrow regarding ordinary gains and loss, only joy in service of the Lord
seeing that criticisms are really from the Lord who controls all	expending no effort in the work of self-protection	
rejoicing that by these criticisms, karma is expended	knowing that gaining the desirable, removing the the undesirable are solely in God's hands	eagerness only for gaining the Lord

As I suggested in chapter 3, Deśika intends texts for meditation, such as are useful giving the "feel" for this new life. His chapter 15 opens with a verse that characterizes this liberated person:

> Just for delight
> among the good people
> he meditates repeatedly on knowledge of the self,
> he ever speaks and teaches good and sweet narratives,
> and until his death keeps choosing flawless and delightful conduct:
> such is the person who has taken refuge,
> who has been granted to see how his burden,
> seen and unseen,[6]
> has vanished.[7]

Deśika introduces the list of quotations with a simple comparison and the lessons to be drawn from it:

> Thus the person who has done what had to be done becomes clear about his proper foundation. During his remaining time in the body, he is like a person who uses only a small portion of a large, fruitful field. The competent person, in one part without any bonds, in another still related, makes his own the portion that is most pleasing, just as liberated souls practice the higher modes of service.[8] And so, such a life is a goal in itself, defined in accord with specific times marked off by scripture. Like links in a chain, acts of service now are linked to the prospect of later acts of service.[9] These are the reason for the master's pleasure, and the effect of that pleasure too.[10]

Throughout, at issue is the single-minded devotion manifest in love throughout the rest of one's life and even over multiple lifetimes. Prescriptions on how to live remain pertinent, but Deśika chooses to stress the radical spirit underlying such details, the interior factors that find visible form in practices (table 5.2).

The chapter's final instruction links "do's and don'ts" with respect to thought, word, and deed.

These particular instances stand in for a larger set of cautions and values pertaining to thought, word, and deed. The things to be avoided are those material, psychological, and social mistakes and errors that divide community; things to be done are those giving form and stability to the community, as it coalesces around its wisest members. To appropriate the truths of the tradition, proper thinking is required; how this will appear is manifest in the lives of the teachers and other exemplary persons who are to be respected in all situations; in between, we need to be listening to words of dedication and praise, and avoiding those of self-aggrandizement.

Consequent upon these fundamental chapters, *Essence* chapters 16–19 go on to characterize the life of this person in community—the bal-

Table 5.2 What Is to Be Avoided and What Is to Be Done after Surrender

	To be avoided	To be done
thought	thinking about sense pleasures	being grateful for the assistance of teachers
word	talking of our own excellence	reciting the Dvaya Mantra
deed	offending those who know Brahman	serving the teacher and all who belong to the Lord

ance of freedom and constraint, what is to be done and what is to be avoided. In these chapters, Deśika seeks to describe what is proper without falling into a situation in which rules predominate or failure is inevitable in the face of impossible standards. Chapters 17 and 18 offer an ethical/spiritual balancing act. The devotee is truly free and yet should, Deśika insists, freely choose to honor orthodox prescriptions regarding caste, behavior, ritual performance, and the set roles of women and men in society. All these norms express the Lord's will (chapter 17). Rules still oblige the devotee socially; penalties apply, and sufferings occur even if the devotee remains immune to the severe and long-term bad effects that accrue to lapses occurring after taking refuge (chapter 18).[11]

Advice given in the seventeenth chapter makes very clear how the discernment of different kinds of persons should govern how we react to those around us. Deśika recalls Rāmānuja's words on how to live safely in a world where different people require different responses:

> Rāmānuja said, the competent person who lives this way must always watch out for these three: people who are well-disposed [to the Lord and the goal of liberation], people who are hostile, and people who are neither. The well-disposed are Śrīvaiṣṇavas; the hostile are those who hate the Lord; most people in this world are neither.[12]

The proper reaction, cultivated over a long period of time, becomes instinctive, even visceral:

> Seeing well-disposed people is like catching the scent of sandal paste and flowers, moonlight and cool breezes, and other pleasing objects, and so you rejoice. Seeing hostile people is like seeing a serpent or fire, and you become afraid. Seeing those who are neither [friendly nor hostile] is like looking at wood or stone, etc., and you should think, "These are like straw to me." If such indifferent people become well disposed, it is appropriate to give them knowledge; if they do not become suitable, it is right to have pity on them—"Ah!"[13]

People who are not properly formed and guided in proper thinking may be hostile, ill-willed toward the community of those who belong to Nārāyaṇa. But almost as distressingly, it seems, they can be indifferent, ill informed, infatuated with inferior values that dim the mind and harden the heart, and thus unable to appreciate a tradition too subtle and demanding for their diminished capacities.[14] For Deśika, the person who depends entirely on God should become practiced in reacting appropriately to these three kinds of persons.[15]

The two other chapters in this ethical section of the *Essence* deserve attention. In chapter 16, Deśika insists that love of God is best expressed by love for other Śrīvaiṣṇavas.[16] Nothing pleases Nārāyaṇa and Śrī more than a community dedicated to mutual service among the people who belong to the Lord:

> When a person acts consciously, even if [her or his] own motives are incidentally involved, what is done must be done ultimately to implement the Lord's own intentions. And when that divine will is pondered, it will be seen that serving His devotees is more pleasing than anything else. . . . Of all forms of service which someone dependent on the Lord may render, service rendered to those devoted to the Lord is most important—just as the fondling of the infant prince is most pleasing to the king.[17]

Chapter 19 praises the holiest temples of Śrīvaiṣṇavism, but Deśika also asserts that what really matters is to live among devotees of the Lord wherever they dwell, however "ordinary" that residence may be.[18]

Deśika envisions a tight-knit community of believers committed to one another and to a life of faith rooted in the belief that taking refuge does truly change one's life. There is every incentive to foster pleasure in this community where God is present and where people live the most important values. Insofar as we understand the *Essence*, we begin to intuit differently where our community actually is, those with whom we belong.

2. *De Sales on Life after Loving Surrender*

After his climactic teaching on abandonment in book 9 of the *Treatise*, de Sales takes up the issue of how people act when they are entirely given over to the will of God. Although he is less concerned in the *Treatise* with the kind of almost legal details that sometimes occupy Deśika's attention, he too finds it appropriate to fill out his discourse on loving surrender with reflections on the interplay of commandment and love. Chapters 10 through 12 may be read as describing the person who has enacted the surrender:

Book 10: "The Commandment of Loving God above All Things"

Book 11. "The Sovereign Authority Which Sacred Love Holds over All the Virtues, Actions, and Perfections of the Soul"

Book 12. "Certain Counsels for the Progress of the Soul in Holy Love"

De Sales thus follows a plan similar to Deśika's, likewise giving great importance to a proper estimate of life after surrender. Like Deśika, de Sales does not see it as his task to rehearse the positive content of the moral life. He too assumes that his readers know the rules from other sources, and he too attempts to reenvision adherence to details and rules in light of the faithful devotee's new state of freedom. He seeks not simply adherence and obedience—although these do matter—but rather more basically the grounding of behavior in the divine love to which one becomes increasingly and more intensely exposed through reflection, through a careful reading of the Bible and classics of the Christian tradition, and through the *Treatise* itself. Like Deśika, de Sales amply describes the spirit underlying the life that not only submits to the commandments of God and community but, more important, is inflamed by love. More specifically, he values the manner of acting, the wisdom, joy, and service that distinguish the Christian living in imitation of Christ.

Several instances will suffice to show us de Sales' positive characterization of the person who has surrendered to God. In chapter 1 of book 10, de Sales praises love and the great commandment to love, since herein lies the force that valorizes the ethical life:

> Man is the perfection of the universe; the spirit is the perfection of man; love, that of the spirit; and charity, that of love. Wherefore the love of God is the end, the perfection, and the excellence of the universe. In this, Theotimus, consists the greatness and the primacy of the commandment of divine love, which the Savior calls *the first and greatest commandment.*[19] This commandment is as a sun which gives luster and dignity to all the sacred laws, to all the divine ordinances, and to all the Holy Scriptures. All is done for this heavenly love, and all has reference to it. On the sacred tree of this commandment depend all the counsels, exhortations, inspirations, and the other commandments as its flowers, and eternal life as its fruit; and all that does not tend to

eternal love tends to eternal death. The Great Commandment, the perfect fulfillment of which lasts through eternal life, and which indeed is nothing other than eternal life![20]

After biblical examples adduced to remind us that it is meaningful to admit that God can *command* love,[21] de Sales adds that obeying God's love commandment is also a most pleasurable adherence, a harmony palpably enjoyed as well as observed:

> O good God, how delicious is the *sweetness* of this commandment. Theotimus, if it pleased the divine will to give it to the damned, they would in a moment be delivered from their greatest misery, while the Blessed are blessed only by the practice of it! O heavenly love, how *lovable* you are to our souls! And blessed be forever that Goodness that so earnestly commands us to love him, though this love is *so desirable and so necessary* to our happiness that without it we can but be miserable![22]

Obedience, we saw in chapter 4, is most profoundly an expression of deep pleasure and growing intimacy with God; similarly, the obligations God imposes on us are sweet and desirable, the very things that we most willingly seek to do.

In the eleventh chapter of book 10, de Sales reprises the unity of the great commandments to love God and love neighbor; in words that might as well come from chapter 16 of Deśika's *Essence*,[23] he sees the energies of the two loves as convergent:

> And therefore the same charity which produces acts of the love of God, produces at the same time those of love of our neighbor. . . . Theotimus, to love our neighbor in charity is to love God in man, or man in God; it is to hold God alone dear for his own sake and the creature for the love of him.[24]

Much of *Treatise*'s book 10 is given over to examples of the moral life lived most deeply in and for love. It climaxes (in its seventeenth chapter) with a turn to the perfect example, by a meditation on the twelve modes in which Jesus "practiced all the most excellent ways of love."[25] After detailing them one by one, de Sales closes his contemplation by appealing to the heightened sensitivities of the reader who can understand the logic of the "love-death" (*mort amoureuse*) of Jesus, wherein death is also an intense heightening of life and pleasure:

> Yet beware of saying, Theotimus, that this loving death of the Savior took place by manner of a ravishing; the object for which his charity moved him to die was not lovable enough to ravish unto itself this divine soul—which departed from his body by way of ecstasy, driven and pushed along by the flood and might of love. Even as we see the myrrh tree send forth its first juice simply by its abundance, without its being pressed or drawn in any way. . . . *No man takes from me* nor ravishes *my soul, but I give it freely* [John 10:18].

Consequently, the reader's own life should be a fire whence arise her or his good deeds:

> O God! Theotimus, what burning coals are cast upon all our hearts to inflame us to do exercises of holy love for our completely good Savior, seeing that he has so lovingly practiced them for us who are so evil! *This charity of Jesus Christ* thus *presses us* [Phil. 2:8]![26]

While this understanding of the moral life raises the standard for behavior to a very advanced level, it seems too, from de Sales' emphasis on the integration of the commandments in love, that the ideal Christian is not just ethical in a narrow sense, but also is a kind of ecstatic, living the extremes of love. De Sales values most of all this free yet passionate person, advanced in love, able to enjoy God, and joyful even in obedience.

In the ninth chapter of *Treatise*'s book 11, de Sales emphasizes that adherence to the Ten Commandments characterizes the Christian life, but here too obedience is a response to love:

> Our Savior ever joins the fulfilling of the commandments to charity. *Whoever keeps my commandments, says he, and observes them, he it is that loves me; he that loves me not keeps not my commandments. If any one love me, he will keep my words* [John 14:23–24]. Now he who has all virtues will keep all the commandments. He that has the virtue of religion will keep the first three commandments; he that has piety will observe the

> fourth; he that has the virtue of mildness and gentleness will observe the fifth; by the virtue of chastity, one will observe the sixth; by liberality, one will avoid the breach of the seventh; by truth, one will effect the eighth; by frugality and purity, one will observe the ninth and tenth.[27]

With a firm stance on the commandments in place, de Sales too has more subtle points to make, concerning rather the interior life of the person who has surrendered to God. Just as Deśika explores the state of the person who has left grief behind for the sake of joy, de Sales draws us to a place where discernment is required if we are to "read" the person behind the behavior. All observances of virtue depend on charity, as bees depend on honey. Charity gives to the devout "the strength to fly in God, and to collect from his mercy the honey of true merit and the sanctification of hearts in which they are found."[28]

In book 11, chapter 21, de Sales fills out his teaching on sorrow and joy. After identifying three causes for sadness in this imperfect life—the devil, natural predispositions, inevitable sufferings—de Sales distinguishes a different sadness that is appropriate to the Christian who does trust in God:

> Indeed, the sadness of true penitence is not so much to be named sadness as displeasure, a sentiment and detestation of evil. This is a sadness which is never troubled nor vexed; a sadness which does not dull the spirit, but makes it active, ready and diligent; a sadness which does not weigh the heart down, but raises it by prayer and hope, and causes in it the impulses of the fervor of devotion; a sadness which in the heaviest of its bitternesses ever produces the sweetness of an incomparable consolation.[29]

Reflection on sadness requires that we differentiate its modes and roots; the debilitating sadness arising in evil is far from the sadness connected to penitence, consolation, and the transformation of life:

> "The sadness," says Cassian, "which effects solid penitence, and that desirable repentance of which one never repents, is obedient, affable, humble, mild, sweet, patient, as a child and descendant of charity: so that spreading over every pain of body and contrition of spirit, and being in a certain way joyous, animated and reinvigorated by the hope of its benefit; it retains all the sweet-

> ness of gentleness and longanimity, having in itself the fruits of the Holy Spirit. . . ."[30] Such is true penitence, and such is a good sadness, which surely is not really sad or melancholy, but only attentive and disposed to detest, reject and hinder the evil of sin, past and future.[31]

Love alone matters, not because it is the only value, but because it infuses the positive and negative norms of tradition with greater strength and vitality, and shapes the various dimensions of the moral realm into an integral, complete life. After loving surrender, we continue to live by the same norms as other Christians, in accord with doctrine and commandment, but now with a different spirit infusing this adherence and a different manner of experiencing our choices.[32]

If this wholeness is the true fruit of loving surrender, it is not surprising to see that de Sales, like Deśika, has little sympathy with those whose behavior, however laudable in terms of the practice of virtue, does not arise from love; and here we may briefly return to de Sales' judgment on pagan virtue, which I discussed briefly in chapter 2.

In the first chapter of book 11, de Sales takes up once more the theme of the pagans, and here they mirror a shallow Christianity misidentified with an array of virtues not rooted in the love of God. Pagans do practice "certain human and moral virtues, which were not by their nature placed above the powers of the rational spirit," but this virtue has no enduring value because it is mainly a matter of public pretense and vanity, resulting in such "trifling acts" as "mutual courtesy, aid [to] their friends, living sober lives" and decisions "not to steal, to serve masters faithfully, to pay workers wages."[33] Despite the modest, flawed nature of such efforts, "God was grateful to those poor people, and recompensed them abundantly."[34]

In the course of a longer reflection on the relation of love to the virtues in chapter 10, de Sales offers "a digression upon the imperfection of the virtues of the pagans," in which he insists that such virtues cannot guide the moral life:

> Those ancient sages of the world long ago made glorious discourses in honor of the moral virtues, yea, even in behalf of religion: but what Plutarch observes of the Stoics suits still better the rest of the pagans. We see ships, says he, which bear the grandest titles: some are called the Victory, others the Valor, others the Sun; yet, for all that, they remain dependent on the

> winds and waves: so the Stoics boast of being exempt from passions, without fear, without grief, without anger, people unchanging and unchangeable. Yet are they in fact subject to trouble, disquiet, impetuosity, and other follies. For God's sake, I ask you, Theotimus, what virtues could those people have, who voluntarily, and of set purpose, overthrew all the laws of religion?[35]

For one who has surrendered all to God, though, a new affective disposition subtly alters all instincts about how to act and react, and, as a result, the person's actions change; as Altieri suggests, this shift is not reducible to reasons and stated motives, but has to do with the manner in which the surrendered one experiences his or her options and responds to them. As was the case with Deśika and his community, for de Sales too, understanding the subtle shifts that are at stake requires attentiveness and discernment; by such understanding, we can make sense of the lives of those we meet and recognize the source of their vitality and joy in love. Discerning such inner movements of the heart does shift law and doctrine into the background, but it does not leave us with merely interior dispositions. De Sales' focus too is on the attitudes people form in shaping their visible lives by affective instincts and not just in accord with particular reasons. This "adverbial" shift[36] most adequately captures the stance of the believer as a new person. Such a shift from sorrow to joy—from harmful sorrow to a deeper spiritual grieving that is the fruit of love—may seem a rather minimal, even "soft" mark by which to distinguish those who have surrendered to God from those who have not, or one religion from another. But both de Sales and Deśika find joy to be a reasoned, imaginative, affective state that is the benchmark for life after surrender, a sure sign by which to recognize the persons in whom tradition is most alive.

II. On Being a Religious Reader and Writer after the *Essence* and *Treatise*

It is here that the analyses of our chapters 2–4 come together most integrally. Achieving a state of readiness for surrendering everything to God means learning to reason properly and in accord with the values of the community (chapter 2); acquiring the basic formation in tradition that infuses our thinking, speaking, and imagining of life's possibilities with the insights and words of scripture and of the teachers who have lived our traditions (chapter 3); clearing out the center of our lives, so as to recognize that it is possible to live for love even to the extreme, in entire dependence on God (chapter 4). Such truths, known by Deśika and de Sales alike and disclosed to their readers, coalesce visibly in persons who live the joy that arises upon loving surrender. As readers become able to recognize such persons and affirm the wholeness of their living example, they begin to live what they are reading. And so too, analogously, we who have ventured to think upon the *Treatise* and *Essence* together can learn how to live in accord with what Deśika and de Sales teach us. And so *we ourselves* become the topic of this book's final section.

1. *On Becoming the Right Person*

We have seen the importance of affective as well as intellectual transformation—of the solitary individual into the participant in tradition and community, the spectator into the participant, the ignorant into the wise, the anxious into the joyful. We have also noted the diminishment that occurs when imaginative and affective maturation is ignored and a person thinks upon spiritual topics as if neutrally, without a history and without any obligation to previous generations of religious practitioners and writers. Given the fruitfulness of integral learning rooted in patient religious reading, we can turn the question upon ourselves, asking what kind of persons we become by reading the *Treatise* and the *Essence*, individually and then together, open to the intellectual, imaginative, and affective powers of such practice.

Even before the necessary further experiments that will deepen and correct the manner of double reading practiced here and clarify its meaning, we are still able to reflect in a preliminary way on its implications for ethics and spirituality, making explicit points from earlier in this chapter and elsewhere in this book. Ideal humble reading, deeper learning, refined expectations, unsettling, intensified intellectual and affective commitment—all stand in harmony with earlier conceptions of commentary and religious reading in both de Sales' Catholic tradition and Deśika's Śrīvaiṣṇava tradition. But this new reading also places us in relation to two traditions read together, in a single learning. Religious traditions seem often enough to abhor comparison as almost necessarily superficial, a distraction from true learning—or as a learning that tempts us to take the Other too seriously; yet tradition can actually guide more fruitful interreligious reading, showing how it can best be practiced by humble readers who know the text *and* also know the past, and learn with gratitude for prior readers who have preserved and passed down the texts we study. By our double reading we enter a world that keeps evolving after we abandon the innocence of knowing only one tradition well, and we also forgo the immunity that comes from a merely dispassionate study of sacred texts. Such a reading marks a case where one plus one—the *Essence* plus the *Treatise*—add up to more than two. The synthesis gives us unexpectedly more words, images, desires, emotions, and deeds that we can consider and respond to in new patterns. "Interreligious literacy" has a richer meaning and impact in light of this more intense practice; properly enacted, this new learning opens nearly endless possibilities.

That this new situation can be interpreted as potentially of great religious importance is hardly a bold claim; one might expect that someone reading two religious classics by an act of attentive religious reading will be deeply affected by the experience. But the reading practice I urge in this book should make it more difficult for us to enjoy the securities that oddly envelop people who talk about surrender to God *within* their own tradition and yet continue to cherish their tradition's intellectual and affective safety net. Here, instead, the *Essence* and *Treatise* work powerfully together, even as the relevant communities may be disturbed by these texts' being read together and their being taken to heart, either directly or through works such as this book—and all without letting new affinities shatter original commitments and loyalties.

I close by drawing together some of the more important insights gleaned from the experiment that is this book, so as to situate ourselves better at the conclusion of this particular reading. Below I discuss reasoning in its reconfigured role (chapter 2), the educative deepening of the imaginative and affective dispositions of the interreligious reader (chapter 3), and the situation of the reader whose double reading opens the possibility of a radically changed way of living (chapter 4).

2. Reason Humbled and Restored (Chapter 2)

We must agree with Deśika and de Sales that reasoned communication—teaching, writing, argument, persuasion—is essential. Reasoning always has a role to play in religious matters, and this role is particularly fruitful when our reasoning proceeds with attention to the complexities of human persons, our limited but real knowledge of God, and the limitations inherent in how we speak and write of what we know. Despite their misgivings about autonomous reason, Deśika and de Sales insist that there is great power in reasoned insights that show us the world as it is as opposed to how we assumed it to be. And so we must learn and speak even of the most complex spiritual realities.

The reflective reader who has engaged in a project such as this becomes consciously and deliberately informed about, and disciplined in, two traditions; she or he learns to be respectful of both; resistant to the grandiose rhetoric of either about its uniqueness; and positioned to think with discipline about how we are to think, read, and write after this exercise. Reason in need, sometimes at a loss, requiring guidance and limit, is a humbler reasoning, the kind that de Sales and Deśika admire greatly; and a complex double reading accentuates the difficulty, the need for humility, and the potential benefits. Even if our religious reasoning is dependent, partial, and prone to error, we should be proactive in identifying the positive possibilities and in acknowledging how precious reasonable inquiry can be when it is located within traditional contexts and is committed to an exploration of two traditions at once. Intentional discourse on God and our relationship to God can be fruitful once reason is honest, disciplined, attentive to particulars, and, in all of this, humble—cognizant of the fact that no reader, however expert, can make credible judgments about a tradition merely from outside it, without the corrective influence of ongoing dialogue with members of that tradition. This is a matter of respect due to those we venture to judge, and it is a matter too of self-respect, knowing enough of a topic to speak intelligently about it—or at least to know when to stop talking.

We can also acknowledge the real strengths and consequent duties of the "religious intellectual"—a category including the scholar but also a wider group of thoughtful, attentive readers and writers—as a particular instance of the religious reader equipped with a focused competence and therefore particular duties. This religious intellectual can stand forth as a plausible defender of the interreligious reading. By rigorous academic reasoning, rooted in the study of texts, she or he may come to protect the integrity of traditions, helping to enhance their resistance to efforts to co-opt them for extraneous purposes, for this religious intellectual knows that each tradition is distinctive and resistant to easy amalgamation and generalization. Even within the boundaries of particular traditions, the most careful of readers can sort out developments and changes, ignoring none while yet resisting the potentially bland overlay of a piety that is more a preservative than a vital force. A professional respect for detail and distinctiveness can also be more richly reimagined as a resource in defending the notion that learning across religious boundaries is possible and beneficial. When traditions are respected in their distinctiveness and particular internal intelligibility, they become more and not less accessible, more able to be studied and appreciated in their myriad small details. While an academician can research and write without a personal commitment to any of the religious traditions involved, we are all better off when some are explicitly religious intellectuals and religious readers well versed in the discipline, costs, and benefits of belonging to a tradition but also blessed with a deep and unsettling openness to other traditions.

3. *The Grounded, Liberated, Passionate Reader (Chapter 3)*

Just as we can learn to balance skepticism and hope regarding reasoning and our words with respect to the power of religious reading as an intelligent spiritual practice, we can also have hope for the efficacy of that reading in the transformation of the reader. This reader, committed to thinking honestly and rigorously about powerful religious texts and to learning from them over time, is flooded with old and new ideas, words, themes, images, and affective possibilities, and is drawn into encounter with exemplary persons ancient and modern. By this learning, the reader gradually gains the psychological and spiritual freedom to accept the discipline of this new learning and flourishes in accord with it, becoming well disposed toward extraordinary religious goals such as loving surrender.

This integral education occurs with particular intensity and clarity in the study of religious classics such as the *Essence* and *Treatise* read individually and then too together as texts potent with rich religious meanings passed down through the generations. As I have illustrated frequently in the preceding chapters, each section of the *Essence* and the *Treatise* provides us with words and ideas, images, memories, and exemplars by which to reenvision our relationship to our own situation. De Sales and Deśika believe, and seek to demonstrate in their writing, that if we have attentively read the *Essence* and the *Treatise*, we can also be in touch with the underlying spiritual, even divine, power that graciously energizes their writing. Both texts are filled with passion; what de Sales achieves by stories of love, Deśika makes real in the simple power of words finely chosen and employed with an utter precision that is tantamount to an enlightenment. De Sales' grand narrative of love, enriched by citations, anecdotes, the lives of saints, means to lead readers from material and instinctive desires toward more reflective choices, and gradually into the greater good and beauty that is the love of God. His great story of love should, when understood and richly imagined, make it very hard indeed for the attentive reader to turn away from the text without recognizing new possibilities or without responding to them with new affective energy. In his concise and intense analyses, Deśika offers interpretations, strings of citations, prose expositions, and imaginative verses that work together in clarifying and then illumining the world, self, and God, such that it becomes nearly impossible to not be deeply affected, not to start living differently, with a real prospect of loving surrender.

Reading either the *Essence* or the *Treatise* first, turning then to the other, and thereafter reading them together, back and forth, is therefore a process of education and formation that unfolds page by page, one book next to the other, in a nearly endless sequence of small, mundane moments of patient reading. We find ourselves going deeper into one tradition, only to be drawn into the other as well. We learn to submit to both traditions and to be instructed by them, even as we earn the freedom to move back and forth from one to the other. Productive spiritual words, verses, and narratives such as we read in the *Treatise* and the *Essence*, heard over and again, imagined, retold, and practiced, become communicative on many levels and ever more demanding with respect to what is possible in our present moment. Such reading instructs and disciplines us, and gradually produces a more expansive understanding that is also more freely imaginative and intensely emotional, all for the sake of deeper spiritual practice. Loving surrender to God, though a most radical adjustment of how we are to live, begins to appear as a real life possibility that we can make our own.[37]

Here too the religious intellectual has a constructive role to play as an especially alert and acute reader who ventures to protect the rich particularity and multidimensionality of religious texts against the prospect of a more aggressive consumption for purposes alien to the text and its tradition. The self-conscious and studiously attentive reader can make sure that we are reading texts as wholes comprehensively and in their multiple dimensions, appreciative of their concreteness and the ways in which they have educated and changed readers in the past. Cognizant of the demands of close reading, the religious intellectual can insist that we should read more slowly and carefully than we usually do, surrendering ourselves to such texts, with attention to the range of imaginative and affective possibilities that become available as we learn from them. This most careful reader can make clear to us the price of this better reading, the implications of an education that promises to transform us in not one but two traditions. Perhaps unexpectedly, the religious intellectual, like the teachers and mystical theologians of old, can play the role of defender and transmitter of text and tradition, insisting that they be properly studied, appreciated, and internalized before anyone should venture to evaluate or write about them.

4. *The Vulnerability and Safe Haven of the (Inter)Religious Reader (Chapter 4)*

Neither Deśika nor de Sales was satisfied with a deeper contextualization of reason or a more ample appreciation of reading as educative, as if these were goals in themselves. For both authors, the real point is the decision for abandonment and approach for refuge, loving surrender into the hands of God or at the feet of Nārāyaṇa with Śrī. As far as their words can reach, they made the case that so radical a choice is better than other still viable choices; by the *Essence* and the *Treatise* they have, ideally, prepared readers to imagine making this choice themselves. Deśika and de Sales are on solid ground in insisting that very much more is at stake than learning something from a book that then might be put aside. The reader who has stayed with the *Treatise* and *Essence* is rendered vulnerable to intellectual, imaginative, and affective transformation; she gains the capacity to engage and respond to these traditions in a fuller way, with honesty regarding their potentially radical effects on how she lives. This prospect of more radical appropriation becomes a paradigm for how to read and learn from religious texts, well beyond the necessary interim stage of detached objectivity.

Deśika and de Sales expect more of their audience than a casual or even moderately interested religious reader is likely to commit to. But if a reader does become vulnerable in this process, and if reading becomes more personal than anticipated, then he or she becomes part of a small, self-selecting (but not necessarily elitist) audience.[38] Small because there is little reason to expect that many readers will be enthusiastic at the prospect of taking both texts seriously, opening themselves to the power of both and to where both sets of insights might lead them. "Surrender lovingly to the love of God" is a recognizable religious appeal, but grounding this appeal in attention to one's own tradition and another together is an acquired taste for which communal sustenance will surely be fragile. I return to this fragility below.

In the intervening time, as our texts offer us possibilities we are not entirely ready to accept, the religious intellectual again has a role to play, this time as guardian and guarantor of the possibility that there is more. It is easy to read texts such as the *Essence* and the *Treatise* inadequately, in a piecemeal fashion, for their details but without regard for the final theme and purpose, loving surrender; it is easy to focus on their themes and to evade the full force of their influence on those who have become susceptible to their appeal. And it is easy to bind such texts in their histories, as if reliquaries of times past, no longer vital. Against all of this, the religious intellectual is the one who can insist that these texts can expand the intellectual, imaginative, and affective capacities of a contemporary reader, even to the extent of inspiring a radical life change. Knowing both traditions and respecting the force of reason, imagination, and affective intensification in each, this honest, stubborn reader can reject truncated readings that would halt the learning process or even pass over in silence the potential for transformation innate to the *Essence* and *Treatise*. She can politely admonish those who draw conclusions without ever having read the texts of the traditions of which they speak. Such a reader may also question those who do know but still seem to be evading, or endlessly deferring, the consequences of religious learning in its transformative power.

When we take into account the demands placed on readers who take two traditions and two texts seriously, then the paucity of readers willing to undertake a double reading is unsurprising. The careful reader engaging the two texts in their two traditions comes to know more than expected, and in a way that cannot be predictably controlled by either tradition. This reader becomes distant from the totalizing power of both texts, precisely because she or he knows both, cannot dismiss either, and does not submit entirely to either. As we learn more about religious traditions in their depth than has been possible before, we know more deeply the possibilities of several traditions and where they lead us, while yet we also lose the intensity and devotion possible for those who know only their own tradition. We are then left in a vulnerable, fruitful learning state, engaging these powerful works on multiple levels and, paradoxically, learning more while mastering less; we have more teachers and fewer masters. It may appear that by this practice we acquire a surfeit of scriptures, yet have no Scripture; multiple languages and words and images, yet no tested, effective manner of speaking; a wealth of theological insights, yet no sure doctrine; not one but two rich religious traditions from which to benefit, and yet—because we know too much—no single, normative tradition that commands our attention. Although this situation will not be to everyone's liking, it is something that a smaller group of readers can do for the communities involved. Though fewer in number, readers speaking, writing, and acting from these more intense sensitivities may in the long term have a deeper and more enduring influence on the communities involved.

Granted, when we contemplate a more specifically academic context, we can readily admit that it is not the business of the scholar to urge loving surrender upon students and readers. But if she or he is deeply affected by the reading, writing and teaching also change. She may find herself on the verge of participation, as experience passes beyond simple intellectual acquisition; she may become an intellectual *prapanna*, prone to the practice of religious self-abandonment I introduced already the beginning of chapter 1. This vulnerable reading becomes then the stuff of writing and teaching, full of indications where an attentive reading together of texts such as the *Essence* and *Treatise* might lead. Religious and academic communities alike may worry that such a religiously vulnerable scholar has gone too far, compromising either professional objectivity or primary religious commitment, or both. But such concerns, however legitimate, do not stand on their own; they are themselves a matter for further conversation, primarily among those willing to undergo such learning and to see firsthand where it leads.

Whatever the procedure, at stake is a more vital engagement, by each reader but inevitably by still broader communities of readers who learn to see loving surrender to God as an intelligible and imaginable way of life that can be pursued with passion and abandon, even in the twenty-first century. In our pluralist, postmodern world this ancient challenge still has power and may become still more irresistible, as we commit ourselves to an interreligious practice of reading with an awareness that neither the Way nor the Goal resides in a book—certainly not in mine, but neither in the *Treatise* nor the *Essence*. Eventually, our reading may open again into joy, as constrained rationalism and detached writing, relativism and fragmentation, fear and neglect all give way to the more intense insight and love that arises when we know two (or more) traditions together, in a learning that proceeds without limit or guarantee, unafraid, growing still more intense, a consolation beyond compare.

III. A Final Word

In all of this, we can envision ideal readers with the qualities of respect for tradition, loyal participation in community, freedom, equanimity, joy and fearlessness—all richly interwoven with diligent yet impartial attentiveness in reading, acute questioning, skill in moving back and forth across religious boundaries. Such persons are often defined as deeply rooted in a single tradition—just Catholic, just Śrīvaiṣṇava—or, in the counterexamples, as smartly beyond dogmas and orthodoxies or as detached scholars for whom the more intense questions of religious meaning simply do not arise. But now we see an alternative, since the virtues imagined here flourish in the deep, doubly complex loyalties that grow out of practices that inculcate the wisdom of traditions, in what must be integral thinking, imagining, and feeling: the Catholic who remains a Catholic through reading the *Essence*, the Śrīvaiṣṇava who retrieves Śrīvaiṣṇava identity by listening seriously to what the *Treatise* tells us about loving God. Such Catholics and Śrīvaiṣṇavas will form a rare but needed community.

There is much work to do, but in the short run it is therefore prudent simply to keep reading the *Essence* and the *Treatise* over and again, making sense of each text, and then of both together, thereby becoming able to reassess what I have made of them in the preceding pages. Or, if we wish to proceed more modestly, a commentary such as this one may itself provide a basis for the initial reflection. As I confessed in chapter 1, the most notable profligacy of this book is its (over)abundance of quotations from the two authors, all of them meticulously referenced in the original and in translation. I have wanted to root my insights in their words, and also to step back and allow them to speak for themselves. After all, such deference before authoritative texts was favored by de Sales and Deśika themselves. Both of them infused their texts with the presence of older, wiser words, never allowing themselves to be the center of attention. As commentator, I needed to bring forward as many of their words as decently possible in "my" book. Now, at the end, this abundance of their voices can be a resource for readers who want to begin searching both texts on their own; one might reread this book simply for the quoted passages, as if it were a compendium of holy, passionate words prized for their own sake, a bridge back to their original texts. This is the point of reading *through* my book.

Or we might begin rather at the far end of the process, not with whole treatises and large ideas, but with those highly distilled and small mantras that Deśika focuses on for most of the *Essence*, the small mantra-like prayers that de Sales calls to the attention of his readers, words that say everything that needs to be said (table 5.3).

The simplest act of listening, reading, memorizing, and reciting becomes the way of keeping our reading attentive and alive, particularly if we see this remembrance and recitation as the beginnings of a practice

Table 5.3 The Two Prayers in Harmony

I approach for refuge the feet of Nārāyaṇa with Śrī; obeisance to Nārāyaṇa with Śrī.	Father, into Your hands I commit my spirit.

returning us to the realities of which Deśika and de Sales speak, concisely and perhaps cryptically inscribed in these few words. All of this then becomes both prayer and intellectual practice, a grace that we might spend the rest of our lives exploring.

Notes

Chapter 1

1. *Tiruvāymoḻi* VI.10.10, my translation. Throughout, I cite and translate the works of the āḻvārs from the original Tamil; given the variety and relative inaccessibility of the printed editions, however, it does not seem necessary to cite particular editions of the original.

2. In 1970, in the Thomas More Chapel of the University Church at Fordham University, Bronx, New York.

3. The formula is found in *Practica Quaedam* 51, p. 14 (1997 edition).

4. Loyola, *Spiritual Exercises*, 80.

5. Or, if the reader does not identify with a religious tradition, simply a tradition to which that reader is new, from the outside. Although I realize that the difference in the location of readers in other religious traditions and readers who choose not to make "belonging to a religious tradition" part of their work, I generally focus on readers with religious commitments who are engaging other traditions.

6. Clooney, *Hindu Wisdom for All God's Children*; *Hindu God, Christian God*; and *Divine Mother, Blessed Mother*.

7. By "spiritual theology," I have in mind classics of religious writing that are substantively grounded in and reflective of their traditions, carefully delineated theologically but also and primarily with respect to prayer and spiritual progress, and open to consequent actual practice and the spiritual transformation and advancement of community members, most immediately the readers of such works.

8. There is no authoritative modern biography of Deśika, but major features of his life have been detailed in Singh's 1958 *Vedānta Deśika: His Life, Works, and Philosophy* and in Hopkins's 2002 *Singing the Body of*

God, a translation of selected verses of Deśika. For insights into Deśika's religious-cultural context, see Mumme, *Śrīvaiṣṇava Theological Dispute;* and Venkatachari, *Śrīvaiṣṇavism: An Insight,* 250–65.

9. The other school is the "southern," *teṅkalai.* Both flourished and still flourish in South India. They are distinguished by social and theological differences, but have in common the far greater part of their faith and practice. I do not in this book refer systematically or frequently to the Teṅkalai tradition's views, which require and deserve full study. On some major theological differences between the schools, see Mumme, *Śrīvaiṣṇava Theological Dispute.*

10. Throughout, I translate *ācārya* (as here) and *guru* as "teacher."

11. These *Sūtras,* attributed to the sage Bādārāyaṇa (ca. sixth century) are a synthesis, in some 450 short verses, of the meaning and method of the ancient Upaniṣads; Rāmānuja and other Vedānta thinkers established their credentials with their commentaries on the *Sūtras.*

12. Singh, *Vedānta Deśika,* 147.

13. Ibid., 148–49. Viśiṣṭādvaita is Śrīvaiṣṇavism in its more philosophical and Sanskritic form. *Sādhanas* are ways of practice. *Vidyās* are texts taken as resources, contexts for meditation. Śaṅkara and Madhva are usually introduced as the leading teachers of two other schools of Vedānta.

14. In modern times his story is retold in Tamil in the *Ācāryavaibhavam,* 116ff., and in secondary sources such as Singh, *Vedānta Deśika,* and Ramaswamy, *Hinduism Rediscovered,* 634–646. These stylized accounts emphasize his greatness as a teacher, dominance in debate, personal piety, and dedication to the well-being of the Śrīvaiṣṇava community.

15. Śaṭakōpaṉ.

16. Deśika, *Lineage,* 4/1. References to Deśika's *Essence* are first to Ramadesikacaryar's edition, and then to the Ayyangar translation, thus: 4/1 = Ramadesikacaryar, p. 4, and Ayyangar, p. 1. Although I give my own translations of the *Essence* throughout, the references to Ayyangar may also be of use to readers. Here and throughout, too, italicization in quoted texts from Deśika and de Sales is my own. In addition to the italicization of the names of texts, I also italicize direct scriptural quotations in de Sales (and indent them in Deśika). I occasionally italicize other words for emphasis.

17. Deśika, *Lineage,* 17–18/5.

18. He goes into some detail regarding Rāmānuja: "Emperumāṉār [Rāmānuja] studied the meanings of the mantras at the feet of Tirukkoṭṭiyūr Nampi; he heard *Tiruvāymoḻi* at the feet of Tirumālai Āṇṭāṉ; after reciting *Tiruvāymoḻi* at the feet of Āḻavantār Āḻvār, he heard the hymns of praise and the rest, and also the gracious good comments [on the hymns] from him. At the feet of Tirumālai Nampi he studied the *Rāmāyaṇa.* Emperumāṟāṟ's writings are nine: *Śrī Bhāṣya, Vedānta Dīpa, Vedānta Sāra, Vedārtha*

Saṃgraha, Bhagavad Gītā Bhāṣya, Ciriya Gadya, Periya Gadya, Vaikuṇṭha Gadya, and the *Nityam*" (*Lineage*, 18–19/6). For information on these works, see Carman, *Theology of Ramanuja.*

19. Deśika, *Lineage*, 18–19/5–6.

20. Probably Deśika's own teacher Ātreya Rāmānuja, who may also be intended in the reference to "this one" at the end of the verse.

21. Deśika, *Lineage*, 23–24/8. Senānāthan is the commander of the celestial host. I have added the names Rāmānuja, Śrī, and Nārāyaṇa, which were left implicit by Deśika.

22. See chapter 3 for these verses.

23. For an ample explication of the three mantras, see Clooney, *The Truth, the Way, and the Life.*

24. It is not historically certain when and how these three mantras came to be seen as the three mantras. Certainly each has its own history, most clearly the Carama Śloka, which is verse 18.66 of the Bhagavad Gītā. The Tiru Mantra (and similar mantras combining a divine name with *namaḥ* ["obeisance"], a word expressive of praise and worship) can be found widely in Sanskrit and even Tamil literature. As I will note in chapter 4, the Dvaya Mantra is harder to trace and may be best understood as an intentional, though very old, theological encapsulation of the theology of the tradition. Although I have had a number of conversations with Śrīvaiṣṇavas in India and the United States about the mantras and the practice of taking refuge, I leave to others the important fieldwork that is also required to understand the full meaning of the mantras for Śrīvaiṣṇavas today and their actual use in devotional practice; but it is clear that the theology and commentary remain deeply related to that practice, even today.

25. The exception is chapters 23–26, which appear as a kind of "response to my critics" in which Deśika defends and clarifies points made elsewhere in the *Essence.*

26. Although I have not done any systematic study of the reception of the *Essence* in today's Śrīvaiṣṇava community, my conversations with Śrīvaiṣṇavas over the years suggest that those who do study the text are intellectually and spiritually transformed by this practice.

27. And not "reread," since I had not read the *Treatise* before learning Deśika's text first.

28. Of which books 10–12 may in some ways fulfill the goals anticipated for the second treatise.

29. Ravier, preface to *Oeuvres*, 323. Translations from the French, other than the *Treatise* itself, are my own.

30. On the history of the publication of the *Treatise*, see Ravier, *Francis de Sales: Sage and Saint*, 321–27. As he suggests, it overlaps in composi-

tion and completion with the "earlier" *Introduction to the Devout Life,* from which it should not be sharply divided.

31. Liuima, *Aux Sources du Traite de L'Amour de Dieu,* 1:9. Translations from Liuima are my own.

32. See Ravier, *Francis de Sales: Sage and Saint,* 1761: "The *Treatise* could end here; the subsequent three books appear as a supplement or summation of the work. But Francis de Sales will return later on to his ideas, and this will transform the three books into a magnificent conclusion." Ravier adds that de Sales intimates found in book 9 the portrait of de Sales himself. Ravier notes, p. 1762, that de Sales also shows signs of struggling to decide where some of the materials in books 10–12 belonged in relation to the more settled books 1–9.

33. Most notably, the *Treatise* includes no parallel to the exegetical chapters of the *Essence,* 27–29.

34. Ravier's preface includes a detailed chronology of de Sales' life, listing in parallel columns "Histoire Generale," "Histoire de la Savoie," and "Biographie de Saint François de Sales."

35. In his book *French Moralists,* Anthony Levi points to authors such as de Sales' friend and disciple Jean-Pierre Camus, author of a large *Traité des Passions* (1614) and a similarly large *L'Esprit du Bienheureux François de Sales,* as well as Lorenzo Scupoli's *Le Combat Spirituel.*

36. Levi, *French Moralists,* 125.

37. Ibid., 126.

38. Regarding de Sales' place in tradition, Liuima, in *Aux Sources du Traite de L'Amour de Dieu,* meticulously identifies the books that de Sales read and refers to in the *Treatise* and the persons with whom he was in contact while writing it. He reviews his education and his familiarity with Ignatian spirituality, classical and contemporary humanism (chap. 2), and mystical authors (chap. 3). In Liuima's judgment, de Sales' wide reading did not determine his outlook as a spiritual writer: "Indeed, regarding these advisers who 'pushed' him along, we cannot say that they formed or even inspired him. If they contributed powerfully to making him undertake this work at this date, without a doubt they still would hardly have had any influence on the manner in which he realized it or even conceived it." Accordingly, he asks: "We are thus led to push the inquiry still further: how did he arrive at the idea itself, this precise idea? Divine inspiration? Some thought arising from his reading or a spiritual conversation? Or, on the contrary, did it evolve slowly?" (13). Liuima sees gradual development as most likely. At the end of Volume 1, he returns once more to the originality of de Sales: "The first fact which imposes itself is the originality of his personality. His zealous heart, inflamed with the love of God, is undoubtedly the first and most direct source of the *Treatise on the Love*

of God. He writes with inspiration, most often, however, not from direct inspiration such as gives light to the intellect or fervor and devotion to the will . . . but rather an inspiration that penetrates his soul, that impregnates itself in the most intimate recesses of his heart, and expresses itself not in the will, but in the ecstasy of his life; that is to say, the entire action of grace expresses itself first by its works, penetrating his own living of the truths, and then suggesting to him reflections, the search for explanations, systems, and formulas" (1:337–38).

39. De Sales, preface to *Treatise*, 336–37/4. Throughout, pagination indicates first the French edition of Ravier and then the translation by Mackey, which I use with slight adaptations. I have also on occasion consulted Ryan but do not give page references to his translation.

40. Ibid., 337/4–5.

41. Ibid., 338/6.

42. Ibid.

43. Another and more direct influence was his regular contact with the nuns of the Visitation Convent, particularly the future saint Jeanne de Chantal. These nuns represented an ideal audience:

> "For you must know that we have in this town a congregation of maidens and widows who, having retired from the world, live with one mind in God's service, under the protection of his most holy Mother, and as their purity and piety of spirit have oftentimes given me great consolation, so I have striven to return them the like by a frequent distribution of the holy word which I have announced to them as well in public sermons as in spiritual conferences, and this almost always in presence of some religious men and people of great piety" (de Sales, preface to *Treatise*, 347–48/14–15).

44. De Sales, "Dedicatory Prayer," 334/2.

45. I am therefore not only proposing that there is a strong analogy between total surrender to God as conceptualized in the *Essence* and the *Treatise*. Also and more important, I am pointing to what happens in the reading, the (ideally) irreversibly changed situation of the reader who, through interreligious study, becomes intensely involved in both traditions and yet at the same time detached from both because each is so vividly and insistently nearby to the other. Consequently, the reader is intellectually and spiritually enriched and yet too distanced from her or his own home tradition. This excess of learning that arises in the double reading is therefore deeply unsettling yet at the same time deeply satisfying.

46. In this way I am also defending the place of such texts and the enduring efficacy of their authors' intentions even in our pluralistic world, where traditions so frequently and powerfully jostle against one another, seeming at times only to neutralize each other's power. My hope is to show, by example, a way to "read pluralism" not as diminution or relativism, but as an opportunity for an intensification of precious truths, revered spiritual paths, and ultimate religious acts as known and written in multiple traditions. While the communities of de Sales and Deśika could hardly be expected to anticipate such a reading-together with such a result, we can, I suggest, come to recognize this new situation as consonant with truths, values, and goals basic to each community.

47. Much has been written on the ideal of surrender, but good starting points are Viller ("Abandon") on abandonment or surrender in the Christian tradition, and both Narayanan (*The Way and the Goal*) and Raman ("Self-Surrender") with reference to the Śrīvaiṣṇava and Hindu traditions. For a powerful modern consideration of the role of surrender in religion properly understood, see Wolff, "Religion and Surrender."

48. A helpful clarification regarding the kind of comparison undertaken here can be made by noting a work that is in some ways quite similar: *The Sense of Antirationalism: The Religious Thought of Zhuangzi and Kierkegaard*, by Karen L. Carr and Philip J. Ivanhoe. My book and theirs explore how select religious intellectuals balance a deep suspicion of reason with a need to identify the spiritual path intelligently and how they write so as to encourage people to traverse that path. In introducing their study, Carr and Ivanhoe predict their threefold goal: "a unique opportunity for greater self-understanding," assistance in understanding and appreciating other traditions, and an enhancement of our "understanding of the general phenomenon of religion" (xii). Though these goals are certainly relevant to my own project, I see as primary here another implication of close, complex reading that they do not articulate: namely, the way in which texts with affective and intellectual power—the *Essence* and the *Treatise*, but also Kierkegaard's *Fear and Trembling* and the *Zhuangzi*—educate their readers and incrementally confront them with choices regarding how to relate to the tradition represented in the text, and how to respond to its challenges. Carr and Ivanhoe conclude their comparative study with a personal reflection on the fruitful dynamic of collaborative scholarship and writing. My own concern has rather to do with whether we can live up to the expectations of the *Treatise* or *Essence*, and then both of them, with respect to the ideal of loving surrender they impress upon us as a real religious choice.

49. See also the website for the online *Journal of Scriptural Reasoning*: http://etext.virginia.edu/journals/SSR.

50. Pecknold, "Editorial Preface," 339.
51. Quash, "Heavenly Semantics," 404.
52. Ibid., 412.

Chapter 2

1. Carr and Ivanhoe, in *Sense of Antirationalism,* usefully employ the term "antirationalism," distinct from the more anarchic and probably self-contradictory "irrationalism," to describe this wise skepticism toward reason:

> Antirationalism is a philosophical position about how one grounds certain kinds of truth claims, particularly those concerned with establishing the proper ends of human life. While antirationalism does not deny the value of reason even in this project, it denies that reason alone will enable one to choose and pursue the proper goal of life. Antirationalists believe in alternative sources of guidance. They maintain that we have a tendency to place too much trust in abstract, apersonal forms of reasoning and that this leads us to lose contact with these important, alternative sources of wisdom. (31)

2. De Sales, preface to *Treatise,* 339/7. Somewhat obscurely, de Sales alludes in the same passage to contemporary expectations: "I have taken into consideration, as I must, the state of the minds of this age: it is important to remember in what age we are writing."
3. De Sales, *Treatise,* bk. 2, chap. 1, 409/63.
4. Ibid., 410/64.
5. Ibid. I use Mackey's enumeration of biblical chapter and verse, but variations in enumeration occur in various editions of the Bible.
6. De Sales, *Treatise,* bk. 2, chap. 1, 410/64.
7. Ibid., 411/64–65.
8. De Sales, *Treatise,* bk. 2, chap. 2, 412/66.
9. Ibid., 412–413/66.
10. De Sales, *Treatise,* bk. 2, chap. 4, 421–22/74–75.
11. Ibid., bk. 2, chap. 8, 431/83.
12. Ibid., 432/85.
13. De Sales, *Treatise,* bk. 1, chap. 11, 385/45. My emphasis.
14. De Sales, *Treatise,* bk. 1, chap. 11, 386/45.
15. Ibid., 386/45–46. De Sales' identification of "spirit" with the "mental part of the soul" in this passage is notable. De Sales does not limit himself to a single fixed vocabulary; the terms "reason," "soul," "spirit," and

"heart" bear a certain fluidity. This is not because he is loose with words but because the realities to which those words refer cannot be fully separated; words denoting the spiritual, the intellectual, and the heartfelt refer to the same lived experience.

16. Ibid., 386–87/46. Some, he adds, are guided "by particular illustrations, inspirations, and heavenly motions."

17. De Sales, *Treatise*, bk. 1, chap. 12, 389/48.

18. Ibid., 389–90/48–49.

19. Ibid., 390/49.

20. Ibid.

21. Ibid.

22. De Sales, *Treatise*, bk. 2, chap. 14, 450–51/101.

23. Ibid., 451/102.

24. Ibid.

25. Ibid., 452/102–3.

26. Ibid., bk. 2, chap. 15, 455/105–6.

27. Ibid., bk. 6, chap. 4, 620/243. In the second volume of his *Aux Sources du Traite de L'Amour de Dieu*, Liuima nicely catches the balance between theological certainty and a lively affective excess:

> If, out of consideration for his readers, he [de Sales] does not make theological demonstrations, nor address himself directly to reason, he is rather seeking, by multiple examples and comparisons, to infiltrate the soul, to take hold of it from the inside. In that way, he can appear, at first glance, to pass beyond some questions which he leaves unanswered. But this omission is only apparent. In reality, he is sure of himself. He is the teacher and master of his art, he knows the goal to be attained, the paths that lead there, and the pitfalls one has to live with. But he is equally the director and guide, and he seeks to spare his reader not only detours, but also steps that are useless. (678)

28. De Sales, *Treatise*, bk. 6, chap. 4, 619/242.

29. Ibid., bk. 6, chap. 1, 609/233.

30. Ibid., 611/234.

31. An additional passage from book 6 of the *Treatise* further clarifies "mystical theology": "In the holy Scripture, the word meditation is ordinarily applied to the attention which we have to divine things to stir us up to love them, [nevertheless] it has, as one might say, been canonized by the common consent of theologians, like the name, angel, and, zeal; as on the contrary the words, craft (*dol*), and, demons have been stig-

matized: so that now when we say, meditation, we mean that which is holy, and that by which we begin mystical theology" (bk. 6, chap. 2, 612/235).

I cannot help but add a comment of de Sales from book 5, chap. 2:

> Milk, which is a food provided by the heart and entirely of love, represents mystical knowledge and theology, that is, the sweet relish which proceeds from the loving deep pleasure taken by the spirit when it meditates on the perfections of the divine goodness. But wine signifies ordinary and acquired knowledge, which is squeezed out by force of speculation under the press of diverse arguments and discussions. Now the milk which our souls draw from the breasts of our Savior's charity is incomparably better than the wine which we press out from human reasoning; for this milk flows from heavenly love, who prepares it for her children even before they have thought of it; it has a sweet and agreeable taste, and the odor thereof surpasses all perfumes; it makes the breath fresh and sweet as that of a sucking child; it gives joy without immoderation, it inebriates without stupefying, it does not excite the senses but elevates them. (571/202)

De Sales hopes that his writing bears something of this milk that is truly nourishing, truly a grace. Although Deśika does not make the same distinction between ordinary and mystical knowing, in the next section of this chapter we will be able to see resemblances to his distinctions among the kinds of yoga and the higher devotion, higher knowledge, and supreme devotion. In de Sales' terms, the *Essence* can be counted a work of mystical theology, for it nourishes the human soul and enables its students to experience the realities of which Deśika writes.

32. De Sales, *Treatise*, bk. 1, chap. 17, 400–401/58–59.

33. Ibid., 401/59.

34. Ibid.

35. De Sales, *Treatise*, bk. 9, chap. 2, 763/368.

36. Deśika shows himself to be a very great proponent of reasoned argument and reasoning's religious value, and devotes four chapters of the *Essence*, 23–26, to the ascertainment of the correct position on disputed issues. He devoted several large works—the *Nyāya Pariśuddhi*, *Nyāya Siddhāñjana*, *Tattva Mukta Kalāpa*, and *Paramata Bhaṅga*—to a proper and corrected exposition of the philosophical foundations of Viśiṣṭādvaita Vedānta, which is the philosophical and theological version of the Śrīvaiṣṇava faith.

37. De Sales, *Treatise*, bk. 3, 50–51/22–23.

38. Ibid., 57/29. That is, all beings depend entirely on the Lord, but only humans and similar beings can choose to live accordingly, in service.

39. Both chapters find precedent in the writings of Deśika's older contemporary, Piḷḷai Lokācārya, even if Deśika organizes and integrates his treatment distinctively.

40. Deśika, *Essence,* chap. 4, 88/47.

41. Ibid.

42. Deśika, *Essence,* chap. 5, 94/48.

43. Ibid., 123–24/71. This refers to the double take that occurs when we see a tree stump in the distance and mistakenly think it to be the silhouette of a person. "Stump" (*sthānu*) may also refer to the deity Śiva, and in this case, the shift would be from seeing Śiva (*sthānu*) to seeing Nārāyaṇa (the true person, *puruṣa*).

44. Deśika, *Essence,* chap. 6, 158/86.

45. Or perhaps "the Two" are the Dvaya Mantra and the Carama Śloka.

46. Deśika, *Essence,* chap. 2, 46/21.

47. Deśika, *Essence,* chap. 58–59/31.

48. Deśika, *Essence,* chap. 23, 415/233.

49. Throughout, "instructive scriptures" translates *śāstra.*

50. Here and for all references in Deśika, I use Ramadesikacaryar's citations of chapter and verse, but variations in enumeration will occur in both Sanskrit and Tamil originals, and in translations.

51. Deśika, *Essence,* chap. 23, 416–17/233–34. *Pāṣaṇḍi* is interpreted variously, often translated as "heretic"; here, I follow Professor Jack Hawley, who, in an e-mail, suggested "schismatic." Loosely, the term refers to those denying orthodox views, practicing defective rites, breaking away from the correct faith in the correct God. See O'Flaherty, "Origin of Heresy." It may also, as commentators suggest, refer to those who deny that Nārāyaṇa is the true God and worship some other deity instead. Deśika warns that even innocent conversation with such people may rob one of wisdom, and for this he cites Bhagavad Gītā 7.15: "The worst of men, those fools, evil-doers, do not approach Me; their wisdom removed by *māyā,* they rather take refuge in asuric [demonic] nature."

52. Deśika, *Essence,* chap. 23, 417–19/234–35.

53. "Hari" and "Mādhava" here refer to Nārāyaṇa. Deśika, *Essence,* chap. 23, 420–21/236.

54. Deśika, *Essence,* chap. 23, 441/253.

55. For example, Deśika mocks those who insist on denying full status to Śrī while insisting that the Lord eternally possesses good qualities—as if it were acceptable to say that Nārāyaṇa "needs" good qualities but unacceptable to say that he "needs" Śrī; such people are stubborn in refusing to accept scriptural testimony. Since the refined exegesis of texts related to Śrī is clearly an issue that mattered inside the community, we must assume that the skeptics attacked by Deśika in chapter 23 were

learned Śrīvaiṣṇavas, people all the more disappointing because they have not taken advantage of the resources of their own tradition.

56. Deśika, *Essence*, chap. 23, 443/254.

57. Ibid., 451–52/259. This may be an allusion to *Chāndogya Upaniṣad* 8.3.2, where men walk over a hidden treasure without knowing it is there.

58. Deśika, *Essence*, chap. 28, 720–21/422. On the power of the Dvaya Mantra, see also chapter 4.

59. Clooney, *Seeing through Texts*, chap. 1. On the rich and important relationship between Rāmānuja and the commentarial tradition, see Raman, *Self-Surrender (prapatti) to God in Śrīvaiṣṇavism*, chaps. 1 and 2.

60. See Clooney, *Seeing through Texts*, chap. 3.

61. Deśika, *Essence*, chap. 9, 191–92/105. The technical point at the beginning of the quotation pertains to two uses of the act of taking refuge: as a subordinate contributor to growing devotion, or as a complete and final religious act in itself. Deśika respects both possibilities, but in the *Essence* he privileges the latter.

62. Deśika, *Essence*, chap. 9, 192/105–6.

63. Ibid.

64. Ibid., 192/106.

65. De Sales, *Treatise*, bk. 9, 194–95/107–108.

66. Only the first words are cited by Deśika.

67. Deśika, *Essence*, chap. 9, 195–96/108.

68. I close this section with one other passage that usefully illumines the interplay of knowledge and love. In *Essence*, chapter 15, Deśika describes the life and attitudes of the person who has already taken refuge. After recommending meditation on twenty-five texts praising knowledge (268–75/147–49), Deśika reminds the reader that proper knowledge must be cultivated even after loving surrender:

> A person should not, merely on the excuse, "I have already done all that should be done," become careless regarding things that should be clear in accord with his firm establishment in refuge, but nonetheless are not yet clear. For clarity as well as love is essential to full experience [of the Lord]. As it says, "One should never beg of Viṣṇu [Nārāyaṇa] anything but knowledge and love for his holy feet. If a person begs otherwise, he will surely perish." This shows that there is nothing improper in desiring both knowledge and love of the Lord. In order to create a mental affection toward the one upon whom he depends entirely, in accord with the text, "Know this, by obeisance, by questioning, by service; the wise ones who see reality will teach you such knowledge" (Bhagavad Gītā 4.34),

> the person who has taken refuge should properly ask for clarity from focused persons who already have that clarity. It is about them that it says, "Our Lord dressed in his yellow raiment came as a Brahma teacher. . . . " (*Periyāḻvār Tirumoḻi* 5.2.8. 15, 275/150)

If the Lord comes as a teacher, then learning still matters, even after taking refuge and in God's presence. Mere learning and mere thinking do no good, but the properly disciplined mind—dedicated to learning integrated with loving service—never has enough of the deeper mysteries of God.

69. By "conversion" I therefore do not mean primarily conversion from one religion to another, even if in some cases that might occur. Neither de Sales nor Deśika anticipates that he has readers who might change religions. I have stressed too the "moment" of conversion, but this does not rule out a long preparation for that moment.

70. In introducing this brief reflection on "conversion," I concede that this is a general term that has to be nuanced distinctively with respect to Deśika and de Sales, even if both propose the absolute centrality of deeper union with the gracious God and the radical transformation that implies. As we shall see, for Deśika the required conversion has to do with clarification of vision and realization of one's own true identity such that these promote a radical change of life. For that same goal, de Sales draws on a vocabulary of sin and repentance, alienation from God and return to God. Even if de Sales values the cognitive element of repentance, that is less central than it is in Deśika; even if Deśika might appreciate the importance of regret and tears, he does not so vigorously stress the affective dimension because, in his view, conversion follows almost necessarily from clear insight. Pondering together these differently patterned views of reason and conversion constitutes a double reading that intensifies and sharpens not only our sense of differences, but also our awareness that both authors stress reason's limitations, its need to reach beyond itself and beyond the fragile capacity of human words, if we are to grasp the realities of God and change our lives accordingly.

71. See also Clooney, "Forms of Philosophizing" and chapter 3 of this book.

72. Deśika, *Essence,* chap. 7, 162/88.

73. Ibid., 163/88.

74. Ibid. The reflective process aims to foster a different attitude and a different way of living, as another scriptural citation shows: "All the instructive texts are enjoined by humans in order to quiet the mind, and so the one whose mind is always quieted should be considered the one who knows all the instructive texts" (*Itihāsa Samuccaya* 12.37).

75. Deśika, *Essence*, chap. 7, 169/92.

76. Ibid., 169/93; the quotation is *Laws of Manu* 4.18.

77. *Nācciyāṟ Tirumoḻi* 11.3; De Sales, *Treatise*, bk. 1, 38/15.

78. Deśika, *Essence*, chap. 1, 38–39/15–16.

79. Ibid., 39/16.

80. The kauṣṭubha gem rests on Nārāyaṇa's chest, where Śrī (Tiru) also resides.

81. Deśika, *Essence*, chap. 1, 39–40/16–17.

82. Ibid., 40/117.

83. See also Liuima, *Aux Sources du Traite de L'Amour de Dieu*, 1:9, on the same point.

84. Ibid., 1:337–38.

85. De Sales, *Treatise*, bk. 6, chap. 4, 620/243.

86. De Sales, *Treatise*, bk. 6, chap. 1, 608/231–32.

87. Ravier, introduction to *Oeuvres*, lxxxiii–cvi.

88. Ibid., lxxxv.

89. De Sales, *Treatise*, bk. 1, chap. 15, 395/54. Herein we find a summation of the whole; as Ravier comments, "It is perhaps in these few words that Francis de Sales has best caught the whole of his *Treatise*" (introduction to *Oeuvres*, lxxxvii).

90. Ravier, introduction to *Oeuvres*, lxxxviii.

91. Ibid., lxxxiv At the end of De Sales, *Treatise*, bk. 1, chap. 14, de Sales glosses the title of his work to accentuate the performative connotation of *amour*: "Therefore the word love [*amour*], as the most excellent, has justly been given to charity [*charité*], as to the chief and most eminent of all loves [*de tous les amours*]; so that for all these reasons, and because I intend to speak of the acts of charity rather than of its habit, I have entitled this little work *A Treatise of the Love* [*amour*] *of God*." As Ravier explains, de Sales is concerned less with the "habitual grace" that makes a person into a child of God than with the "actual grace" operative in that person's history, "the love of God in act, inspiring and transfiguring each act of the Christian" (*Francis de Sales: Sage and Saint*, 1707 n. 4).

92. De Sales, *Treatise*, bk. 2, chap. 18, 465–66/115.

93. Ibid., bk. 2, chap. 20, 468/117.

94. Ibid., 471–472/120.

95. Ibid., bk. 2, chap. 9, 435–36/87–88.

96. Ibid., bk. 12, chap. 13, 971–72/554–55.

97. In keeping with my focus on the "inner context" of the *Treatise* and *Essence*, I do not address the social dimensions of the authority that Deśika and de Sales assumed as leading religious figures—an ācārya, a bishop—in their religious communities. Though this social context is surely relevant to the reception of their teaching and their self-

conception as authors, neither author explicitly draws on such authority in these texts.

98. That is, *écrit d'amour.*

99. De Sales, *Treatise,* Dedicatory Prayer, 333–34/1–2.

100. The reference is of course to Pentecost, Acts 2; preface to *Treatise,* 335/3.

101. De Sales, preface to *Treatise,* 336/3–4.

102. Ibid., 342/9–10.

103. Ibid, 347/14.

104. Ravier, *Francis de Sales: Sage and Saint,* 1734.

105. De Sales, preface to *Treatise,* 342–43/10.

106. De Sales insists that his book will be of value to his readers in ways discernible only in the reading: "It even seems to me that my design is not the same as that of others except in general, inasmuch as we all look towards the glory of holy love. But the reading itself will convince you of this" (preface to *Treatise,* 338/6).

107. Deśika, *Lineage,* 4/1.

108. Deśika thus states the thesis of his *Lineage*: "It is said, 'Kṣatrabandhu, the worst of sinners, and Puṇḍarīka, the merit-doer, both were liberated due to having a teacher. Therefore, you must have a teacher.' This confirms that for every one having a teacher is the cause for liberation" (9/2). There is no one who does not require a teacher, neither the saint (Puṇḍarīka) nor the sinner (Kṣatrabandhu); merit does not gain liberation, nor does sin make it impossible. Having a teacher is the decisive difference.

109. Deśika, *Lineage,* 9/2.

110. On Deśika's understanding of the role of the teacher and tradition in the *Guruparaṃparāsāra,* see Clooney, "From Person to Person."

111. Deśika, *Lineage,* 23/7.

112. Ibid. Deśika adds that remembrance is a remedy even for dealing with outsiders, who are a perennial threat to those cherishing insider status: "This meditation on the teachers is also expiation for having conversed with those who are forbidden: 'Having conversed [with improper people], let him meditate mentally on those who act virtuously.'"

113. Deśika, *Essence,* chap. 30, 967/573.

114. Ibid.

115. The deity with the "horse face" is Hayagrīva, an avatar of Nārāyaṇa as teacher. Hayagrīva is honored in a temple in Deśika's hometown, Tiruvahindrapuram. See Singh, *Vedānta Deśika,* 12.

116. Deśika, *Essence,* chap. 31, 982–83/580.

117. Deśika, *Essence,* chap. 32, 1008/591.

118. That is, by eavesdropping.

119. Of this verse and the following *Viṣṇu Purāṇa* verse, Deśika cites only the first line.

120. The mention of Parāśara's fidelity to ritual heightens the propriety of the scene.

121. The death effigy is given away and might conceivably be worn—but custom and sensitivity make it impossible to conceive of actually doing so.

122. Deśika, *Essence,* chap. 31, 978–79/577–78.

123. Another of Deśika's texts is relevant. The opening prose section of his *Śrī Sampradāya Pariśuddhi* ("On the Perfect Purity of the Auspicious Tradition") illumines his attitude here:

> By means of the tradition of good teachers, one must inquire into the specific meaning of the scriptures related to the self. This is well known in the Upaniṣads and in related supporting texts. When people do not have the capability to articulate the meaning of the scriptures, then nothing but the tradition of those who know the scriptures offers the desired analysis. As it says, 'Knowing Hari because of teaching . . .' Inquiry into meaning by way of scripture but without the benefit of the tradition of the good is too difficult. Regarding objects beyond the senses, tradition not rooted in scripture and tradition contrary to respected scriptures both foster error or deceit; these are like heterodox traditions, not to be trusted. (Vol. 1, p. 3)

See also, in the same volume, the commentary on this paragraph by Srirama Desikacarya Swami, pages 1–3 in the second and separately paginated part of the volume, and also the translation in Srinivasaraghavan.

124. Deśika, *Essence,* chap. 30, 965–66/572.

125. Deśika seems to be claiming that his verses are received from his teacher; if so, then by implication the prose of the text is his own reflection, written as it were around the verses.

126. That is, that state of union, heavenly bliss.

127. Deśika, *Essence,* chap. 32, 1007/590–91.

128. Works such as Henri de Lubac's *Medieval Exegesis: The Four Senses of Scripture* and Jean Leclerq's *The Love of Learning and the Desire for God* confirm the rich contextualization possible for learning that is intentionally rooted in scripture, tradition, and religious practice.

129. Griffiths, *Religious Reading,* 41–42.

130. See also McGhee, *Transformations of Mind,* and Stalnaker, *Overcoming Evil,* both of which exemplify aspects of Hadot's insight into lived philosophy, its role as spiritual exercise. Fowl's *Engaging Scripture* offers

a specifically Christian reflection on the interplay between reading-engaging the Bible and the theological dispositions one generates from and brings to that reading. Highlighting virtues that we can recognize as applicable to Deśika's Śrīvaiṣṇava tradition as well, Fowl explores the communal, educational (catechetical), and liturgical context of becoming a properly engaged reader of the Bible. He assesses the tensions and divergences between a Christian theological reading and the professional scholarly analysis of biblical texts such as occurs in academic settings.

131. Hadot, *Philosophy as a Way of Life*, 74.

132. Davidson, introduction to Hadot, *Philosophy as a Way of Life*, 26.

133. Ibid., from Hadot's "Présentation au Collège International de Philosophie."

134. Hadot, *Philosophy as a Way of Life*, 267.

135. Hadot adds that in ancient Greece and in cultures consequent upon Greek culture, study itself could be valorized as an essentially philosophical and religious act, a kind of exegetical reasoning quite at odds with the expectations regarding "system" that would become common in early modernity: "It is not the case that every properly philosophical endeavor is 'systematic' in the Kantian or Hegelian sense. For two thousand years, philosophical thought utilized a methodology which condemned it to accept incoherences and far-fetched associations, precisely to the extent that it wanted to be systematic. But to study the actual progress of exegetical thought is to begin to realize that thought can function rationally in many different ways, which are not necessarily the same as those of mathematical logic or Hegelian dialectic" (76). A real shift occurred, says Hadot, when later philosophers (those of the seventeenth century and thereafter) "refused the argument from authority and abandoned the exegetical mode of thinking" (76). For not only was authority called into question, but so too the received, time-honored modes of study and models that had been established for teacher and student.

Chapter 3

1. Here too, Carr and Ivanhoe (*The Sense of Antirationalism*) catch the right note, remarking that both Zhuangzi and Kierkegaard exhibit "a concerted refusal to speak from an absolute or God's-eye perspective. While both thinkers are moral realists and gesture toward sources of higher ethical guidance, they consciously avoid the construction of a philosophical system to justify or demonstrate their normative visions." Rather, they seek to "undermine the, in their eyes, pretentious illusion of the search for

philosophical completeness and finality. Instead of constructing a single philosophical model that informs and underwrites their thought, both employ concrete authorial strategies designed to expose the inadequacy of conventional beliefs, attitudes, and ways of thought," and attempt "to elicit and engender new ways of perceiving, evaluating, and acting in the world, ways regarded by them as spiritually both more profitable and authentic" (90–91).

2. For fuller treatments of their literary practices, see Liuima's *Aux Sources du Traite de L'Amour de Dieu* regarding the *Treatise,* and, regarding Deśika in general, Singh's *Vedānta Deśika,* Hopkins's *Singing the Body of God,* and Venkatachari's *Śrīvaiṣṇavism: An Insight.*

3. Liuima, *Aux Sources du Traite de L'Amour de Dieu,* 2:566–67.

4. In the main sections of Volume 2, "Les Sources des Moyens d'Expression de l'Idée d'Amour de Dieu," Liuima covers de Sales' indebtedness to classical authors (chap. 1); to the Christian tradition, including the church fathers, hagiographies, theologians, spiritual writers, church councils, and liturgical texts (chap. 2); and to scripture (chap. 3).

5. Liuima, *Aux Sources du Traite de L'Amour de Dieu,* 2:552.

6. Ibid., 2:559.

7. In the second part of Volume 2, "L'Ecriture Sainte, Source de Moyens Litteraires."

8. Liuima, *Aux Sources du Traite de L'Amour de Dieu,* 2:615ff. See also 2:650.

9. Ibid., 2:627.

10. Ibid., 2:673.

11. As noted in chapter 2, the preface begins (335/3) with a contemplation of Pentecost and the outpouring of the Holy Spirit as fundamental to the life and meaning of the church.

12. De Sales, preface to the *Treatise,* 336/3–4.

13. Ibid., bk. 8, chap. 10, 741/350–51.

14. Ibid., 741/350.

15. Ibid., 741–42/351.

16. Ibid., bk. 8, chap. 3, 720/331.

17. Even if "meditation" and "contemplation" are not exclusively linked to reading; see below.

18. De Sales, *Treatise,* bk. 6, chap. 2, 612/235–36.

19. Ibid., 612/236.

20. Ibid.

21. Ibid., 612–13/236.

22. Ibid., 614–15/238.

23. Ibid., 613/236.

24. Ibid., 615/239.

25. Although this image of the bee seems appropriate to the Song of Songs, it does not appear in the text itself.

26. De Sales, *Treatise,* bk. 6, chap. 2, 615–16/239.

27. Bk. 6, chap. 6, 625–26/248–49.

28. Bk. 6, chap. 12, 644/265.

29. In *Essence,* chapter 18, Deśika identifies hardness of heart as a problem even *after* taking refuge. See Clooney, "For Your Own Good."

30. De Sales, *Treatise,* bk. 6, chap. 12, 644/265.

31. Ibid.

32. Ibid., 644–45/265–66.

33. "Lover" in this passage is first in the feminine, and then in the masculine gender.

34. De Sales, *Treatise,* bk. 6, chap. 12, 645/266.

35. Ibid.

36. Ibid.

37. Ibid.

38. Ibid., 645–46/266–67.

39. Ibid., 646/267.

40. Ibid., 647/267–68. De Sales seals his argument by recollecting that saints—models for the reader who is willing to take to heart what she or he has read—let themselves be absorbed by God, hovering for now on the edge between life here and life with God: "Such, I think, were the feelings of the great Blessed Philip Neri and Francis Xavier, when, overwhelmed with heavenly consolations, they petitioned God to withdraw himself for a space from them, since his will was that their life should a little longer appear unto the world—which could not be while it was wholly hidden and absorbed in God" (bk. 6, chap. 12, 647/268).

41. This is true even if "scripture" is a more complex notion for Deśika. There is no single, strict analogue to the Bible, and he draws on a wide array of Sanskrit and Tamil sources that are not all of the same rank, but rather ordered in accord with gradations of authority. In the *Essence,* various sources are used profusely and in close proximity to one another, to intensify whatever theme is being discussed. In citing Tamil and Sanskrit sources together so regularly, he demonstrates his mastery of all relevant scriptures, and testifies to his conviction that the relevant Sanskrit and Tamil sources—theologically linked, as a single body of testimony to the truths and values of the tradition—cooperate in confirming the truth of his Śrīvaiṣṇava synthesis and the efficacy of its doctrinal and practical teachings.

There is, to my knowledge, no full study of Deśika's use of scripture, and the comments I make in this section are provisional in lieu of that wider research.

42. Thus my approximate count of the texts footnoted in Ayyangar's translation. As with the *Treatise*, however, there are many more implicit allusions to scriptural passages, and additional manners of speaking that richly resonate with scripture without quoting a particular text.

43. For the sake of widest accessibility, it seems, he rarely quotes the most sacred revelatory texts (*śruti*).

44. Or "I have left You for them."

45. The "hard-to-fathom" joy is the delight in the self, by itself, apart from the senses and from God.

46. *Essence* 165–67/90–99. I give only the first thirteen of the twenty-one quotations. The commentators systematize the purposefulness of the quotations, correlating them with the seven flaws. Thus each flaw, though rooted in observation of human experience, also correlates with one or more of the passages cited: experience and scripture confirm each other.

47. Deśika, *Essence,* chap. 7, 168/92.

48. Research needs to be done to ascertain changes over generations in the use and interpretation of such quotations.

49. Deśika, *Essence,* chap. 15, 275/150. The twenty-four quotations are on 268–75/147–50.

50. That is, a permanent dwelling in a place holy to Nārāyaṇa is preferable to the divine powers of the gods Brahmā and Rudra.

51. Numbers 35 and 36 of the verses of Vaṅkivaṃśeśvara (also known as Vaṅkipuruttunampi or Śrīranga Nārāyaṇācārya, a disciple of Rāmānuja; see Singh, *Vedānta Deśika,* 135). The preceding quotations are from chapter 15, 274–75/149–50. Here are the remaining instructions:

2. "Having gained clarity in the proper way," that is, spiritual knowledge from proper teachers (3 quotations);
3. "Having become possessed of purified knowledge" (1 quotation);
4. "Having come near to those who are established in these truths" (1 quotation);
5. "In their actions they should be determined to what must be done in accord with their religious class, stage of life, birth status, and qualities, etc., and should have the attitude, 'We are to do these things,' reflecting on the greatness of others and their own lowliness, thus looking ahead of themselves to avoid falling into holes" (1 quotation);
6. "They should focus on their helplessness in accord with what is said to them" (13 quotations);
7. "Immersing themselves in the holy waters of the mysteries of

the avatāras, etc., having understood clearly the most pleasing teachings, most salutary like mother's milk" (2 quotations);

8. "Having not lost the experience of service that comes in following the [divine] commands and permissions in conformity with their state, as if building a dam for waters" (5 quotations);
9. "Changing their attitudes toward unworthy objects, instead immersing their senses in appropriate experiences of pure food, service, etc." (1 quotation);
10. "They should rejoice, consuming this word like those who are healthy and drink milk not as medicine" (no quotations);
11. "They should be those who have taken the remedy for the confusion of mind that comes due to the force of the fruits of reasons related to the three means of authoritative learning, perception, etc." (5 quotations);
12. "Meditating on the excellence of the one beyond word and mind who nonetheless is dependent on those who take refuge with him" (3 quotations);
13. "Having acted in accord with the accessibility and transcendence of the divine relationships [with humans]" (1 quotation);
14. "They should think upon the protection a wife devotes herself to, protecting her wedding—thread, etc."
15. "They should keep faith [in their teachers] and remain grateful, meditating on the service, etc., coming to them due to [the teachers'] excellence" (4 quotations);
16. "They should understand clearly that natural compassion and be grateful toward [the Lord]" (6 quotations). (15, 275–89/150–58)

52. The *śrīvatsa* is a mark—perhaps curl of hair—on the chest of Viṣṇu, who is "the beloved of Śrī" (Śrīvatsa); she too is represented as forever on his chest.

53. Here Trijāta the demoness is speaking to other demonesses about the situation they find themselves in—holding Sītā prisoner yet needing her protection.

54. Deśika, *Essence,* chap. 4, 63–64/33–34.

55. Ibid., 66–67/35. Much more could be said about the entire list of quotations, since the commentators find specific points highlighted by individual quotations or small clusters of quotations. Quite apart from its function in the list, each quotation has its own narrative or meditative context and conjures its own images and affects. Quotations 1–5 offer a vision of the eternal Viṣṇu, seen always and only with Śrī; quotations 6–

10 invoke the story of the *Rāmāyaṇa* and the deeds and experiences of Śrī and Viṣṇu as Sītā and Rāma on earth; the Tamil verses portray Nārāyaṇa and Śrī as the meditator's true destiny. Further nuances can be added: The quotations from the *Liṅga Purāṇa* and *Harivaṃśa* stress the eternal relationship of Śrī and Nārāyaṇa, even in the transcendent realm, before and beyond this world; the quotations from the *Yuddha Kāṇḍa, Viṣṇu Purāṇa, Āraṇya Kāṇḍa,* and *Sundara Kāṇḍa* highlight the role of Śrī as mediator (a theologically significant role not entirely clear in many sources). Lakṣmaṇa's words from the *Ayodhyā Kāṇḍa* indicate that Sītā as well as Rāma is the object of his total devotion. *Tiruvāymoḻi* 4.9.10 and 6.9.3 emphasize Śrī's beauty, and *Tiruvāymoḻi* 6.10.10 affirms her intention never to be apart from Nārāyaṇa—and thus always to be present, when anyone comes for refuge. Such texts, when meditated on, gradually clarify and make present for the devotee how God actually is. Each quote suggests its own emotional response, while speaking to the truth that Nārāyaṇa is never without Śrī.

56. Deśika, *Essence*, chap. 4, 77/41.

57. Deśika also correlates the truth of the self to what is taught in the three mantras, and advises readers to turn also to other chapters of the *Essence*.

58. Perhaps "covering them" without healing them.

59. Only the last two lines are quoted by Deśika.

60. Only the second line is quoted by Deśika.

61. On interpretations of (seeming) divine absence according to Śrīvaiṣṇava commentators, see Clooney, "Divine Absence."

62. The "Song of Surrender."

63. There are, in accord with a standard theory, scriptures tainted with passion (*rajas*) and/or a kind of dark lethargy (*tamas*). See Clooney, *Hindu God, Christian God*, chap. 3.

64. The second and third constituents of matter, *rajas* (passion) and *tamas* (lethargy, decay), define the character of such people. For the Bhagavad Gītā text, I have adapted Zaehner's translation.

65. Deśika, *Essence*, chap. 4, 79–81/44.

66. Attachment to the body is not the only temptation. Even yogic asceticism and detachment too become distractions, and in fact no human practice is free of the danger of attachments and the concomitant alienation from Nārāyaṇa and Śrī. Yet as Deśika asserts in an allusion to the Bhagavad Gītā 6.40 ("Pārtha, neither here nor hereafter is there destruction of such a person; for no one who has done what is auspicious travels an evil path, friend"), no good effort is entirely wasted, even if our best still falls short of the higher goal. Because God is as God is, obstacles are never insurmountable.

67. The *Śrī Bhāṣya* is Rāmānuja's very influential commentary on Bādārāyaṇa's *Brahma Sūtras* (or, *Uttara Mīmāṃsā* or *Vedānta Sūtras*), which in turn are a systematization of the teaching of the Upaniṣads.

68. Deśika, *Essence,* chap. 4, 86–87/46. The web of quotations is thus by implication rendered more complex. For Deśika knows that Rāmānuja, in explaining *Kaṭha Upaniṣad* 3.10–11 in the *Śrī Bhāṣya,* backs up his reference to taking refuge with yet another citation, one from the Bhagavad Gītā: "The Lord abides in the heart of all things, Arjuna; He whirls them about by His marvelous power (*māyā*), mounted on a machine (*yantra*); to Him alone go for refuge (Bhagavad Gītā 18.61–62a). See *Śrī Bhāṣya,* tr. 356–57. For the Bhagavad Gītā text, I have adapted Zaehner's translation.

69. De Sales, *Treatise,* bk. 7, chap. 8, 690/306.

70. Ibid., bk. 7, chap. 9, 690/307.

71. Ibid., 692/308–309.

72. Ibid., 693/310.

73. Ibid., bk. 7, chap. 10, 695/311.

74. Ibid., bk. 7, chap. 11, 695–96/312.

75. De Sales fills them out by additional reflections on the deaths of Francis of Assisi and Basil, and more briefly those of Mary Magdalene and Teresa of Avila.

76. De Sales, *Treatise,* bk. 7, chap. 12, 700–701/316–17.

77. Ibid., bk. 7, chap. 14, 707/322.

78. Ibid., 708/324.

79. Ibid., bk. 9, chap. 15, 801–2/404.

80. Ibid., 802/405.

81. De Sales also finds spiritual lessons in such natural phenomena as plants and animals. To take just one example: He is fond of certain "footless" birds—*apodes*—that cannot fly but can glide once lifted by the wind. After describing them in some detail with a kind of scientific precision, he moralizes:

> Most of us humans rather resemble apodes: for if it chance that we, quitting the air of holy divine love, fall upon earth and adhere to creatures, which we do as often as we offend God, we die indeed, yet not so absolute a death but that there remains in us a little movement, besides our legs and feet, namely, some weak affections, which enable us to make some essays of love, though so weakly, that in truth we are impotent of ourselves to detach our hearts from sin, or start ourselves again in the flight of sacred love, which, wretches that we are, we have perfidiously and voluntarily forsaken. (Bk. 2, chap. 9, 435/87)

See also book 2, chapters 12, 13, and 21.

82. De Sales, preface to *Treatise,* 342/9.

83. De Sales, *Treatise,* bk. 7, chap. 8, 687–88/304.

84. Ibid., bk. 9, chap. 16, 805/407.

85. Ibid., bk. 12, chap. 12, 970/553.

86. "Secular" stories tend to deal with kings and their courts—for example, the parable of the prince lost in the forest (*Essence,* chap. 1) and the many accounts of kings' dealings with their courtiers, wives, and family members—or with the business world.

87. Deśika, *Essence,* chap. 31, 982/580.

88. See for example Clooney, *Seeing through Texts,* 227–42.

89. The older Śrīvaiṣṇava commentaries on *Tiruvāymoḻi* and related resources, already in place before Deśika's time, contain vivid anecdotes from the lives of saintly Śrīvaiṣṇavas and recollections of moments when the teachers engaged their students in vivid, emotional terms. By contrast, Deśika includes almost no such recollections or pious accounts of persons living the life of loving surrender.

90. Deśika, *Essence,* chap. 17, 310/169.

91. Interestingly, their songs are described as "gracious deeds," presumably the deeds of the saints and also of the Lord whom they praise.

92. On Deśika the poet, see Singh, *Vedānta Deśika,* part IV; and Hopkins, *Singing the Body of God.* Though de Sales writes beautiful prose and enjoys quoting biblical poetry—the Psalms and the Song of Songs—there are very few verses of his own in the *Treatise.*

93. See also the verses cited in chapter 1.

94. Probably Ātreya Rāmānuja.

95. Deśika, *Lineage,* 23–24/8.

96. Ibid., 24/8.

97. Ibid., 25/8–9.

98. A play on his name, *āḷa vantāṟ,* "he came to rule."

99. Deśika, *Lineage,* 9–10/25–26.

100. Plus an additional thirty-third verse at the end of the entire work.

101. Ramadesikacaryar indicates the three kinds of literature in Tamil: poetry, music, drama (*iyal, icai, nāṭakam*).

102. The Vedas.

103. Deśika, *Essence,* chap. 32, 1004/588–89.

104. "Hidden" or "secret" knowledge.

105. Ibid., 1005/589.

106. Cited also in chap. 2.

107. That is, devotion: It works, but its demands make us doubtful whether we can perform it.

108. An image probably drawn from *Kaṭha Upaniṣad* 1.3.3–6, a detailed analogy between the embodied self and a chariot.

109. That the tradition does give special attention to the verses in the *Essence* was signaled by the release in 2000 of a small pamphlet, *Śrīmadrahasyatrayasārattil swāmi deśikar aruḷi cceytuḷḷa ślokaṅkaḷum pācuraṅkaḷum* ("The Verses and Stanzas of Swami Deśika in the Śrīmad Rahasyatrayasāra"), which in its forty pages includes the seventy-eight Sanskrit verses found in the *Essence,* particularly at chapters' beginnings and ends, and fifty-six Tamil verses, most of which end chapters. In addition, the pamphlet also contains the 173 two-line *kārikas* that are found throughout the *Essence* (and referred to here simply as "verses"). The pamphlet has no introduction, but presumably was published in recognition of the importance of these verses even on their own.

110. Altieri, *Canon,* 17. Throughout, in citations from Altieri's texts, the emphases are mine.

111. Ibid., 45

112. Ibid.; see also p. 55.

113. Altieri also has in mind drama, poetry, and visual works of art.

114. Altieri, *Particulars,* 33.

115. Ibid. At the opening of his first chapter, Altieri writes that his book

> originated as a reaction against dominant tendencies in my field of literary criticism. I had always hated criticism that preferred context to text and insisted on situating works in relation to historical forces and sociopolitical interests. But the imperative to work intensely on the affects came from recognizing that even criticism sharing my overall values seemed to me too eager to equate texts with the interpretive frameworks we could put around them. (1)

Altieri's attitude may be taken as informing my own work here as well.

116. Altieri, *Particulars,* 186. Altieri explicates each of these states as follows. In the moment of *intensity,* "there emerges a vivid awareness of particulars," while "the will is called into some kind of decisive action, if only to persist in what is extraordinary or to turn from that to the comfort of more habitual behaviors" (187). As *involved,* "the soul's concentrative powers also provide means of appreciating how we are modified by our connections with other people and with the natural world. . . . This awareness can be cultivated as a direct identification with a dramatic situation, or it can depend on second-order investments in how the text asks us to envision our relationship to other readers" (194). *Plasticity* marks "the capacity of a psyche or work of art to establish satisfaction in holding together without collapsing diverse aspects of experience which all have substantive claims on us" (205).

117. Altieri, *Particulars,* 110–11.

118. Ibid., 118.
119. Ibid., 125.
120. Ibid., 125–26.
121. Ibid., 126.
122. Ibid.

Chapter 4

1. See Ravier, preface to *Oeuvres de Saint François de Sales,* xxviii–xxxiii.

2. See Levi's *French Moralists* and Bremond's *Literary History of Religious Thought.*

3. De Sales, *Treatise,* bk. 2, chap. 12, 444–45/96.

4. Ibid., chap. 21, 474/122. De Sales appeals to the authority of the Council of Trent to confirm the orthodoxy of his views on divine initiative and human freedom:

> And meantime we remain in full liberty, to consent to the divine appeals or to reject them; for as the sacred Council of Trent has clearly decreed: "If any one should say that man's freewill, being moved and incited by God, does not in any way co-operate by consenting to God, who moves and calls him that he may dispose and prepare himself to obtain the grace of justification, and that he is unable to refuse consent even if he should so wish," truly such a man would be excommunicated, and reproved by the Church. (Bk. 2, chap. 12, 444–45/96)

The boundaries drawn by Trent are definite and stern, de Sales implies, because subtle and important Christian truths and values are at stake: Loving surrender is a gift of grace, but humans must have the freedom to accept this gift.

5. In bk. 12, chap. 10, "An exhortation to the sacrifice which we are to make to God of our free will."

6. De Sales, *Treatise,* bk. 12, chap. 10, 967/550–51.

7. Chapters 23–26 of Deśika's *Essence* are devoted to the clarification of controversial issues discussed earlier and later in the book. On the distinctions between devotion and taking refuge, see my chapter 2.

8. In his translation, pp. 263–96, Ayyangar does not divide the objections in the same way.

9. That is, as if contrary to the idea that all saving activity is the Lord's alone.

10. Deśika, *Essence*, chap. 24, 511/298.

11. None of this is quite like Deśika's understanding of great faith (see below), which here too has more strongly intellectual overtones.

12. *Śrīmannārayaṇacaraṇau śaraṇaṃ prapadye; Śrīmate Nārāyaṇāya namaḥ*. *Śrī* = Śrī, the goddess; *man* [*mat*] = with; *Nārāyaṇa* = Nārāyaṇa; *caraṇau* = feet; *śaraṇam* = refuge; *prapadye* = I approach; *Śrīmate Nārāyaṇāya* = to Nārāyaṇa with Śrī; *namaḥ*—obeisance.

13. The Dvaya Mantra must necessarily be interpreted, in a full study, along with the Tiru Mantra and Carama Śloka. On the three mantras, see chapter 1 of this book, and see also my commentary *The Truth, the Way, and the Life*.

14. The entire "Song of Surrender" is no more than five or six pages in ordinary printed editions without commentary.

15. Here and below, my translation, but see also the text and translation available in Ayyangar 2002, to which I will give page references here and below: Sanskrit p. 38, translation p. 12.

16. The tree that fulfills the wishes of those eating its fruit.

17. "Song," Sanskrit 39, translation 15.

18. Deśika, *Essence*, chap. 28, 717/420.

19. Ibid., 719–20/421.

20. "Song of Surrender," Sanskrit 41, translation 19. Deśika cites only the first line.

21. Deśika, *Essence*, chap. 28, 720–21/422.

22. Ibid., 721/422. See also chap. 2 of the present book.

23. By this reconstruction I do *not* mean that the mantra itself evolved in this fashion.

24. Deśika, *Essence*, chap. 28, 737/437. See also my book *The Truth, the Way, and the Life*, chap. 2.

25. Ibid., chap. 27, 672–74/389–92. For the 108 characteristics of Nārāyaṇa, see Clooney, *The Truth, the Way, and the Life*, chap. 2.

26. Ibid., chap. 28, 737–41/436–40.

27. Thus showing that together they are the means (in the first clause) and the goal (in the second clause); chap. 28, 736/435.

28. Deśika, *Essence*, chap. 28, 736/435–36.

29. Ibid., 736/436.

30. Ibid., 742/441.

31. Ibid., 743/441. "Pure-matter" (*śuddha sattva*) is a special form of matter that is free of the defects of ordinary matter.

32. Both "meditation" and "means" refer to devotion (*bhakti*).

33. Deśika, *Essence*, chap. 28, 750–51/447–48.

34. The basic word for movement, *gati*, which here glosses *pra-pad*, may also indicate the movement of the mind.

35. Deśika, *Essence*, chap. 28, 751–52/449.

36. Ibid., 752/449.

37. Ibid., 752–53/449.

38. Cited also in *Essence*, chap. 24, where it is attributed to Bhārata Muni.

39. Deśika, *Essence*, chap. 28, 753/450.

40. Deśika here echoes claims made elsewhere in the *Essence* about the once-for-all nature of the act of taking refuge indicated by *I approach for refuge*. He insists that the present tense of the verb simply indicates the moment of the action. It is not to be construed, he says, as indicating an ongoing, even lifelong action, nor one that requires constant repetition. Repetition is permissible, but only for enjoyment, not necessity.

41. Deśika, *Essence*, chap. 28, 757/456.

42. That is, possessed of the powers and good qualities of a true Lord.

43. Deśika, *Essence*, chap. 28, 757/455.

44. That is, the *śeṣi-śeṣa* relationship, "possessor and possessed," between God and the individual self.

45. Deśika, *Essence*, chap. 28, 758–59/456–57.

46. Ibid., 759/457.

47. In this section I retain the word *namaḥ*, a departure from my usual practice of translating every word. Although *namaḥ* does mean obeisance or praise, key to its meaning is also its division into na + mama, impossible to produce in English without using the *namaḥ* and *na + mama* tension.

48. Unusually, Deśika includes here a Tamil translation of the Sanskrit word, hence the apparent repetition in English.

49. Deśika, *Essence*, chap. 28, 759–60/457–58.

50. Ibid., 754/451–52.

51. He draws a ritual analogy:

> Just as a person offering an oblation says, "This is for Indra, not for me," so too here one offers up the very source of the burden, saying, "I am for Nārāyaṇa with Śrī," and then breaks the connection with oneself by asserting [in the second clause], "This is not mine." This is the proper sentiment that makes the offering coherent. Accordingly, the first clause is about the five aids subsidiary [to the act of taking refuge], while the second expounds that primary reality [toward whom everything points]. (Chap. 28, 761/459)

52. Deśika, *Essence*, chap. 28, 760–61/458–59.

53. The self that is surrendered is precisely what needs to be protected; it is surrendered so that it can be protected.

54. Deśika, *Essence*, chap. 28, 761/459.

55. That is, the utterance of the mantra effects the taking of refuge, which occurs in the recitation.

56. Deśika, *Essence*, chap. 28, 761/460.

57. Deśika, *Essence*, chap. 12, 232–33/128–29.

58. Ibid., 237/131.

59. Ibid., 238/132.

60. Ibid., 239/133.

61. De Sales, *Treatise*, bk. 1, chap. 7, 369/30–31.

62. Ibid., 370–71/32.

63. Ibid., bk. 1, chap. 8, 375/36.

64. Ibid., 376/36. At the end of chapter 7, de Sales concedes that love itself is a kind of deep pleasure:

> For not only does the movement of love take its origin from the deep pleasure which the heart feels at the first approach of good, and find its end in a second deep pleasure which returns to the heart by union with the thing beloved,—but further, it depends for its preservation on this deep pleasure, and can only subsist through it as through its mother and nurse; so that as soon as the deep pleasure ceases love ceases. (371/32)

65. De Sales, *Treatise*, bk. 1, chap. 7, 370/31–32.

66. Ibid., bk. 1, chap. 10, 380/40. De Sales also distinguishes "three sorts of actions of love: the spiritual, the reasonable, and the sensitive"; intensified, these ignite in "a prodigious flash."

67. De Sales, *Treatise*, bk. 1, chap. 10, 382/42.

68. Ibid., bk. 1, chap. 12, 390/49.

69. Ibid., 390/49.

70. In *Treatise* book 5 de Sales further explores the relationship between love and deep pleasure, this time distinguishing "the two principal exercises of love," deep pleasure (chaps. 1–5) alongside benevolence (chaps. 6–10). Here, deep pleasure takes pleasure in the other, and benevolence brings pleasure to that other. Whereas God's act begins in benevolence (creation) and becomes his deep pleasure (joy in created realities), for humans what comes first is deep pleasure, an instinct for and pleasure in God, and that in turn prompts benevolent action (chap. 6).

71. De Sales, *Treatise*, bk. 5, chap. 2, 568/199.

72. Ibid., 569/199–200.

73. Ibid., 569–70/200. As the soul matures in mystical theological insight, it enters more intimate unity with the Lord, quite passionately:

> Has not this fair soul reason to cry: O my king how lovable are your riches and how rich your loves! Oh! which of us has more joy, you that enjoy it, or I who rejoice thereat! *We will be glad and rejoice in you remembering your breasts* so abounding in all excellence of sweetness! [Song of Songs 1.3] I because my well-beloved enjoys it, you because your well-beloved rejoices in it; we both enjoy it, since your goodness makes you enjoy my rejoicing, and my love makes me rejoice in your enjoying. (bk. 5, chap. 2, 570/200–201)

It is hard for the reader—the double reader—to avoid finding here echoes of Deśika's sentiment, when he quotes Tirumaḻicai Pirāṉ: "The meaning of Nārāyaṇa is in accord with [what the āḻvār says]: 'I am not, without you; but see, Nārāyaṇa, you without me are not' (*Nāṉmukaṉ Tiruvantāti* 7). This was the experience of the people of the Kośala land [distressed at Rāma's departure] and the emperor's son [Rāma, distressed at leaving the people]" (*Essence*, chap. 3, 55/28).

74. De Sales, *Treatise*, bk. 5, chap. 2, 571–72/202.

75. Ibid., bk. 8, chap. 1, 713/325.

76. Ibid., 713–14/326.

77. Ibid., 714/326. See chapter 9 of Deśika's *Essence* on the expansion of knowledge (*jñāna-vikāsa*) in liberation.

78. De Sales, *Treatise*, bk. 8, chap. 1, 714–15/326.

79. Ibid., 715/327.

80. "The conformity of submission which proceeds from the love of benevolence."

81. Ibid., bk. 8, chap. 2, 716/327–28. That this conformity in obedience is more than intellectual assent or extrinsic subordination of the will was shown earlier:

> This soul then being thus *mollified, softened and almost melted away* in *this love-full pain*, was thereby extremely disposed to receive the impressions and marks of the *love and pain* of his sovereign lover; for his memory was wholly steeped in the remembrance of this divine love, his imagination forcibly applied to represent unto himself the wounds and livid bruises which his eyes then saw so perfectly expressed in the picture [of the crucified Jesus] before him; the understanding received those most vivid images which the imagination furnished to it; and, finally, love employed all the forces of the will to enter into and conform itself to the passion of her well-beloved; whence

> without doubt the soul found herself transformed into a second crucified. (Bk. 6, chap. 15, 658/278)

It is contemplation, compassion (as suffering-with), the intimately shared experience of lovers, even if in the model of a ruler and one ruled over.

82. De Sales, *Treatise,* bk. 8, chap. 2, 717/328.
83. Ibid., 717/329.
84. Ibid., bk. 8, chap. 13, 753/361.
85. Ibid., bk. 9, chap. 4, 768/373.
86. Ibid., 770/374–75.
87. Ibid., bk. 9, chap. 1, 761–62/367. In chapter 5, de Sales adds that this "holy indifference extends to all things." He has in mind the various troubles that face us in ordinary life, even aside from those more particular sufferings that arise in serving God and preaching the Gospel.
88. Ibid., bk. 9, chap. 11, 791/394.
89. Ibid.
90. Ibid., bk. 9, chap. 12, 792–93/395–96.
91. Ibid., 793/396.
92. Ibid., 794/397.
93. Ibid.
94. Ibid.
95. Ibid., bk. 9, chap. 13, 795/398.
96. Ibid., 796/399.
97. Ibid., 797/400.
98. Ibid., bk. 9, chap. 15, 800–801/403.
99. Ibid., 803/405.
100. Ibid., 804/406.
101. Ibid.
102. Ibid., bk. 9, chap. 16, 804–805/407.
103. Ibid., 807/409.
104. Ibid., bk. 7, chap. 9, 693/310.
105. Ibid., bk. 7, chap. 11, 697/313–14.
106. Ibid., bk. 9, chap. 13, 796/399.
107. As above. So too, in book 10, chapter 17, a kind of summary claim appears:

> "Love was not content to have only made him subject to death for us unless it made him dead. It was by choice, not by force of torment, that he died. . . . And therefore it is not said that his spirit went away, forsook him, or separated itself from him, but, contrariwise, *that he gave up his spirit, breathed it out,*

yielded and commended it into the hands of his eternal Father. (867/462–63)

108. On Hadot and Griffiths, see chapter 2.

109. Similarly Carr and Ivanhoe, in *The Sense of Antirationalism,* are very attentive to likenesses between Kierkegaard's and Zhuangzi's attitude and style, but they do not hesitate in concluding that although "these two thinkers shared important concerns and approaches, they took these in remarkably different directions." Indeed, "their antirationalisms are distinct in form, function differently, and lead toward profoundly dissimilar religious goals" (57).

110. On the refusal to resolve rationally the paradox of the highest religious truths and values, see Carr and Ivanhoe, *The Sense of Antirationalism,* pp. 90ff., and my mention of that text in an endnote early in chapter 3. On the challenge and difficulties of an interreligious understanding that seems likely to lead to direct address and prayer in an unfamiliar tradition that the reader has studied, see chapter 5 of Clooney, *Divine Mother, Blessed Mother.*

Chapter 5

1. This profile is best read in light of my characterizations of exemplary persons in chapter 3.

2. The person who "has done what had to be done."

3. Deśika, *Essence,* chap. 13, 246/136–37.

4. Ibid., chap. 11, 219/121.

5. Some of these quotations also appeared in chapter 3.

6. "In its seen and unseen parts:" Ramadesikacaryar indicates that this means changes evident in this life ("seen") and those that will be evident not now, but only in the state of liberation.

7. Deśika, *Essence,* chap. 15, 267/147.

8. That is, here on earth this person chooses only things related to God, just as the liberated selves in heaven make a similar choice there.

9. That is, service here on earth enables a life of service in heaven after death.

10. Deśika, *Essence,* chap. 15, 268/147.

11. On chapter 18 of the *Essence,* see Clooney, "For Your Own Good."

12. Deśika, *Essence,* chap. 17, 310/169–70.

13. But without having any more to do with them; Deśika, *Essence,* chap. 17, 310/169–70.

14. The nuance is different in chapter 18, "On Avoiding Transgressions after Taking Refuge." There Deśika argues for a balance between

an acknowledgment of weakness and sin on the one hand, and absolute faith that taking refuge has decisively changed everything, on the other. Even after taking refuge, he admits, one may sin. He refers several times to the obdurate, those who are hard of heart and unable to live out fully the new freedom that is theirs, in utter detachment and trust in God. Such "failures" indicate that they lack the affective transformation to make their new way of life complete and vital. Knowledge has not been freed up, so as to change their hearts. And yet, because they are in the community and in some real even if minimal way committed to its truths and values, they are not like people who entirely lack the resources to improve their lives spiritually. See Clooney, "For Your Own Good."

15. Deśika cites the Bhagavad Gītā to characterize the virtues of those properly formed:

> Fearlessness, purity of heart, steadfastness in the exercise of wisdom, generosity, restraint, sacrifice, the recitation of one's Vedic text, ascetic practice, rectitude, non-violence, truth, lack of anger, renunciation, peacefulness, aversion to calumny, compassion for all beings, absence of greed, gentleness, modesty, steadiness, ardor, forbearance, endurance, cleanliness, lack of treachery and lack of arrogance: such are the qualities of a person born to a godly destiny, O Bhārata. (Adapted from the Zaehner translation)

The Bhagavad Gītā 16.4 (only alluded to by Deśika) describes the person who, by contrast, is unworthy, indeed demonic: "Hypocrisy, pride, an excessive opinion of oneself, anger, harshness and ignorance: such are the qualities of a person born to a demonic destiny, O Pārtha." In 16.5, the Gītā adds that a person of the first kind is destined to liberation and a person of the second to continuing bondage. It seems that Deśika is putting this ethical choice before his own community. Such differences in behavior and reaction are what separates the community from those outside it, and a liberated person learns to respond differently but also "naturally" to different people.

16. See Clooney, "In Joyful Recognition."

17. Deśika, *Essence*, chap. 16, 298–300/161–62. Deśika cites three texts: "Of all forms of homage, reverence for Viṣṇu is the best, but it is said that superior even to this is reverence for Viṣṇu's devotees" (*Padmottara Purāṇa* 29.81); "I have great affection to those who are devoted to my devotees. Therefore, the devotees of my devotees should be specially reverenced"; (*Mahābhārata, Aśvamedhika Parva* 116.23); and "Devotion to me is of eight forms: tender affection for those who love Me, joy in their worship" (*Garuda Purāṇa* 219.6.9).

18. As we learn still more specifically in *Essence*, chapter 30, the teachers of the tradition are, in a sense, *the* place to be: They are the primary exemplars of the new life that is to be lived, embodying the truths and values of the community; where they are, the community comes together, survives, and flourishes.

19. That is, to love God completely, as in *Matthew* 22:37: "You shall love the Lord your God with all your heart, and with all your soul, and with all your mind."

20. De Sales, *Treatise*, bk. 10, chap. 1, 811/410.

21. Similarly, Deśika argued that properly understood, taking refuge could be understood to be enjoined: "Come to me alone for refuge" (*mām ekaṃ śaraṇaṃ vraja*).

22. De Sales, *Treatise*, bk. 10, chap. 1, 813–14/412–13.

23. Even if the interconnection of the two loves differs; for de Sales, one loves God through loving the neighbor; for Deśika, one loves the neighbor in whom God takes delight.

24. De Sales, *Treatise*, bk. 10, chap. 11, 844/440–41.

25. Ibid., bk. 10, chap. 17. I offer here a very concise summary, close to de Sales' own words:

1. He loved us with a love of complacency, for his delights were to be with the human race (Prov. 8.31) and to draw humans to himself, making himself human.
2. He loved us with a love of benevolence, bestowing his own divinity upon what is human, so that a human was God.
3. He united himself unto us by an incomprehensible union, whereby he adhered to our nature and joined himself so closely, indissolubly, and supereminently to it that never was anything so strictly joined and bound to humanity as is now the most holy divinity in the person of the Son of God.
4. He flowed out into us, and as it were melted his greatness, to bring it to the form and figure of our littleness—whence he is styled a source of living water, dew, and rain of heaven.
5. He loved us to ecstasy, not only because, as Saint Denis says, by the excess of his loving goodness he goes in a certain manner out of himself, extending his providence to all things and being in all things, but also because he has in a sort forsaken and emptied himself, dried up his greatness and glory, resigned the throne of his incomprehensible majesty. . . .
6. Love often led him to admiration, as of the centurion and Canaanite woman.

7. He contemplated the young man who had till that hour kept the commandments and now desired to be taught perfection.
8. He took up a loving rest within us, even with some suspension of his senses, in his mother's womb, and in his infancy.
9. He had wondrous movements of tenderness toward little children, toward Martha and Magdalen, toward Lazarus, over whom he wept, as he wept also over the city of Jerusalem.
10. He was animated with an incomparable zeal. . . .
11. He had a thousand languors of love.
12. Finally, this divine lover died among the flames and ardors of love, by reason of the infinite charity which he had toward us, and by the force and virtue of love. (865–68/460–63)

26. De Sales, *Treatise*, bk. 10, chap. 17, 868/463.

27. Ibid., bk. 11, chap. 9, 899/489.

28. Ibid., 900/490.

29. Ibid., bk. 11, chap. 21, 943/530.

30. Saint John Cassian (360–435) was a monk and theologian who was a disciple of John Chrysostom and a strong advocate of Eastern monasticism in the West. Quotations are from his *Monastic Institutes* 9.11.

31. De Sales, *Treatise*, bk. 11, chap. 21, 944/531. Here we can recall Deśika's teaching on the difference between grief before and grief after taking refuge; only the former is consistent with proper spiritual growth because the person who has lovingly surrendered to God is characterized by cessation of grief.

32. On de Sales' parallel judgment on the lives and behavior of those who fail to ground their virtue in love, see chapter 2.

33. De Sales, *Treatise*, bk. 11, chap. 1, 871/464.

34. Ibid.

35. Ibid., bk. 11, chap. 10, 901–902/491–92. Drawing again on Augustine, de Sales next pushes forward his sharp analysis of the gap between writing and living, next criticizing a Stoic captain who, though honest and noble and brave, nevertheless clearly fell short of a truly virtuous life. This was manifest in his suicide, committed out of fear or envy of Caesar: "He may have the praise of having a stout, perhaps a great heart, but not of being a wise, virtuous and constant soul. The cruelty that is exercised without emotion and in cold blood is the most cruel of all. It is the same with despair; for the most slow, deliberate, and determined is the least excusable and the most desperate" (902–903/492). De Sales likewise condemns Lucretia for her suicide, and censures otherwise esteemed figures, such as Aristotle and Seneca, for their toleration of infanticide: "Good God!

Theotimus, what kind of virtuous men were these? And what was their wisdom, who taught a wisdom so cruel and brutal?" (904/493).

36. See chapter 3.

37. Neither de Sales nor Deśika expects loving surrender to result in a visibly, socially marked renunciant or monastic life. Though such is possible, their much more ambitious goal aims at the transformation of monk and lay person alike.

38. Recall Vaugelas' comment, cited in chapter 2, regarding the *Treatise*: "The book which [de Sales] composed about divine love . . . is a major work admired by those capable of judging it; but it is certain that the price for knowing it well is necessarily to be very devout and very learned; these are two qualities rare enough when separate, and still more rare when conjoined."

Bibliography

François de Sales

On the Love of God. Translated by John Ryan. 2 vols. Garden City, NY: Image Books, 1963.

Traité de l'Amour de Dieu. In *Oeuvres de Saint François de Sales*. Edited and with preface and introductions to the texts by André Ravier. Paris: Éditions Gallimard (Bibliothèque de La Pléiade), 1969.

Treatise on the Love of God. Translated by Henry Benedict Mackey. Rockford, IL: TAN Books and Publishers, [1884] 1997.

Vedānta Deśika

The Minor Rahasyas of Sri Vedānta Deśika. Translated by A. Srinivasaraghavan. Madras, India: Sri Vishishtadvaita Pracharini Sabha, 1993.

Śrīmad Rahasyatrayasāra. Translated by M. R. Rajagopala Ayyangar. Kumbakonam, India: Agnihotram Ramanuja Thathachariar, 1956.

Śrīmad Rahasyatrayasāra. Edited and annotated by Ramadesikacaryar Swami. Srirangam, India: Srimad Andavan Sri Pundarikapuram Swami Asramam, 2000.

Śrīmad Rahasyatrayasāra with the Cetlur Commentary by Tiruvahindrapuram Cetlur Narasimhacary Svami. Chennai, India: Rahasyatrayasara Pracarana Sabha, 1920.

Śrīmad Rahasyatrayasāra with the *Sārasvadinī* of Vedanta Ramanuja (chaps. 1–12) and Gopala Desika (chaps. 13–32) and the *Sāraprakāśikā* of Srinivasa (chaps. 1–32). 2 vols. Edited by Srisaila Venkataranganatha

Mahadesikar and Raghunatha Tatayaryadasar (Kumbakonam, India: Mangalavilasa Press, 1903–1911).
Śrīmad Rahasyatrayasāra with the *Sāravistaram* of Uttamur T. Viraraghavacharya. 2 vols. Madras, India: Ubhayavedanta Granthamalai, 1980.
Śrīmad Rahasyatrayasāra with the *Śrīsārabodhinī* of Sri Srirangasankopa Yatindramahadesika. Ahobila, India: Ahobila Math, 1954.
Śrīmadrahasyatrayasārattil Swāmi Deśikaṉ aruḷi cceytulla Ślokaṅkaḷum Pācuraṅkaḷum. Chennai, India: Sri Pundarikapuram Swami Asrama Veliyitu, 2000.
Śrīsampradāyapariśuddhi. In *Cillarai Rahasyaṅkal*. Srirangam, India: Srimad Andavan Poundarikapuram Swamy Ashramam, 1978. Edited with annotations by Srirama Desikacarya Swami.

Other Sources

Acaryavaibhavam. Mylapore, India: Śrī Vishistadvaita Research Center, 1992.
Altieri, Charles. *Canons and Consequences: Reflections on the Ethical Force of Imaginative Ideals*. Evanston, IL: Northwestern University Press, 1990.
———. *The Particulars of Rapture: An Aesthetics of the Affects*. Ithaca, NY: Cornell University Press, 2003.
———. "Reading for an Image of the Reader: A Response to Block, Caraher, and Mykyta." *Reader* 9 (1983): 38–44.
Bremond, Henri. *Devout Humanism*. Vol. 1 of *A Literary History of Religious Thought in France from the Wars of Religion down to Our Own Times*. Translated by K. L. Montgomery. London: Society for Promoting Christian Knowledge, 1928.
———. *The Coming of Mysticism (1590–1620)*. Vol. 2 of *A Literary History of Religious Thought in France from the Wars of Religion down to Our Own Times*. Translated by K. L. Montgomery. London: Society for Promoting Christian Knowledge, 1930.
Carman, John B. *The Theology of Rāmānuja: An Essay in Interreligious Understanding*. New Haven, CT: Yale University Press, 1973.
Carr, Karen L., and Philip J. Ivanhoe. *The Sense of Antirationalism: The Religious Thought of Zhuangzi and Kierkegaard*. New York: Seven Bridges Press, 2000.
Clooney, Francis X. "Divine Absence and the Purification of Desire: A Hindu Saint's Experience of a God Who Keeps His Distance." In *Science and Religions: Knowing the Unknowable about God and the Universe*, ed. John Bowker. London: I. B. Tauris, forthcoming.

———. *Divine Mother, Blessed Mother: Hindu Goddesses and the Virgin Mary*. New York: Oxford University Press, 2005.

———. "Exegesis, Theology, and Spirituality: Reading the Dvaya Mantra according to Vedānta Deśika." *International Journal of Hindu Studies* 11.1 (2007): 27–62.

———. "For Your Own Good: Suffering and Evil in God's Plan according to One Hindu Theologian." In *Deliver Us from Evil*, ed. M. David Eckel, forthcoming.

———. "Forms of Philosophizing: The Case of Chapter 7 of Vedānta Deśika's *Srimad Rahasya Traya Sara*." *Satya Nilayam* 8 (August 2005): 21–33.

———. "From Person to Person: A Study of Tradition in the *Guruparaṃparāsāra* of Vedānta Deśika's *Śrīmat Rahasyatrayasāra*." In *Boundaries, Dynamics, and Construction of Traditions in South Asia*, ed. Federico Squarcini, 203–24. Florence, Italy: University of Florence Press, 2006.

———. *Hindu God, Christian God: How Reason Helps Break down the Barriers among Religions*. New York: Oxford University Press, 2001.

———. *Hindu Wisdom for All God's Children*. Maryknoll, NY: Orbis Books, 1998.

———. "In Joyful Recognition: A Hindu Formulation of the Relationship between God and the Community, and Its Significance for Christian Theology." *Journal of Ecumenical Studies* 25.3 (1988): 358–69.

———. "In Ten Thousand Places, in Every Blade of Grass: Uneventful but True Confessions about Finding God in India, and Here Too." *Studies in the Spirituality of Jesuits* 28.3 (May 1996).

———. *Seeing through Texts: Doing Theology among the Śrīvaiṣṇavas of South India*. Albany: State University of New York Press, 1996.

———. *The Truth, the Way, and the Life: A Christian Commentary on the Three Holy Mantras of the Śrīvaiṣṇavas*. Brussels, Belgium: Peeters Publishers, 2008.

Crowe, Frederick E. "Complacency and Concern in the Thought of St. Thomas," *Theological Studies* 20.1–3 (1959): 1–39, 198–230, 343–95.

Davidson, Arnold. Introduction to Pierre Hadot, *Philosophy as a Way of Life: Spiritual Exercises from Socrates to Foucault*. Edited by Arnold L. Davidson and translated by Michael Chase. Malden, MA: Blackwell, 1995.

de Lubac, Henri. *Medieval Exegesis: The Four Senses of Scripture*. Translated by Mark Sebanc. Grand Rapids, MI: W. B. Eerdmans, 1998.

Fowl, Stephen. *Engaging Scripture: A Model for Theological Interpretation*. Malden, MA: Blackwell, 1998.

Griffiths, Paul. *Religious Reading: The Place of Reading in the Practice of Religion.* New York: Oxford University Press, 1999.

Hadot, Pierre. *Philosophy as a Way of Life: Spiritual Exercises from Socrates to Foucault.* Edited by Arnold L. Davidson and translated by Michael Chase. Malden, MA: Blackwell, 1995.

Hopkins, Steven P. *Singing the Body of God: The Hymns of Vedantadesika in Their South Indian Tradition.* New York: Oxford University Press, 2002.

Kepnes, Steven. "A Handbook for Scriptural Reasoning." *Modern Theology* 22.3 (July 2006): 367–83.

Leclerq, Jean. *The Love of Learning and the Desire for God: A Study of Monastic Culture.* 3rd ed. Translated by Catharine Misrahi. New York: Fordham University Press, 1982.

Levi, Anthony. *French Moralists: The Theory of the Passions 1585 to 1649.* Oxford, England: Clarendon Press, 1964.

Liuima, Antanas. *Aux Sources du Traite de L'Amour de Dieu de Saint François de Sales.* Premiere Partie: Les Sources de L'Idée d'Amour de Dieu. Deuxieme Partie: Les Sources des Moyens d'Expression de l'Idee d'Amour de Dieu. Libraire Editrice de l'Universite Gregorienne. [Collectanea Spiritualia Vols. 5, 6] 1959, 1960.

Loyola, Ignatius. *The Spiritual Exercises.* Translated by Thomas Corbishly. London: Burns and Oates, 1963.

McGhee, Michael. *Transformations of Mind: Philosophy as Spiritual Practice.* New York: Cambridge University Press, 2000.

Mumme, Patricia Y. *The Mumukṣuppaṭi of Piḷḷai Lokācārya with Maṇavāḷamāmuni's Commentary.* Bombay: Ananthacharya Indological Research Institute, 1987.

———. *The Śrīvaiṣṇava Theological Dispute: Maṇavāḷamāmuni and Vedānta Deśika.* Madras, India: New Era Publications, 1988.

Narayanan, Vasudha. *The Way and the Goal: Expressions of Devotion in the Early Śrī Vaiṣṇava Tradition.* Washington, D.C.: Institute for Vaishnava Studies; Cambridge, MA: Center for the Study of World Religions, Harvard University, 1987.

O'Flaherty, Wendy Doniger. "The Origin of Heresy in Hindu Mythology." *History of Religions* 10 (1971): 271–333.

Pecknold, C. C. "Editorial Preface: The Promise of Scriptural Reasoning." *Modern Theology* 22.3 (July 2006): 339–43.

Practica Quaedam: Norms for Correspondence with Father General and Other Business Matters. Rome: General Curia, 1997.

Quash, Ben. "Heavenly Semantics: Some Literary-Critical Approaches to Scriptural Reasoning." *Modern Theology* 22.3 (July 2006): 403–20.

Raman, Srilata. *Self-Surrender (prapatti) to God in Śrīvaiṣṇavism*. London: Routledge, 2007.

Rāmānuja. *Sree Gadhyathrayam*. Translated by M. R. Rajagopalan Ayyangar (Iyengar). Chennai, India: Śrī Nrsimhapriya Trust, 2002.

———. *Vedānta Sūtras with Rāmānuja's Commentary*. Translated by G. Thibaut. Sacred Books of the East, Vol. 48. Delhi: Motilal Banarsidass, 1976 [Oxford University Press, 1904].

Ramaswamy, Anbil. *Hinduism Rediscovered: A Contemporary Study of Hindu Thought*. Kuwait: Tiruvenkatam Group, 2004.

Ravier, André. Preface to *Oeuvres de Saint François de Sales*, edited and introduced by André Ravier, pp. ix–cix. Paris: Éditions Gallimard (Bibliothèque de La Pléiade), 1969.

———. *Francis de Sales: Sage and Saint*. Translated by Joseph D. Bowler. San Francisco: Ignatius Press, 1988.

Singh, Satyavrata. *Vedānta Deśika: His Life, Works, and Philosophy*. Vārānasi, India: Chowkambha Sanskrit Series, 1958.

Stalnaker, Aaron. *Overcoming Evil: Spiritual Exercises in Xunzi and Augustine*. Washington, D.C.: Georgetown University Press, 2006.

Strowski, Fortunat. *Saint François de Sales: Introduction a L'Histoire du Sentiment Religieux en France au Dix-Septiéme Siécle*. Paris: Librairie Plon, 1928.

Venkatachari, K. K. A. *Śrīvaiṣṇavism: An Insight*. Mumbai: Ananthacharya Indological Research Institute, 2006.

Viller, Marcel. "Abandon." In *Dictionnaire de Spiritualité*, ed. Marcel Viller. Vol. 1, cols. 2–25. Paris: Gabriel Beauchesne et Ses Fils, 1937.

Wolff, Kurt H. "Religion and Surrender." *Journal for the Scientific Study of Religion* 2.1 (1962): 36–50.

Zaehner, R. C. *The Bhagavad Gītā*. Oxford: Oxford University Press, 1968.

Index